T0305558

Public Relations as Emotional Labour

Inextricably linked to neoliberal market economies, public relations' influence in our promotional culture is profound. Yet many aspects of the professional role are under-researched and poorly understood, including the impact on workers who construct displays of feeling to elicit a desired emotional response, to earn trust and manage clients. The emotionally demanding nature of this aspirational work, and how this is symptomatic of "always on" culture, is particularly overlooked.

Drawing on interviews with practitioners and agency directors, together with the author's personal insights from observations in the field, this book fills a significant gap in knowledge by presenting a critical-interpretive exploration of everyday relational work of account handlers in PR agencies. In underscoring the relationship–driven, highly contingent nature of this work, the author shows that emotional labour is a defining feature of professionalism, even as public relations is reconfigured in the digital age. In doing so, the book draws on a wide range of related contemporary social and cultural theories, as well as critical public relations and feminist public relations literature.

Scholars, educators, and research students in PR and communications studies will gain rich insights into the emotion management strategies employed by public relations workers in handling professional relationships with clients, journalists, and their colleagues, thereby uncovering some of the taken-for-granted aspects of this gendered, promotional work.

Liz Yeomans was a Reader in Public Relations and Communication at Leeds Business School, Leeds Beckett University, UK, until her retirement in January 2018. She continues to supervise doctoral work and is a peer reviewer for journals in the fields of public relations and communication management. She remains interested in the emotional dimension of organisations and public relations' role in society and culture, which continues to influence her research and writing projects.

Routledge New Directions in Public Relations and Communication Research

Edited by Kevin Moloney

Current academic thinking about public relations (PR) and related communication is a lively, expanding marketplace of ideas and many scholars believe that it's time for its radical approach to be deepened. *Routledge New Directions in PR & Communication Research* is the forum of choice for this new thinking. Its key strength is its remit, publishing critical and challenging responses to continuities and fractures in contemporary PR thinking and practice, tracking its spread into new geographies and political economies. It questions its contested role in market-orientated, capitalist, liberal democracies around the world, and examines its invasion of all media spaces, old, new, and as yet unenvisaged. We actively invite new contributions and offer academics a welcoming place for the publication of their analyses of a universal, persuasive mind-set that lives comfortably in old and new media around the world.

Books in this series will be of interest to academics and researchers involved in these expanding fields of study, as well as students undertaking advanced studies in this area.

Social Media, Organizational Identity and Public Relations
The Challenge of Authenticity
Amy Thurlow

Protest Public Relations
Communicating Dissent and Activism
Edited by Ana Adi

Public Relations in the Gulf Cooperation Countries
An Arab Perspective
Edited by Talal M. Almutairi and Dean Kruckeberg

Public Relations as Emotional Labour
Liz Yeomans

For more information about the series, please visit https://www.routledge.com/Routledge-New-Directions-in-Public-Relations--Communication-Research/book-series/RNDPRCR

Public Relations as Emotional Labour

Liz Yeomans

Routledge
Taylor & Francis Group

LONDON AND NEW YORK

First published 2019 by Routledge

2 Park Square, Milton Park, Abingdon, Oxon OX14 4RN

605 Third Avenue, New York, NY 10017

Routledge is an imprint of the Taylor & Francis Group, an informa business

First issued in paperback 2021

Publisher's Note
The publisher has gone to great lengths to ensure the quality of this reprint but points out that some imperfections in the original copies may be apparent.

British Library Cataloguing-in-Publication Data
A catalogue record for this book is available from the British Library

Library of Congress Cataloging-in-Publication Data
Names: Yeomans, Liz, author.
Title: Public relations as emotional labour / Liz Yeomans.
Description: Abingdon, Oxon ; New York, NY : Routledge, 2019. |
Series: Routledge new directions in public relations and
communication research | Includes index.
Identifiers: LCCN 2019008480 (print) | LCCN 2019010712 (ebook) |
ISBN 9781315687162 (E-Book) | ISBN 9781138920309 (hardback)
Subjects: LCSH: Public relations—Psychological aspects. |
Emotions.
Classification: LCC HM1221 (ebook) | LCC HM1221 .Y46
2019 (print) | DDC 659.2—dc23
LC record available at https://lccn.loc.gov/2019008480

ISBN: 978-1-138-92030-9 (hbk)

ISBN: 978-1-03-217801-1 (pbk)

DOI: 10.4324/9781315687162

Typeset in Bembo
by codeMantra

Contents

List of figures

List of tables

Acknowledgements

A number of people have contributed to this project, providing inspirational sources, discussions, practical advice, and feedback on chapters. Thanks especially to Neil Washbourne, Chris Till, and Clea Bourne.

Thanks to Kevin Moloney, who believed in the project and provided encouragement throughout.

Thanks also to my husband John who provided support in numerous ways but most of all the motivation, and numerous refreshments, to keep going.

Thanks to Leeds Beckett University for supporting my fieldwork through an Early Career Fellowship (2015–2016).

I would also like to thank the PR practitioners who participated in the research, for their generosity and insights.

1 Introduction and guide to chapters

•

Introduction: 'It's PR, not ER'[1]

Public relations (PR) is inextricably linked to the zeitgeist of neoliberal market economies. Its influence in promotional culture, linking consumer lifestyles with products through diverse media outlets, is profound; yet the emotional effort, or labour, that goes into producing PR work has received little serious attention. Emotional labour is a global phenomenon (Brooks and Devasahayam, 2011) within the New Economy that requires a high level of social interaction involving workers managing their own emotions and displays of feeling to elicit a desired emotional response in other people. Hochschild (1983) was concerned with the psychologically alienating effects of this interactive, gendered work. Recent studies present complex depictions of how workers negotiate the emotional demands of their jobs. Such demands are likely to become intensified as they seep into workers' personal lives and are symptomatic of 'always on' culture reinforced by 'tethering' technological developments (Turkle, 2008) in time-pressured contexts (Wajcman, 2015).

PR scholars are not alone in ignoring emotional labour. For a profession which prides itself on building organisation-public relationships through strategic communication, the PR industry has been reticent in acknowledging the emotional effort expended behind the scenes on high profile, award-winning campaigns. PR is pathologically driven to celebrate success rather than seriously reflect on the emotional effort it has taken to achieve it. This not only suggests a lack of self-awareness about the consequences of PR service work but also a lack of maturity within the profession. In 2017, there were signs in the United Kingdom that PR had belatedly recognised the problems arising from 'always on' culture. It is a culture which takes much for granted: at the most punishing end are the spokespeople who 'are on call' 24/7, whose every statement and defence is visible through numerous media outlets and platforms. One only has to think of the US President Donald Trump's beleaguered press secretary Sean Spicer for whom relentless public scrutiny, trolling, and criticism were an ongoing effort in emotion management, albeit atypical of everyday agency experience.

And yet, turning to typical experience, PR is an industry with an annual staff turnover at 25%, according to one UK survey, where PR workers are choosing to leave high-pressured workplaces rather than discuss the problems of coping with the stress of 'unrealistic expectations' and 'ridiculous deadlines' (Hall and Waddington, 2017). Further evidence of stress experienced within the UK PR industry is offered by a European-wide survey of communication practitioners. In 2018, over one-third of UK practitioners reported 'serious stress problems', placing the UK fourth highest in Europe for workplace stress. Among the top reported issues related to stress (across Europe) were 'constant availability outside working time' and 'too heavy a workload' (Zerfass et al., 2018). The problem of 'over-servicing' clients for low fees, a common theme in my research, has contributed to stress. Therefore, despite the 'enormous' growth of the PR agency sector, predicted more than a decade ago (Holmes, 2007, p. 22), industry growth has accelerated at considerable cost to those who have entered its labour force. Competition is 'fierce' among agencies, according to the former WPP chairman Martin Sorrell. He goes on to say that, 'as image in trade magazines, in particular, is crucial to many, account wins at any cost are paramount' (Sudhaman, 2017). Poor mental health in PR is frequently ignored by the industry or regarded as a performance issue (Hall and Waddington, 2017). Indeed, the CIPR (2019, p. 7) concluded from its 2018/2019 annual survey that there was a 'mental health epidemic' within the UK PR industry. A mental health crisis, endemic across a range of institutions and occupations, would suggest that people from all walks of life are required to manage their emotions, both in their personal lives and at work; but when the illusion of being 'in control', positive and successful, is crucial to an occupation such as PR, then denial of these pressures may prevail. Although the tweet at the beginning of this section: 'It's PR, not ER' suggests humility about the stressful labour of PR work in comparison to the perceived life-preserving and highly expert labour of the A&E or 'emergency room' surgeon, it also speaks of denial in this intensive service work.

This book is primarily intended for scholars, educators, and research students, although practitioners may find the title interesting enough to dip into its contents. While much of the book focuses on the UK context, there are some very good reasons why the UK PR industry is important. For example, the size of the UK market is estimated at £13.9 billion (PRCA, 2018) and the United Kingdom has a well-developed agency landscape, based on continuous expansion since the 1980s, based on neoliberal economic policies, as documented by Miller and Dinan (2000) and Davis (2013). In sum, there is rich material for exploration in focusing on the UK agency sector alone. However, to widen the book's geographical scope and interest, I have brought in international studies for comparison, particularly in examining the phenomenon of emotional labour; gender and feminisation in occupations; as well as relevant international PR studies.

To clarify the scope of this book: it is *not* about stress in PR work, even though stress and burnout are symptomatic of emotionally intensive occupations and there are many studies that take this line of questioning (e.g. Brotheridge and Grandey, 2002). Rather, this book seeks to examine how, when, and why emotional labour is deployed in everyday PR agency practice, as well as who is typically engaged in this work. My central argument, drawing on empirical data, is that in common with many professional service occupations, emotional labour constitutes much of the PR role. I argue that emotional labour constitutes much of the PR role because PR must repeatedly legitimise itself (Waeraas, 2009) to clients in order for its efforts to be taken seriously, alongside the more established management disciplines such as marketing and human resources. Although there is a high demand for PR services, clients do not always know much about the service they are buying, nor do some clients know what they want from PR, except, for example, positive media coverage and certainly an improved reputation. But the 'backstage' work is hidden from view (Goffman, 1959). Therefore, legitimisation of the PR role is partly accomplished through intensive interactions with clients, potential clients, and other stakeholders that serve to instil their confidence and earn trust. On an everyday level, relationships in PR involve complex performances of individual identity management and emotion management of others' expectations, all of which constitute emotional labour, transformed into an emotional competence, a form of expertise.

I choose to examine PR agency (or PR consulting) practice because it exemplifies the competitive nature of PR service work, where emotional labour could be said to be at its most intense. Agencies operate at the sharp end of PR practice, often vying for a favourable position at the client's top table alongside the related promotional disciplines of marketing, advertising, and the new specialisms of digital marketing/SEO. Agencies also rely on a largely female workforce to undertake the everyday relationship handling with clients, journalists, and suppliers. Emotional labour is gendered and both women and men tend to enact the gender roles required by the situation. Therefore, gendered performance and 'identity work' is a feature of emotional labour in PR (Yeomans, 2013).

In contributing to PR scholarship, my stance is that of a critical-interpretive scholar examining the broader, socio-cultural context of PR as intrinsically linked to market ideology and promotional culture, as well as the micro-level of everyday 'lived experience' of agency practitioners whose interactions I view as playing a part in structuring the broader context. However, unlike some critical scholars, the aim of my book is not to condemn PR's existence, but to examine not only why it has become one of the defining occupations of the late twentieth and early twenty-first centuries but also to lift the veil on PR practice. By focusing on the micro-level 'backstage' emotion work – something that every agency public relations practitioner (PRP) is aware of doing but may not talk openly about – I aim to expose some of the contradictions of this work afforded by emotional labour theory. In other words, we can love our labour, but this comes at a cost when we are engaged in intensive social interactions that impact the bottom line. ('Love for the job' also applies to academic work: Charlotte Bloch (2012) writes about the paradox of passion and pressure in academic life.) In nursing, by contrast, there is considerable knowledge about emotional labour as an occupational hazard (e.g. Smith and Gray, 2000; Elliott, 2017). Therefore, the purpose of this book is emancipatory, providing a critical examination of the socio-cultural context of PR labour as well as illustrations of everyday emotion management in PR practice which is used as the basis for theory-building.

The public relations industry: UK context

In their detailed analysis of the rise of the PR industry in the United Kingdom during the 1980s, critical scholars Miller and Dinan (2000, p. 12) argued that within the United Kingdom, a crucial turning point for PR growth was the 'tilt to the market in government policy' arising from the election of a Conservative government under Margaret Thatcher in 1979. At the time, PR expertise of various kinds was required: first to support policies that would privatise the national utilities; second to provide promotional support that would enable the newly privatised companies to compete in national and international markets; and third to support deregulation of City financial institutions and their associated professions such as law and accountancy.

During the past 30 years, PR (or 'strategic communication') has become institutionalised across business, government, and non-profit sectors. I regard it as an 'institutional practice that is widely distributed and is based on a set of governing mechanisms, including taken-for-granted activities, rules, norms and ideas that can together be described as a public relations logic' (Fredriksson et al., 2013, p. 194). In other words, the 'logics' of PR (for example, the management of reputation) are embedded in institutional thinking. Furthermore, the PR agency sector is a leading player among the marketing services that sustain 'promotional culture', which is defined as the 'intensive and extensive development of the market as an organizing principle of social life' (Wernick, 1991, p. viii).

The PR industry is significantly larger and established in the United States and the United Kingdom than in other countries (Miller and Dinan, 2000; Holmes, 2007). The significance of PR services to the UK economy may be judged according to financial contribution, estimated at £13.8 billion (PRCA, 2018). PR firms are known interchangeably as 'consultancies' or 'agencies' (Verčič, 2012). These firms provide services to a wide range of business sector clients as well as the public sector, health, and charities (CEBR, 2005). In 2018, the majority of PR agency client work in the United Kingdom came from the technology, consumer, and business services sectors (PRCA, 2018).

In 2017, some of the top performing agencies achieved growth in revenue of around 10% or more (McKinley, 2018).

An estimated 86,000 are employed in the UK PR sector in total (PRCA, 2018). The sector comprises in-house practitioners, agency/consultancy employees, and freelancers. Fifty-two per cent or 44,720[2] are employed in agencies or consultancy firms (PRCA, 2018). The agency sector comprises small- to medium-sized enterprises, with the majority of firms employing 11–25 staff (PRCA, 2018). Larger PR firms employ between 100 and 500 staff, reflecting the size of revenues (McKinley, 2018). For example, in 2018, the top-ranking firm was Edelman PR, which generated a revenue of £60,701,000.

Client work involves media relations strategy planning, media relations, and digital and social media duties (PRCA, 2016). Although media relations work is progressively decreasing, digital and online communications is increasing and this has contributed to agency growth (PRCA, 2018). Everyday PR work, therefore, involves fostering good relationships with clients in order to win and keep their business, but also maintaining relationships with journalists and other stakeholders. Although PR is a female intensive profession, only 36% of female PR agency practitioners held board level positions in 2016 (PRCA, 2016). Much of the day-to-day relationship handling is undertaken by White British female practitioners, working in account executive, account director, and associate director roles, a profile which has typified the practice for a number of years (CEBR, 2005; PRCA, 2018).

PR agency work is both competitive and intensive. Agency employees within the communications industry typically work well beyond the standard 35 full-time hours (Clarke, 2013), with around 40% continuing to work out of hours every single day to pick up emails or phone calls (PRCA, 2016, 2018). As already discussed, over 30% of practitioners in the United Kingdom experience 'serious stress problems' and this affects job satisfaction, although PR agency workers report higher job satisfaction than those working in non-profit, joint stock, government or private companies (Zerfass et al., 2018). Clients of PR firms, especially small firms, have high expectations concerning the level of interaction as well as of who is performing the service (Mart and Jackson, 2005); therefore the practitioner who embodies such expectations is paramount to a good service.

Emotional labour theory

Goffman (1959, p. 17) was the first to conceptualise 'face work', or managing one's own and or another's emotional performance as a 'central "competence" against which a commercial transaction or service stands or falls'. In recent years, in parallel with the rise in service industries in Western economies, the concept of emotional labour (Hochschild, 1983) has received renewed attention. Defined as the 'the management of feeling to create a publicly observable facial and bodily display; emotional labor [sic] is sold for a wage and therefore has exchange value' (Hochschild, 1983, p. 7). In *The Managed Heart: Commercialization of Human Feeling*, Hochschild (1983), a sociologist, estimated that roughly one-third of American workers had jobs that subjected them to high demands for emotional labour, and that half of all women's jobs call for emotional labour. Hochschild also identified that the middle classes (certainly in Anglo and Northern European cultures) were traditionally socialised for jobs involving a high degree of emotion management. Further, Donato (1990 p. 139), also a sociologist, argued that employers preferred to recruit women to PR because it 'increasingly involves emotional labour' and emotion work is seen as 'women's work'. Studies suggest that the relationship building and communicative aspects of PR work are indeed constructed as women's work by women (Fröhlich, 2004; Fröhlich and Peters, 2007; Tsetsura, 2009; Yeomans and Mariutti, 2016). Furthermore, this type of labour is not perceived as labour, but as 'love' (i.e. for the job), thereby rationalising stress-inducing conditions such as long working hours and tight deadlines (Hesmondhalgh and Baker, 2011; Rodino-Colocino and Beberick, 2014).

Feminisation of PR

The increase in the number of women entering PR in the United Kingdom took place during the 1970s and 1980s, rising to 40% in 1991 (Yaxley, 2013). The 'standard white' (Aldoory, 2001), middle-class female practitioner today comprises just over two-thirds of the profession (CIPR, 2017; PRCA, 2018). Characterised as a female intensive profession involving high levels of client interaction, PR warrants closer examination from both emotional labour and feminist perspectives. Yet since Donato's sociological observations, PR scholarship, with a few exceptions, has remained relatively silent on the emotional dimension of PR work. It is useful to examine possible reasons why emotion work has been neglected in PR scholarship. A starting point for this discussion is the development of PR research and theory since the 1980s. Such a discussion is necessary to locate this book within the field, specifically as part of the 'socio-cultural turn' of PR inquiry (L'Etang and Pieczka, 2006; Ihlen et al., 2009; Edwards and Hodges, 2011; Ihlen and Fredriksson, 2018).

Beyond systems approaches to PR

Systems theory was the dominant approach during the second half of the twentieth century, at the time when PR education was established (Edwards, 2009). The systems approach was proposed by Grunig and Hunt (1984) in their influential text *Managing Public Relations* in which they presented a typology of PR (four models of PR practice), thus introducing the concepts of one-way communication (or press agentry); public information; two-way asymmetric and two-way symmetric communication. The purpose of this work was to improve practice or PR effectiveness through normative theories 'describing how a profession ought to behave' (Edwards, 2009, p. 158). Two-way symmetric communication practice was regarded as the most effective model of PR, in its emphasis on long-term relationships between organisations and their publics (Grunig, 1992). Grunig and his colleagues' long-term 'excellence in PR' study of PR practice, funded by the International Association of Business Communicators Research Foundation across three countries, led the way in spawning similar studies in other countries to discover whether the same models of communication practice could be applied to non-Anglo-American cultures.

Ledingham and Bruning went on to develop the systems approach in their 'relationship management' perspective of PR (Ledingham and Bruning, 2000). The emphasis was still on improving practice but the focus was on the quality of the relationship, or exchange, between organisations and publics. A measurement scale for assessing public perceptions of an organisation (OPRA) was based on four dimensions of relationships: trust, relational commitment, relational satisfaction, and control mutuality. A fifth variable, derived from Chinese culture: 'face' and 'favour', was developed to help practitioners measure the health of cross-cultural organisation–public relationships (Huang, 2001). However, while 'face' (which is close to Goffman's (1959) 'face work') held potential for exploring the concept of emotional display in cross-cultural contexts, the OPRA approach was quantitative, limiting the study of relationships to numeric predictions of relationship quality and conflict resolutions.

Inspired, it would seem, by the emphasis on 'relationships', Coombs (2001, p. 112) sought to get closer to the relational aspects of PR by reviewing literatures on interpersonal communication and proposing a research agenda divided into 'variables, taxonomies and models, and theories' of interpersonal communication. Coombs' research agenda was nevertheless a further response to the 'excellence' model of PR and therefore an attempt to identify better ways for practitioners to build and manage relationships, for example, by identifying 'specific traits that should affect the practitioner's ability to function effectively' (p. 113). A trait-based approach to relationships tends to favour psychological, quantitative research which overlooks socio-emotional processes of interaction.

Much of the systems research has focused on the role of the practitioner (e.g. Broom and Smith, 1979; Broom and Dozier, 1986). This body of research has identified two basic roles for the PRP: the communications technician who writes and executes PR programmes and the communications manager who operates at a more strategic level creating PR strategy and dealing with client briefs. The roles research is considered important because practitioners enacting the communication manager role have a stronger chance of being part of the 'dominant coalition', an organisation's group of decision-makers (Grunig, 1992). As a member of the dominant coalition, PR is more likely to contribute to organisational effectiveness (e.g. helping to shape the organisation's goals). The communication technician role, on the other hand, has become 'women's work' which feminists argue disadvantages women; women then find it harder to be seen as managerially competent (Creedon, 1991; Fröhlich, 2004; Fröhlich and Peters, 2007).

Systems research, driven largely by North American PR scholars in a quest for 'excellence' and 'effectiveness', has been preoccupied with process models of communication. The 'relationship management' perspective emphasises information and resources exchanges or transfers (Broom et al., 1997, 2000), while 'roles' research understands PR roles in the form of tasks to be accomplished by the communication technician or communication manager – a functionalist perspective rather than one that focuses on social and cultural processes. While this brief review summarises a substantive and influential body of research that has formed the basis of the university PR curricula in English-speaking countries, it is also clear that a functionalist, systems understanding of PR and PR work has limitations when it comes to understanding relationships and emotion.

Criticisms of the systems approach

Criticisms of the systems approach to PR research and theory development started with a critique of Grunig's 'excellence' theory and symmetric communication. L'Etang (1996) and Cheney and Christensen (2001) highlighted the self-interested nature of PR practice, while Pieczka's (1996) in-depth analysis of Grunig's 'excellence' theory drew attention to its contradictions. Further to this line of criticism, Robert L. Heath's *Handbook of Public Relations*, published in 2001, drew together for the first time in one volume a diverse range of PR scholarship, including critical voices from outside the mainstream North American academy. McKie (2001, p. 75), for example, identified a restriction in the 'traffic in ideas between public relations and other areas of knowledge', and, at times, isolation from other disciplines signifying an occupational field that was 'out of touch'. McKie traced the 'theoretical lateness' of PR to outmoded (reductionist) ideas of science, scientific management, and methodology (McKie, 2001, pp. 80–81). While advocating 'new science' perspectives such as chaos theory and complexity theory, McKie provided a range of alternative perspectives for researchers to consider in developing new PR theory.

New directions in PR scholarship

Following McKie's plea for 'new science' approaches, and in parallel to this, PR scholarship has adopted a range of theoretical approaches, including postmodern (e.g. Holtzhausen, 2012); social and cultural (e.g. L'Etang and Pieczka, 2006; Ihlen et al., 2009; Edwards and Hodges, 2011); and gender perspectives (Daymon and Demetrious, 2013). A landmark gathering in stimulating some of these developments was the *Radical PR Roundtable*, hosted in 2008 by the University of Stirling and organised by David McKie, Jesper Falkheimer, Jordi Xifra, Magda Pieczka, and Jacquie L'Etang. This group set out an agenda which was to: 'reform and liberate the field of public relations and hope to establish a distinct network with a clear identity that can redress the problems of isolation that can afflict scholars in our field, especially those that espouse critical perspectives' (Radical PR website, 2008). Rather than merely critiquing the dominant paradigm in PR research, scholars associated with this grouping have sought to develop new knowledge by drawing on interdisciplinary approaches. Bringing PR into central debates concerning the present modes of society and culture, including the endemic nature of 'promotional culture' (Wernick, 1991), is a necessary task for PR scholars in order to bring structural and ethical issues to the attention of other scholars, educators, and practitioners. This is not the focus of social critics outside the field who are in general examining PR at a distance from the profession and are largely uninterested in 'field' debates.

Routledge's *New Directions in Public Relations and Communication Research* series, of which this volume is part, has facilitated a flourishing of alternative perspectives to the dominant systems paradigm. However, while researchers have begun to address the socio-cultural aspects of PR work by examining the experiences of practitioners to explore power, race, and cultural differ- ence, few have directly addressed the emotional dimension of PR. This is possibly due to theoretical lateness of PR (as observed by McKie, 2001) to concepts already well-established in the social sciences and cultural studies, and unfamiliarity – even discomfort – with the literature on emotion and affect. I review some of this work in the Appendix to provide the reader with an understanding of where emotional labour theory sits within the much broader literature on emotion and affect.

My starting point is that emotion work represents a large proportion of the practice of PR and indeed may be a defining feature of professionalism in PR. Emotion work, or emotional labour, while common to many occu- pations that require face-to-face or voice-to-voice contact, is relevant to the work of practitioners, especially women, employed by PR firms where the client's demands influence the level of service provided. Unlike other busi- ness consultancy services, however, PR firms have other demands requiring emotion work: those of handling the media, and increasingly, social media influencers (SMIs). These relationships are mediated within the agency set- ting, which itself has 'feeling rules' or socio-emotional norms for the practi- tioner to negotiate.

Guide to chapters

Chapter 2 critically examines Hochschild's (1983, 2003) emotional labour theory and its framework of feeling rules, surface acting and deep acting, and, in particular, the relevance of the subjective experience of emotion.

The chapter questions whether emotional labour *is* the site of alienation in contemporary service work – or more complex and contradictory. The relevance of 'performance' and 'identity' in understanding the motivations of professionals in willingly doing emotion work in pursuing status, material rewards, and legitimacy is highlighted (Bolton, 2005). Furthermore, an extended framework of emotional labour that includes 'embodied dispositions' (Witz et al., 2003) and the shaping of emotional expression within open plan spaces as well as through ICT is proposed. Finally, consideration of gender is essential to address Hochschild's concern with female workers as the most suitable candidates for emotional labour.

Chapter 3 begins with an examination of the political, economic, and social conditions that have created the demand for PR as a service in the United Kingdom during the past 30 years. The ideas of neoliberalism (Harvey, 2005) and promotional culture (Wernick, 1991) are explored as being particularly relevant to discussing the significance of PR work in contemporary society and culture. The key relationships in the 'market' for emotional labour (Hochschild, 1983) are discussed, starting with the client, then moving on to examine journalists operating within a changing media environment, including the 'PR-isation' of the media (Moloney, 2006). Within these contexts, this chapter goes on to critically examine the ever-shifting relationships between journalists and PRPs, as well as new entrants to the media ecology: the SMIs.

Chapter 4 argues that a specific gender perspective is essential to understanding relationships between PRPs and their professional contacts from an emotional labour perspective, particularly in the light of the 'feminisation' of PR over the past 30 years, and Hochschild's (1983) contention that emotion work largely falls to women working in service occupations. Gendered interactions are a key focus of this chapter, in which I extend Hochschild's perspective of gendered emotional labour, as well as examine PR as a gendered occupation. I argue that postfeminist theory has utility as a critical lens to generate a more nuanced understanding of PR – for example, as performative emotional labour. Finally, I consider emotions linked to digital labour (Fuchs and Sevignani, 2013), as reflective of the requirement for PRPs to simulate intimacies online through social media platforms. PRPs working in the 'pink ghetto' of PR agencies can be viewed as participating in gendered struggles for legitimacy in day-to-day relations with clients, journalists, colleagues, and online influencers.

Chapter 5 examines Yeomans' (2010, 2013) exploration of emotional labour in PR and reflects on its currency in a rapidly changing PR agency environment. Yeomans proposed that PRPs in her study drew on resources of the 'basic socialised self' in learning to become skilled emotion managers (Bolton, 2005). Through everyday interactions, PRPs became highly attuned to the different expectations of agency directors, clients, and journalists. 'Managing expectations' was central to practitioners' emotion management strategies due to the contingent nature of much PR work where 'results' could not always be guaranteed. 'Empathising' and 'educating' illustrate some of the gendered features of client expectation management. Further, gendered performance (Butler, 1990) could be adapted to perceived relational requirements. Both men and women practitioners were found to engage in identity work (Alvesson and Willmott, 2002) in which they discursively distanced themselves from the 'feminised' and stereotypical aspects of PR work and aligned their performances and identities with a masculine notion of a profession (Bolton and Muzio, 2008). Despite the pressures of the job, PR agency work was a preferred career choice among participants and a perceived means of self-identity expression (Korczynski, 2003) rather than 'alienation' from the self (Hochschild, 1983).

Chapter 6 seeks to identify the emerging socio-emotional norms of interaction in PR agencies. The emotion management of self and others is explored based on interviews with senior practitioners – directors, partners, and owners of PR firms, as well as observational notes at four agencies. Understanding the process of becoming an entrepreneur in PR is essential to gain insights into self-perceptions of identity and leadership and the shaping of entrepreneurial PR identity. The agency's internal environment is examined, including the physical space, technologies, as well as account directors' expectations of attitude, dress, and demeanour in client relationships. The balancing of employee, client, and other professional relationships is of central interest in this chapter, as is the competitive environment, including the agency's pursuit of business growth. While emotional labour theory provides an ongoing interpretive framework, I extend the theoretical focus to the material features of PR, including physical spaces and ICTs, as 'agents' that are likely to play an increasingly important role in mediating relationships in the future. Furthermore, a gender perspective brings in a highly relevant lens to interpret the emotion management of professional relationships in the PR agency.

Chapter 7 concludes the book, drawing together findings and arguments from each chapter to propose a tentative theory of emotional labour in agency PR. This theory is based on empirical findings, developed in relation to the broader themes covered in earlier chapters: neoliberalism, promotional culture, digital capitalism, individualisation, and (post)feminism. In this chapter I provide an agenda for future research on emotion management/emotional labour in PR. In addition, I call for research that addresses the bigger picture of PR and the 'emotional turn' in society and culture.

Appendix: Researching emotions. From theory to methodology

This appendix is in two parts. The first part provides a review of emotion theory, starting with a critique of 'common-sense' theories of emotion that shape everyday discourse. I then move on to categorisations of emotion, including anger, joy, and sadness, including the problem of labelling emotions in isolation from their socio-cultural contexts. Distinctions between the terms 'emotion' and 'affect' are then discussed. A critique of the emotion in organisations literature is followed by an argument in which I advocate social constructionist and social interactionist perspectives of emotion as highly relevant in occupational settings. Finally, I pay particular attention to 'shame' as encompassing a large family of social emotions that are relevant to the workplace (Scheff, 2000).

The second part of the appendix outlines the social phenomenological approach that guides the two empirical studies presented in Chapters 5 and 6. Methodological details are provided including sampling, qualitative data gathering and analysis.

Notes

1 Practitioner tweet, 27 September 2018.
2 Based on 2018 survey data (personal communication, PRCA, 12.10.18).

References

Aldoory, L. (2001) The standard white woman in public relations. In E. L. Toth and L. Aldoory, eds. *The Gender Challenge to Media: Diverse voices from the field*. Cresskill, NJ, Hampton Press, pp. 105–149.

Alvesson, M. and Willmott, H. (2002) Producing the appropriate individual. Identity regulation as organizational control, *Journal of Management Studies*, 39 (5), pp. 619–44.

Bloch, C. (2012) *Passions and Paranoia: Emotions and the culture of emotion in academia*. Farnham, Surrey, Ashgate.

Bolton, S. C. (2005) *Emotion Management in the Workplace*. Houndsmill, Hampshire: Palgrave Macmillan.

Bolton, S. C. and Muzio, D. (2008) The paradoxical processes of feminization in the professions: The case of established aspiring and semi-professions. *Work, Employment and Society*, 22 (2), pp. 281–299.

Brooks, A. and Devasahayam, T. W. (2011) *Gender, Emotions and Labour Markets: Asian and Western perspectives*. London, Routledge.

Broom, G. M. and Smith, G. D. (1979) Testing the practitioner's impact on clients. *Public Relations Review*, 5 (3) pp. 47–59.

Broom, G. M. and Dozier, D. M. (1986) Advancement for public relations role models. *Public Relations Review*, 12 (1), pp. 37–56.

Broom, G. M., Casey, S., and Ritchey, J. (1997) Toward a concept and theory of organization–public relationships. *Journal of Public Relations Research*, 9 (2), pp. 83–98.

Broom, G. M., Casey, S., and Ritchey, J. (2000) Concept and theory of organization–public relationships. In J. A. Ledingham and S. D. Bruning, eds. *Public Relations as Relationship Management: A relational approach to the study and practice of public relations*. Mahwah, NJ, Lawrence Erlbaum Associates, pp. 3–22.

Brotheridge, C. M. and Grandey, A. A. (2002) Emotional labor and burnout: Comparing two perspectives of 'people work'. *Journal of Vocational Behavior*, 60, pp. 17–39.

Butler, J. (1990) *Gender Trouble: Feminism and the subversion of identity*. New York and London, Routledge.

CEBR: Centre for Business and Economic Research/Chartered Institute of Public Relations (2005) *48,000 Professionals; £6.5 Billion Turnover: The economic significance of public relations*. London, Centre for Business and Economic Research.

CIPR: Chartered Institute of Public Relations (2017) State of the profession 2017. London, Chartered Institute of Public Relations. Available from: https://www.cipr.co.uk/sites/default/files/10911_State%20of%20PR%202017_f1.pdf. Accessed 28 October 2018.

CIPR: Chartered Institute of Public Relations (2019) State of the profession 2019. London, CIPR. Available from: https://www.cipr.co.uk/sites/default/files/11812%20State%20of%20Profession_v12.pdf. Accessed 8 April 2019.

Cheney, G. and Christensen, L. T. (2001) Public relations as contested terrain: A critical response. In R. L. Heath, ed. *Handbook of Public Relations*. Thousand Oaks, CA, London, and New Delhi, Sage, pp. 167–182.

Clarke, C. (2013) 70% of marketing and communications agency employees say work affects their health. *The Drum*, 22 May. Available from: http://www.thedrum.com/news/2013/05/22/70-marketing-and-communications-agency-employees-say-work-affects-their-health. Accessed 28 October 2018.

Coombs, W. T. (2001) Interpersonal communication and public relations. In R. L. Heath, ed. *Handbook of Public Relations*. Thousand Oaks, CA, London, and New Delhi, Sage, pp. 105–114.

Creedon, P. J. (1991) Public relations and 'women's work': Towards a feminist analysis of public relations roles. In L. A. Grunig and J. E. Grunig, eds. *Public Relations Research Annual 3*. Hillsdale, NJ, Lawrence Erlbaum and Associates, pp. 67–84.

Davis, A. (2013) *Promotional Cultures*. Cambridge, Polity.

Daymon, C. and Demetrious, K. (2013) *Gender and Public Relations: Critical perspectives on voice, image and identity*. London, Routledge.

Donato, K. M. (1990) Keepers of the corporate image: Women in public relations. In B. F. Reskin and P. A. Roos, eds. *Job Queues, Gender Queues: Explaining women's inroads into male occupations*. Philadelphia, Temple University Press, pp. 129–144.

Edwards, L. (2009) Public relations theories: An overview. In R. Tench and L. Yeomans, eds. *Exploring Public Relations*. Harlow, Pearson Education, pp. 149–173.

Edwards. L. and Hodges, C. E. M. (2011) *Public Relations, Society and Culture: Theoretical and empirical explorations*. London and New York, Routledge.

Elliott, C. (2017) Emotional labour, learning from the past, understanding the present. *British Journal of Nursing*, 6 (19), pp. 1070–1077.

Fredriksson, M., Pallas, J., and Wehmeier, S. (2013) Public relations and institutional theory. *Public Relations Inquiry*, 2 (2) pp. 183–203.

Fröhlich, R. (2004) Feminine and feminist values in communication professions: Exceptional skills and expertise or 'friendliness trap'? In M. de Bruin and K. Ross, eds. *Gender and Newsroom Cultures: Identities at work*. Cresskill, NJ, Hampton Press, pp. 65–77.

Fröhlich, R. and Peters, S. B. (2007) PR bunnies caught in the agency ghetto? Gender stereotypes, organizational factors, and women's careers in PR agencies. *Journal of Public Relations Research*, 19 (3), pp. 229–254.

Fuchs, C. and Sevignani, S. (2013) What is digital labour? What is digital work? What's their difference? And why do these questions matter for understanding social media? *Triple-C*. 11 (2), pp. 237–293.

Goffman, E. (1959) *The Presentation of Self in Everyday Life*. London, Penguin Books.

Grunig, J. E. ed. (1992) *Excellence in Public Relations and Communication Management*. Hillsdale, NJ, Lawrence Erlbaum Associates.

Grunig, J. E. and Hunt, T. (1984) *Managing Public Relations*. New York, Holt, Rinehart and Winston.

Hall, S. and Waddington, S. (2017) Exploring the mental wellbeing of the public relations profession. London, PRCA.

Harvey, D. (2005) *A Brief History of Neoliberalism*. Oxford, Oxford University Press.

Hesmondhalgh, D. and Baker. S. (2011) 'A very complicated version of freedom': Conditions and experiences of creative labour in three cultural industries. *Poetics: Journal of Empirical Research on Culture, the Media and the Arts*, 38 (1), pp. 4–20.

Hochschild, A. R. (1983) *The Managed Heart: Commercialization of human feeling*. Berkeley, University of California Press.

Hochschild, A. R. (2003) *The Managed Heart: Commercialization of human feeling*, 2nd ed. Berkeley, University of California Press.

Holmes, P. A. (2007) The state of the public relations industry: Preliminary report: June 2007, for Huntsworth plc. [Online]. Available from: http://www.huntsworth. com/docs/Paul%20Holmes%20Report%20-%20The%20State%20of%20the%20 PR%20Industry.pdf. Accessed 5 February 2009.

Holtzhausen, D. (2012) *Public Relations as Activism: Postmodern approaches to theory and practice*. New York, Routledge.

Huang, Y.-H. (2001) OPRA: A cross-cultural, multiple-item scale for measuring organization-public relationships. *Journal of Public Relations Research*, 13 (1), pp. 61–90.

Ihlen, Ø., van Ruler, B., and Fredriksson, M. (2009) *Public Relations and Social Theory: Key figures and concepts*. New York and London, Routledge.

Ihlen, Ø. and Fredriksson, M. (2018) *Public Relations and Social Theory: Key figures, concepts and developments*, 2nd ed. New York and Abingdon, Oxon, Routledge.

Korczynski, M. (2003) Communities of coping: Collective emotional labour in service work. *Organization*, 10 (1), pp. 55–79.

Ledingham, J. A. and Bruning, S. D. (2000) *Public Relations as Relationship Management: A relational approach to the study and practice of public relations*. Mahwah, NJ, Lawrence Erlbaum Associates.

L'Etang, J. (1996) Corporate responsibility and public relations ethics. In J. L'Etang and M. Pieczka, eds. *Critical Perspectives in Public Relations*. London, International Thomson Business Press, pp. 82–105.

L'Etang, J. and Pieczka, M. eds. (2006) *Public Relations: Critical debates and contemporary practice*. Mahwah, NJ, and London, Lawrence Erlbaum Associates.

Mart, L. and Jackson, N. (2005) Public relations agencies in the UK travel industry: Does size matter? *PRism* [Online], 3 (1). Available from: http://www.prismjournal. org/vol_3_iss_1.html. Accessed 2 May 2018.

McKie, D. (2001) Updating public relations: 'New science', research paradigms, and uneven developments. In R. L. Heath, ed. *Handbook of Public Relations*. Thousand Oaks, CA, London, and New Delhi, Sage, pp. 75–91.

McKinley, R. (2018) PR Week reveals the top 150 UK PR consultancies in 2018. *PR Week*, 23 April. Available from: https://www.prweek.com/article/1462518/ prweek-reveals-top-150-uk-pr-consultancies-2018. Accessed 28 October 2018.

Miller, D. and Dinan, W. (2000) The rise of the PR industry in Britain, 1979–98. *European Journal of Communication*, 15 (1), pp. 5–35.

Moloney, K. (2006) *Rethinking Public Relations: PR propaganda and democracy*, 2nd ed. London, Routledge.

Pieczka, M. (1996) Paradigms, systems theory and public relations. In J. L'Etang and M. Pieczka, eds. *Critical Perspectives in Public Relations*. London, International Thomson Business Press, pp. 124–156.

Public Relations and Communications Association (2016) *PRCA Census 2016*. London, PRCA.

Public Relations and Communications Association (2018) *PRCA Census 2018*. London, PRCA. Available from: https://www.prca.org.uk/sites/default/files/PR%20 and%20Communications%20Census%202018.pdf. Accessed 23 October 2018.

Radical PR (2008) About radical PR. Available from: http://radicalpr.wordpress. com/. Accessed 23 October 2018

Rodino-Colocino, M. and Berberick, S. N. (2015) 'You kind of have to bite the bullet and do bitch work': How internships teach students to unthink exploitation in public relations. *Triple-C*. 13 (2), pp. 486–500.

Scheff, T. J. (2000) Shame and the social bond. *Sociological Theory*, 18 (1), pp. 84–99.

Smith, P. and Gray, B. (2000) *The Emotional Labour of Nursing: How students and qualified nurses learn to care*. London, South Bank University.

Sudhaman, A. (2017) Q1 2017: Procurement 'dominant' says Sorrell as WPP PR growth leads group [27 April]. Available from: https://www.holmesreport.com/ latest/article/q1-2017-procurement-dominant-says-sorrell-as-wpp-pr-growth-leads-group Accessed 2 October 2018.

Tsetsura, K. (2009) How female practitioners in Moscow view their profession: A pilot study. *Public Relations Review*, 36 (1), pp. 78–80.

Turkle, S. (2008) Always on/always on you: The tethered self. In J. E. Katz, ed. *Handbook of Mobile Communication Studies*. Boston, MA, MIT University Press, pp. 121–138.

Verčič, D. (2012) Public relations firms and their three occupational cultures. In K. Sriramesh, and D. Verčič. eds. *Culture and Public Relations: Links and implications* New York, Routledge, pp. 243–257.

Waeraas, A. (2009) On Weber: Legitimacy and legitimation in public relations. In Ø. Ihlen, B. van Ruler, and M. Fredriksson, eds. *Public Relations and Social Theory*. New York and London, Routledge, pp. 301–322.

Wajcman, J. (2015) *Pressed for Time: The acceleration of life in digital capitalism*. Chicago, IL, and London, The University of Chicago Press.

Wernick, A. (1991) *Promotional Culture*. London, Sage.

Witz, A. Warhurst, C., and Nixon, S. (2003) The labour of aesthetics and the aesthetics of organization. *Organization*, 10 (1), pp. 33–54.

Yaxley, H. (2013) Career experiences of women in British PR (1970–1989). *Public Relations Review*, 39 (2), pp. 156–165.

Yeomans, L. (2010) Soft sell? Gendered experience of emotional labour in UK public relations firms. *PRism*, 7 (4). Available from: http://www.prismjournal.org. Accessed 28 October, 2018.

Yeomans, L. (2013) Gendered performance and identity work in PR consulting relationships: A UK perspective. In C. Daymon and K. Demetrious, eds. *Gender and Public Relations: Critical perspectives on voice, image and identity*. London, Routledge, pp. 87–107.

Yeomans, L. and Mariutti, F. G. (2016) Different lenses: Women's feminist and post-feminist perspectives in public relations. *Revista Internacional Relaciones Publicas*, 6 (12). Available from: http://revistarelacionespublicas.uma.es/index.php/revrrpp/article/view/430. Accessed 28 October 2018.

Zerfass, A., Tench, R., Verhoeven, P., Verčič, D., and Moreno, A. (2018) European Communication Monitor 2018. Strategic communication and the challenges of fake news, trust, leadership, work stress and job satisfaction. Results of a survey in 48 countries. Brussels, EACD/EUPRERA, Quadriga Media Berlin.

2 Emotional labour in a global context

A framework

Introduction

In this chapter I critically examine Hochschild's (1983, 2003) emotional labour theory and its framework of 'scripted' organisational feeling rules that require workers to engage in surface acting and deep acting, leading to an estrangement from the self in interactive service work. To begin with, I discuss the origins of emotional labour theory, highlighting the importance of emotion in social interactions, the subjective experience of emotion and social context. I then move on to analyse the concept of self-estrangement, or alienation, in the light of questions and critiques as to whether emotional labour *is* the site of alienation in contemporary service work – or a more complex and contradictory experience. For example, 'creative labour' with which public relations (PR) is sometimes associated has been described as 'a very complicated version of freedom', indicating that individual's relationship to work can be experienced ambivalently (Hesmondhalgh and Baker, 2011). As I discuss in this and later chapters, young PR executives claim to enjoy their work and there is a sense of personal agency in their client relations, and yet they work long hours which can be emotionally exhausting (Hickman, 2018).

I then go on to critically review the development of emotional labour theory which extends analyses both within and beyond Anglo–American contexts. This includes emotional labour experienced within professional domains. Bolton's (2005) typology of workplace emotion, in particular, highlights the relevance of 'performance' and 'identity' in understanding the motivations of professionals in willingly doing emotion work in pursuing status, material rewards, and legitimacy. This framework is useful in analysing sources of potential conflict or emotional dissonance among public relations practitioners (PRPs). On the other hand, Bolton (2005) adopts a normative view of the professional who operates under explicit codes, rather than one who responds to the 'unwritten' feeling rules and expectations of client organisations (Kaiser et al., 2008; Bourne, 2017). Furthermore, a framework that includes gender is essential to address Hochschild's concern with female workers as the most suitable candidates for emotional labour, as well as understanding PR as service work.

Exploring Hochschild's social theory of emotion management

Hochschild's social theory of emotion draws on the works of Dewey (1922), Gerth and Mills (1964), and Goffman (1959). Hochschild acknowledges that this model 'presupposes [emotion as] biology but adds more points to social entry: social factors enter not simply before and after but interactively during the experience of emotion' (1983, p. 211). Giving the example of a man becoming violently angry when insulted, she raises the question of what would constitute an insult within the man's culture, and what social codes might help or constrain anger. According to Hochschild, Dewey was an early proponent of the interactional model, arguing that the feelings of fear or anger became manifest only in social context. Gerth and Mills who are quoted developed this perspective: 'The social interaction of gestures may thus not only express our feelings but define them as well' (1964, p. 55).

But it is Goffman who provides the main 'vantage point' in identifying the 'affective deviant' who has the wrong feeling for a social situation and '…for whom the right feeling would be a conscious burden…' (Hochschild, 1983, p. 214). Goffman's concept of a situation's 'social logic' or rules which may be tacitly recognised, 'generally agreed upon and unchanging' (p. 216) provides the springboard for Hochschild's social theory of emotion. Hochschild identifies embarrassment and shame as being Goffman's speciality because of his focus on a person's display to other people. Where display to others becomes an 'issue' for the person who is conscious of being watched (that is, producing embarrassment or shame), then the self comes alive in a similar way to actors on a stage. As actors, we 'play characters and interact with other played characters', thereby engaging in surface acting (Hochschild, 1983, p. 216).

In examining performances at work, and especially the performances of PRPs who are themselves in the image and reputation business, Goffman's concepts of self-presentation resonate, since, as I suggest in Chapter 2, professional status or credibility may be at stake within the social situation. Johansson (2009, p. 132) argues that Goffman's concept of 'face' or the public self-image that professionals might want to claim for themselves is an 'important dimension' for studying interactions between PRPs and journalists, especially in examining power differences and respective professional identities.

For Hochschild, however, Goffman falls short. He fails to address the deep acting that takes place in situations where actors are compelled to alter their feelings in accordance with the feeling rules of social and cultural contexts, and specifically, the work setting. PRPs must alter their feelings according to the demands of different social and cultural contexts; however to what extent this adjustment of feeling may be identified as 'deep acting', 'surface acting', or 'impression management' (Goffman, 1959) is a point for debate and further exploration.

Though a rich field of ideas, however, Hochschild's social theory of emotion does reinforce a Western dualism of body and mind; that is, emotion is regarded as a pliant resource that may be manipulated or influenced by external, cognitive forces that subjugate actors' emotional expression to culturally accepted conventions and norms (Lutz, 2007). That emotions also serve to equip emotional labourers with a level of agency to resist, disrupt, or subvert conventions, while skilfully maintaining culturally approved relations with customers or clients is not explored adequately by Hochschild but is the topic of more recent studies. These studies connect emotion management to ideas of the self, identity, and social relations within occupational contexts and reinforce the notion of personal agency of emotional labourers within these settings.

To provide a basis for examining the emotional labour of PRPs working within UK PR firms, I now go on to explore and distinguish Hochschild's concepts of emotional labour, emotion management, and emotion work and critically discuss the development of emotional labour studies and theory to the present. In particular I describe and critique Bolton's (2005) emotion management typology and its utility for analysing the emotion work of PRPs. In addition, I examine arguments about the perceived problem of 'always on' culture (Turkle, 2008; Wajcman, 2015) and its implications for emotional labour in the contemporary digital work environment.

Hochschild's 'emotional labour', 'emotion management', and 'emotion work'

Three related concepts are employed by Hochschild (1983) in *The Managed Heart*: 'emotional labour', 'emotion management', and 'emotion work'. According to Hochschild, emotional labour applies to jobs that: involve face-to-face interaction with the public; the need for actors to manage their own emotions and displays of feelings to elicit a desired emotional response in other people; and allow the employer, through training and supervision, to exercise a degree of control (Hochschild, 1983, p. 147). Emotional labour is defined as 'the management of feeling to create a publicly observable facial and bodily display; emotional labor [sic] is sold for a wage and therefore has *exchange value*' (Hochschild, 1983, p. 7). Hochschild estimated that roughly one-third of American workers had jobs that subjected them to high demands for emotional labour, and that half of all women's jobs called for it. She identified that the middle classes, especially in Anglo and Northern European cultures, were traditionally socialised for jobs involving a high degree of emotion management.

Hochschild (1983) consciously used the term 'emotional labour' synonymously with 'emotion management' and 'emotion work'; however these latter terms, according to her footnote on page 7, refer to the management of feeling in the *private* realm rather than the *commercial* context: i.e. where there is 'use value' or utility instead of 'exchange value'. 'Use value' is not clearly defined but Hochschild appears to suggest that emotion management and emotion work equip the individual with a sense of agency and choice of when to manage emotion in social contexts, whereas emotional labour subjects the individual to an emotional script prescribed by the commercial context. The choice of term, nevertheless, connotes different meanings: for example, Bolton (2005) was criticised by Brook (2009) for preferring the less political term emotion management over emotional labour. Therefore, it is crucial to first examine the genesis of Hochschild's emotional labour concept before moving on to discuss these different terms, which I return to later in this chapter.

Hochschild's position appears to stem from the first line of the first chapter where she references *Das Kapital* in which Marx examined the working conditions of child labourers in the nineteenth-century English factories (Hochschild, 1983, pp. 3–5). She suggests parallels between the physically exhausting conditions of Marx's factories and the instrumental use of emotional labour by twentieth-century commercial institutions, whereby the worker becomes increasingly estranged or alienated from a sense of self. The alienating processes of factory work, referred to by Marx, literally separated workers from the products of their labour (thus rendering them powerless), while the imposed nature of production work took away self-expression or meaning in the labour process (see the discussion on workplace alienation on page 22). The main tenets of her argument are that the strain exerted on the worker by the commercialisation of feeling may lead to a loss of the authentic self, to the extent that commercial systems *appropriate* private emotional 'gift exchanges' that would otherwise have been given freely and spontaneously by the worker. An emotional gift exchange might be a smile, or a thank you, expressed through polite, everyday interaction, but when these everyday gestures are scripted, they become part of the service offer.

In her Preface to *The Managed Heart* (1983, pp. ix–x), Hochschild attributes her interest in emotional labour to three main influences: C. Wright Mills' writings on the use of personality in the labour process; the works of Goffman on the performance of self; and Freud on emotion as a signal function. While these sources were important in the development of emotional labour theory, something 'was missing', as she puts it, to understand what happens to the individual when 'the private management of feeling is socially engineered and transformed into emotional labor for a wage' (Hochschild, 1983, Preface, p. x). Her pioneering study (1983) that detailed the everyday working lives of the Delta flight attendants is now widely recognised as a classic within the social sciences literature (e.g. Reskin and Padavic, 1994; Bolton, 2005; Turner and Stets, 2005; Wulff, 2007; Greco and Stenner, 2008) as well as highly relevant to contemporary media and politics (Wahl-Jorgensen, 2018). The experiences of the flight attendants, for Hochschild, provided the 'missing' element of her theory development. Her study was thus designed to elicit insights into the lives of airline workers who represented a commercial sector that was part of an expanding service economy in the United States. Importantly, jobs in the service sector required the 'capacity to deal with people rather than with things' and yet 'people jobs', she argued, were underexplored and undertheorised in terms of the kind of labour that they entailed. Her enquiry, she argued, had 'special relevance for women' because 'women more than men have put emotional labor [sic] on the market, and they know more about its personal costs' (Hochschild, 1983, pp. 9–11). I now go on to describe and discuss the key concepts of emotional labour.

The key concepts of emotional labour

'Feeling rules' and 'display rules'

Within the neocapitalist economic framework, the individual worker is bound by feeling rules culturally defined by their employer. Feeling rules are the expected attitudes and modes of normative employee behaviour regulated by an organisation's management and communicated through company orientation programmes, ongoing training, and supervisors' surveillance of workers performing the service role. In drawing attention to the culturally acceptable scripts or feeling rules in the performance of a task, and the flight attendants' responses to these feeling rules, Hochschild characterises commercial organisations as socialising institutions engaged in 'massive people processing' [...] 'the advanced engineering of emotional labor' (1983, p. 187).

Feeling rules are most evident, according to Hochschild, by focusing on the gap, or 'emotive dissonance' (p. 90), between how actors *actually* feel and how they *should* feel in meeting the emotional conventions laid down by their employers. How actors *should* feel is translated into display rules. An example of a display rule is 'service with a smile' which is performed as part of an organisation's customer service orientation: pleasing the customer by continuously presenting a friendly attitude when performing the service role with an audience of paying customers who expect nothing less.

While Hochschild asserts that both women and men are expected to be 'nice' as a 'necessary and important lubricant to civil exchange' (1983, p. 166), being nice often involves what Hochschild refers to as 'evocative emotion work' (Hochschild, 2008, p. 122) or consciously working-up a feeling that is initially absent, whereas suppressing a feeling that is already present requires the cognitive focus of control. 'Evocative' emotion work requires 'deep acting' (Hochschild, 1983, p. 36) which requires framing feelings in accordance with the 'feeling rules' (pp. 57–59) or expectations set by a particular social context or work setting. Hochschild asserted in 1983 that half of women's jobs called for emotional labour; therefore women were most subject to its requirements.

'Surface' and 'deep' acting

Surface acting is sometimes not enough in providing the level of service required. Surface acting, or pretending, is something that workers do every day: it is pretending to feel what they do not such as pretending to care or pretending to listen. There is a sense of detachment while going through the motions of showing feeling. Hochschild's flight attendants referred to this as 'going into robot' while consciously not hiding their pretence as a form of protest (p. 129). While 'surface acting' (p. 36) produces a 'false self' (p. 194) that can be left behind at the end of the working day, 'deep acting' involves deceiving oneself as much as deceiving others. To do this, actors must have a store of 'emotion memories' (p. 41) that they can call up to enable them to believe that an imagined happening really is happening – the feeling is 'self-induced' (p. 35). Where there is a marked discrepancy between private feelings and public display, which Hochschild refers to as 'emotive dissonance' (p. 90), feelings of strain arise unless the individual is able to change either what they feel or what they fake.

Hochschild's theorising of emotional labour centred around the study of flight attendants in the 1980s, where the commercial exploitation of their 'feminine' qualities of both mother and 'sexual mate' (1983, p. 182) led to actors' estrangement or alienation from authentic feelings, where their own sense of self, or identity, had yet to be discovered. Critiques of Hochschild's theorising of alienation from authentic feelings are explored later in this chapter; however, the salience of the theme of workplace alienation in sociological thought warrants closer attention and I now examine this.

The relevance of workplace alienation to Hochschild's emotional labour theory

The alienating effect of the labour process under capitalism, conceptualised by Marx in his examination of conditions of the working class in England during the nineteenth century, is a topic that has been pursued within industrial sociology and labour process theory in particular. Marx (1975 in Calhoun et al., 2007, pp. 88–91) proposed four types of workers' alienation or 'estrangement'. These were: first, alienation from the products of labour; second, alienation from the production process; and third, alienation from the worker's 'essential being', so that labour becomes a means to existence, humanity (or 'spiritual aspect') is reduced, and the worker becomes self-estranged. This reduced state of humanity and human potential, fourth, means that co-workers who are positioned in the same relationship to their labour, as well as their 'essential being', become estranged from one other. Du Gay (1996) interprets two main uses of the term 'alienation': first, 'social alienation' which refers to the alienating effects of the human products and processes of the social environment, rendering production workers as powerless; and second, 'spiritual alienation' which refers to production work that lacks self-expression, creativity, or meaning for the worker because his or her labour is externally imposed, illustrated in Marx's words as 'its alien character is clearly shown by the fact that as soon as there is no physical or other compulsion it [work] is avoided like the plague' (Bottomore and Rubel, 1963, pp. 177–178, cited in du Gay, 1996, p. 11).

From the foregoing discussion, Hochschild's alienation argument appears to align with spiritual alienation (or estrangement from one's essential being), although there may be a danger here of transferring ideas from Marx's nineteenth-century paradigm to the modern era: in other words, spiritual alienation may not directly concur with Hochschild's psychological interest in alienation from authentic feelings. Weyher's (2012, pp. 353) extensive analysis of the role of emotion in Marx's theory of human nature and estrangement concludes much the same when he states:

> Hochschild often discusses 'estrangement' in more personal than social terms – as a loss of *'sense* of self'. This places her closer to the more psychological and individual orientation of the sociological 'alienation' literature that flourished from the late 1950s through the 1970s. Missing is any reference to the contemporary Marxist literature on estrangement or alienation [...]

Indeed, Hochschild quotes from the 1950s sociologist C. Wright Mills: 'We need to characterize American society of the mid-twentieth century in more psychological terms...' (Mills, 1956, p. xx, cited in Hochschild, 1983, p. 7) and she acknowledges Freud's influence in her own theorising of emotion management in the Preface.

Du Gay argues that Marx's notion of alienation is an *objective* condition that becomes widespread within society 'without any growing feeling of discontent among those subjected to it' (du Gay, 1996, p. 13; also Weyher, 2012, p. 354). Drawing heavily on Mészáros's [1970] (1986, p. 258) work on Marx's theory of alienation, Weyher (2012) develops this point. He argues that the more 'atomized' and 'individualized' our society becomes as a consequence of capitalism's effects on human beings (i.e. 'self-seeking egoistic fulfilment, promoting the values of "individual autonomy"'), the 'more estranged we are from others around us – in *all* our social relations' (Weyher, 2012, pp. 352–353). Therefore, he argues, in all social relations, we must increasingly engage in emotion work to realise the values of individual autonomy promoted by capitalism. This point is relevant to the work of PRPs, who, I argue, actively engage in emotional labour, in part, as a necessary process to protect their own sense of autonomy and control in their professional relationships.

Du Gay (1996) notes that the inadequacies in theory and methodology of macro-sociological approaches (such as Mills) were addressed more directly through the work of George Herbert Mead (1934) and symbolic interactionism. Mead's approach to investigating the social world rejected the static, macro-sociological versions of social life, seeking instead to understand the *fluid* nature of self and identity developed through discourse (ideas of identity that were developed by Foucault and Butler in 'queer theory'). Importantly, Mead's 'self' is not conceived of as private but as emerging through the social interaction processes of discourse and language. Du Gay cites the work of interactionists such as Roy (1973) as lending weight to the notion that any form of work, no matter how limited or lowly, could be a source from which individuals could appraise their own identity, thus generating some level of meaning.

As du Gay notes, the notion of alienation within the labour process is an enduring concept. As already identified, Hochschild's emotional labour theory is a development of Mills' alienation thesis in relation to middle-class occupations. As discussed, *her* focus on alienation, however, is less concerned with structural features of capitalism (although structural factors shape her assumptions) than the micro-sociological insights of the airline workers discussing feelings about their identity. In making the link between structure and agency Hochschild takes an interactionist approach, drawing on the works of Mead and Goffman to develop a theory which is reflexively grounded in the language and discourse of the flight attendants as well as the discourse of the institutions that shape their working lives. However, her final prognosis is that claims on the 'managed heart' are the site of an ongoing struggle between the worker's authentic, private feelings and company feeling rules (p. 197). Ultimately, then, Hochschild concludes that emotional labour is the 'thing to be engineered' which increasingly belongs 'to the organization and less to the self' (1983, p. 198). In moving the discussion back to structure at the conclusion of *The Managed Heart,* Hochschild evokes her original reference to Marx, asserting that those who:

> perform emotional labor in the course of giving service are like those who perform physical labor in the course of making things: both are subject to the rules of mass production. But when the product – the thing to be engineered, mass-produced, and subjected to speed-up and slowdown – is a smile, a mood, a feeling, or a relationship, it comes to belong more to the organization and less to the self.
> (Hochschild, 1983, p. 198)

Hochschild's conceptualisation of emotional labour laid the foundations for numerous occupational studies in the late twentieth century, and as discussed earlier, opened up new types of investigations within the social sciences. In the Afterword (pp. 199–207) to the twentieth anniversary edition of *The Managed Heart,* Hochschild comments on other employees' reactions to her study as well as the subsequent interest among scholars. In particular, she notes how her study of the flight attendants had articulated the 'anguish' felt by many workers about a phenomenon – emotional labour – previously marked by its 'sheer invisibility' (Hochschild, 2003, p. 200). The twentieth anniversary edition provides an extensive bibliography that includes some of the emotional labour studies published throughout the 1980s, 1990s, and early 2000s. Some of these studies examined the workplace socialisation processes of other occupations (e.g. Pierce, 1995, who examined paralegals; Leidner, 1993 who examined fast food handlers and insurance agents); emotional socialisation by educational institutions (e.g. Smith and Kleinman, 1989, who examined medical schools; Cahill, 1999, who examined mortuary science students); while other studies focused on the consequences of emotional labour such as stress and burnout (e.g. Brotheridge and Grandey, 2002). A further group of studies, meanwhile, examined specific, undertheorised strands of emotional labour theory (e.g. 'collective emotional labour').

Perhaps Hochschild's most significant contribution, however, as Kleinman (2002) argues, is that she legitimised emotions in social research, and as Lively (2006) claimed: 'raised sociological consciousness of how something that is often thought of as being inherently individual – emotion – is shaped, sometimes to individuals' detriment, by the very social structures and organizations in which they are embedded' (Lively, 2006, p. 569). The extent to which Hochschild's emotional labour theory applies in the twenty-first century is the focus of critique and discussion in more recent studies examining the emotional labour process. The themes that emerge from recent studies in emotional labour directly address some of the criticisms and are discussed in the next section.

Emotional labour theory development: critiques and challenges to Hochschild

Emotional labour as a global phenomenon

Emotional labour is now understood to be a global phenomenon within service work: for example, call centre workers in India who have to pretend to be British (D'Cruz and Noronha, 2008); butchers in a Danish supermarket who are expected to communicate the brand (Gyimóthy and Rygaard Jonas, 2010); and different service workers in Singapore who find ways to accommodate their employers' emotional prescriptions (Yun, 2010). However, as Brooks and Devasahayam (2010) point out in *Gender, Emotions and Labour Markets: Asian and Western Perspectives*, emotional labour as a Western concept is linked to a particular kind of Anglo-American socialisation (middle-class, often female). Therefore, it would be interesting to compare these contexts to consider, for example, the cultural norms of Western PR firms and non-Western PR firms in the Middle East, Asia Pacific, and Latin American regions, and how employees experience these contexts from an emotional labour perspective.

As discussed in Chapter 3 (page 97), very few social constructionist studies of PR agencies have been undertaken outside Western contexts. Tse et al.'s (2016) ethnographic study of Hong Kong PR firms is closest to an emotional labour analysis. Developing the themes of Hesmondhalgh and Baker's (2011) study of creative labour in the United Kingdom, Tse et al. (2016) found PR agencies in Hong Kong to be highly exploitative of the labour-power of junior executives. Participants likened their work to 'a factory' where they were closely watched for errors by senior agency staff, worked excessively long hours in the service of clients due to high staff turnover, and were poorly paid compared to other communication professions. The pressure to network to generate business, use social media more extensively, and the need to educate clients about the value of PR contributed to feelings of insecurity and un-certainty among executives as well as agency managers, indicative of a 'high stress industry' in Hong Kong where opportunities for young people had 'stagnated' (Tse et al., 2016). Within the Hong Kong setting, the relatively new and under-regulated PR industry is therefore susceptible to some of the worst labour practices.

Shared emotional labour and 'space'

Hochschild's notion of shared or collective emotional labour is only briefly dealt with in *The Managed Heart*. Here, the focus is on the need for flights at-tendants, working in pairs, to *avoid* sharing emotional difficulties in public so as not to undermine the cheerful mood required to work together effectively. Recent studies in the *shared* nature of emotional labour, however, suggest that the burden of emotion work, rather than being borne privately by the individual alone, is very much shared among service workers in public spaces. This mutual support among service workers or 'communities of coping' (Korczynski, 2003), in turn, enables them to cope with difficult emotional situations more easily. Case study findings of emergency ('911') despatchers showed that actors sought out a shared emotional labour, and specifically the 'comic relief' found in emergency situations (Shuler and Davenport Sypher, 2000). Guerrier and Adib's (2003) study of tour representatives identified that this occupational group actively sought out spaces that allowed them to pursue lifestyles that reflected their authentic selves. This enabled them to accept the negative aspects of leisure work. However, in a situation where the expectations of professional norms are dominant (e.g. displays of emo-tional detachment in nursing), such collectivism may be constrained and not publicly occur but may take place in private spaces away from the workplace (Lewis, 2005; Burkitt, 2014).

The commercially attuned and highly individualist setting of the PR agency might suggest a lack of collective sharing of emotional labour; on the other hand, given that the majority of PR firms are small businesses of be-tween 11 and 25 staff (PRCA, 2018), sharing open plan office spaces, intimate colleague relationships, and 'banter' among a predominantly youthful age profile are likely to coexist within the competitive context. The millennial generation of PR employees, in particular, is identified as seekers of 'fun' in the workplace as well as a 'sense of community' (Porter Novelli, 2008, cited in Gallicano et al., 2012).

How physical space shapes emotional norms, and how these norms are re-interpreted, is a further area to explore. For example, Lewis (2008) ar-gued that gendered emotion work is established through spatial practices, so that dominant forms of emotion work are performed as masculine in some spaces, rendering other spaces as feminine. Hirst and Schwabenland (2018, p. 173) drew attention to how the 'new office' design increased 'visibility' for all occupants, with some women using the open office for the way it was intended – i.e. to be 'themselves', to network and build relationships, while others felt 'watched' and the need to suppress 'tears and hot flushes' to 'reduce the risk of marginalization' in their careers. Either way, female bodies 'stood out' and were subject to scrutiny by the self and others. Drawing on Lefebvre (1991), Hirst and Schwabenland (2018, p. 162) outlined three dimensions in which space can be analysed and interpreted. The 'conceived space' of the office (i.e. undertaken by design professionals) is a dominant form of capitalism because it structures social relations. 'Spatial practices' refer to the 'routes we take through a building, where and how we sit, the selection and arrangement of artefacts on a desk, and our dress, gestures and manners', while 'lived space' links to 'how spaces are construed, interpreted and imagined by people occupying and using them'.

Emotion as a 'gift exchange'

Hochschild's idea (1983, p. 18) is that emotional labour may sometimes be a 'gift exchange' or an act of altruism. She argued that we unconsciously 'keep a mental ledger with "owed" and "received" columns for gratitude, love, anger, guilt, and other feelings' (p. 78). Within the workplace, however, the gift of feeling becomes a commodity which may lead to unequal exchanges where the customer or client 'is king' (p. 86). The concept of feeling as gift exchange is taken up in recent literature (Lewis, 2005; Burkitt, 2014; Duffy, 2016). Lewis (2005) develops the theme of emotion as a gift by relating it to actors' possession of a 'dual consciousness' (Collinson, 1992) whereby a 'masculine' professional script of detachment and the 'feminine' personal script of caring may be in direct conflict within a clinical environment. Burkitt (2014, p. 139) draws out similar points about emotion management in nursing, although preferring to relate notions of conflict to threats to the core professional values embodied in professional nursing practice and self-identity, rather than scripted feeling rules. For example, he argues that the core value of caring and the display of care towards patients is a boundary requiring 'poise' to avoid relationships becoming too involved and personal. A further source of conflict, especially in nursing, is where core values are under threat from structural constraints such as budgetary cutbacks, forcing nurses to speed up and spend less time with patients to provide the attention and care they believe they should provide.

As already noted, PR continuously needs to legitimise itself to clients as the preferred discipline for building trust (Bourne, 2017). PR firms also need to legitimise themselves to wider society through corporate social responsibility initiatives, thereby showing altruism at an organisational level. Popular discourse in PR would also suggest that practitioners frequently engage in emotional gift exchanges on an interpersonal level with their clients and media contacts in order to foster close working relationships; however, to what extent gestures of kindness are sincerely and freely offered is questionable given the instrumental use of emotion that is required of the practitioner in some situations (Yeomans, 2016). Other research examines the gendered 'gift exchanges' that take place online (Duffy, 2016), as discussed in Chapter 4.

Expressing the self through work

Cahill (1999) introduced the concept of *emotional capital*, which, in his study, involved students dealing successfully with the emotional difficulties of working with human cadavers. However, as many were children of funeral directors, they were already socialised to be comfortable with this type of work. Schweingruber and Berns (2005) built on this concept of emotional capital to examine, through an ethnographic study, the experience of people who undertook sales training in an 'attempt to develop a new, better self, which in turn will be better equipped to do emotion management' (p. 680). The study found that trainee salespeople, drawn from a variety of backgrounds, were trained to produce and use emotional capital through 'mining' emotional experiences in their past lives as a bridge to their new selves. The development of emotional training in Schweingruber and Berns' study may be likened to Hochschild's 'deep acting', where 'transmutation of an emotional system' (Hochschild, 1983, p. 19) from a private to an organisational act is often a requirement of service provision. However, the changing of the self in Schweingruber and Berns' study (through training) appears to fulfil the individual's need to become a better person, proving to themselves, their families, and friends that they can be more successful and responsible.

Associated with this is the idea that work can satisfy the expression of self-identity. Korczynski (2003, p. 57) noted that call centre workers were recruited on the basis of possessing pro-customer attitudes, beliefs, and values and that 'it is the pleasurable emotional labour that occurs in service interactions that service workers regard as one of the most significant and satisfying aspects of their jobs'. This further supports the notion that people select jobs that best conform to their ideas of self-identity expression. This is true of PRPs who seek opportunities to express themselves within the job. Within the neoliberal, entrepreneurial PR firm, the expression of the personal brand is encouraged through face-to-face PRP-client relationships (Yeomans, 2010), while online platforms enable the PRP personal brand to be further exploited (Bridgen, 2011).

Drawing on Korczynski's (2003) notion of pleasurable emotional labour, Bridgen (2011) found that PRPs derived pleasure from building online relationships in pursuit of their personal brand. They did not see themselves as exploited when undertaking this type of work at home. Nevertheless, a body of critical work which explores 'creative labour' examines the paradox of this type of work, particularly at the more junior levels where internships, both paid and unpaid, are prized, competed for, and flourish in a variety of settings (e.g. Frenette, 2013; Rodino-Colocino and Beberick, 2015). While jobs such as PR, journalism, and marketing have a glamorous aura and represent certain lifestyles, workers' aspirations mean that exploitation, particularly the self-exploitation that emerges from 'love' for the job, is hidden (Hesmondhalgh and Baker, 2011). Therefore, enjoyment expressed within the job has to be viewed through a critical lens in order to recognise the objective conditions of labour within the context of neoliberal capitalism.

Aesthetic labour and embodied disposition

Witz et al. (2003) argued that 'aesthetic labour' is as much a part of the labour process as emotional labour within an interactive service environment, particularly in labour markets where an embodied, commodified form of 'style' is important to the service offer. In focusing on embodiment, Witz et al. (2003, p. 40) veer away from Hochschild's emotional labour concept of 'surface acting', instead drawing on Goffman's 'impression management' concept which strongly emphasises visible behaviour and Bourdieu's concept of 'embodied disposition'. Embodied disposition involves 'body work' that is more than just physical appearance: it is about alignment with the habitus through the 'inculcation of a corporate "doxa"' (beliefs). The physical body is also imbued with dispositions that are performances of class, such as accent, bearing, and manners, particularly among those in management and professional positions. However, modes of symbolic value change over time and therefore embodied dispositions shift according to social demands in the field (Witz et al., 2003). For example, recent analyses of aesthetic labour in the politics of beauty include modes of femininity that involve women becoming 'aesthetic entrepreneurs' through which they maintain continuous surveillance about their appearance (Elias et al., 2017). Similarly, within PR scholarship, Edwards (2015, p. 76) highlighted the importance of 'accent and voice as embodied indicators of difference' to UK black and minority ethnic practitioners, and how these indicators contribute to racial stereotyping. Embodied indicators such as accent, bearing, manners, skin colour, gender, and so forth should therefore be brought into the analysis of PRPs' labour since specific embodied identity markers may or may not hold symbolic value for PR agencies.

Challenges to preserving 'an authentic self'

The basis of Hochschild's concern is with preserving self-identity: an 'authentic' self. This idea has led to several criticisms, primarily that the concept of the 'private' (or 'true') and 'public' (or 'false') self is flawed when actors' emotional behaviours are already socialised by the family, school, church, and state – more so than commercial institutions (Wouters, 1989). Indeed, it may not be possible to distinguish between private and public life when the boundaries between domestic life and organisational life have become increasingly blurred (van Iterson et al., 2001 in Hughes, 2003). As already suggested in relation to PRPs' use of social media for personal branding (Bridgen, 2011), developments in technology challenge notions of the division between work and domestic life when it is possible to interact simultaneously with personal friends, colleagues, and contacts through mobile devices. Rather than seeing technology as abetting the encroachment of work into the private realm and harming the self and personal relationships, Wajcman (2015, p. 146) argues, in contrast to critics such as Turkle (2008), that the 'always on' character of digital technologies enables people to balance and coordinate their work and family life more flexibly and that the 'social and technical are mutually shaped' meaning that devices help to better organise time spent in work and family domains.

The liquidity of the private and public self merged into a mediated self means that people are better able to adapt to a media-saturated environment (Deuze, 2012). For the media or PR professional, this adaptation is essential to professional survival, since, if everyone is a media producer and consumer (or 'prosumer'), the PRP must be several steps ahead of the game, looking for ever more novel ways to network and use digital platforms to connect brands with consumers. However, while notions of private and public selves can be viewed as outdated for those participating in a digitally fluid society, it is important not to lose sight of time-pressured, high staff turnover professional contexts driven by 'ridiculous deadlines', where poor mental health, according to one PR industry report, is frequently ignored (Hall and Waddington, 2017).

A second perspective which challenges notions of the authentic self is offered by Bolton and Boyd (2003), who present work life as performative. In their large-scale comparative study of cabin crew in three airlines, the authors argue that cabin crew present multiple selves to management and customers, depending on given situations (Bolton and Boyd, 2003). Cabin crew use humour to resist commercially prescribed feeling rules, actively seeking spaces or small moments to create fun and enjoyment within the workplace. From their findings, Bolton and Boyd conceptualise emotional labour as a typology of four manifestations of self-presentation: *pecuniary* and *prescriptive* (summarised as social actors' instrumental adherence to commercial and professional rules and scripts); *presentational* (described as the basic, socialised self used by social actors to conform to social norms); and *philanthropic* which is described as social actors using emotional labour as a gift in helping others out. Bolton and Boyd's study can be viewed as an important development in emotional labour theory in that it recognises multiple selves that have multiple meanings presented by multi-skilled actors. The multiple selves or '4 Ps' model is explored further in Bolton's subsequent work (e.g.

2005) in which prescriptive emotional labour, which she prefers to describe as 'emotion management', is conceived as being synonymous with the professional role.

Emotional labour as professionalism

Hochschild is criticised for focusing on the harmful effects of emotional labour (e.g. Cahill, 1999; Korczynski, 2003; Schweingruber and Berns, 2005) through the transmutation of the private use of feeling for institutional gain. Poynter (2002), for example, argued that there may be positive, negative, and ambiguous outcomes for the individual, depending on factors such as the individual's control over their emotional labour and equality in work relationships. Highly pertinent to the analysis of PR, then, is the emotional labour of the professional.

Hochschild's position on the emotional labour of those in higher-status or professional roles is contradictory. Hochschild claims that 'the social worker, the day-care provider, the doctor and the lawyer: are not emotional labourers due to the level of control they have over how emotional labour is performed' (1983, p. 153). However, as Bolton (2009) points out, Hochschild then refers, in the Afterword to the twentieth anniversary edition, to nurses, professors, and police detectives carrying out emotional labour (Hochschild, 2003, p. 200). It would appear that Hochschild's earlier position changed to acknowledge the evidence that a broad range of service and professional occupations, not just those within the commercial sector, could be subjected to emotional labour. Professionals, according to Poynter (2002), typically *do* enjoy more autonomy and discretion over their engagement with the labour process than, for example, workers in call centres for which feeling rules, or scripts, are often prescribed by management. He argues that if the relationship with the client is more equal, then doing emotional labour can have positive outcomes for the individual. In examining work intensification and emotional labour among 54 university lecturers in the United Kingdom, Ogbonna and Harris (2004) found that this professional group extensively faked their emotions in response to high levels of occupational expectations from senior management (and, in turn, government) and decreasing autonomy. Indeed, lecturers believed that they could not be professional *without* doing emotional labour. For this occupational group, the emotional labour performed had both positive and negative outcomes. While certain appropriate behaviours and emotions brought rewards such as career progression, the same displays of behaviour and emotions also promoted individualism and a lack of teamwork.

Other emotional labour research (e.g. Smith and Gray, 2000; Mann, 2004; Mastracci et al., 2006) suggests that those occupying semi-professional and professional occupations, particularly those in public services, fulfil the tenets of Hochschild's emotional labour which are: first, face-to-face or voice-to-voice interaction with the public; second, the need for actors to manage their own emotions and displays of feelings to elicit a desired emotional response in other people; and third, they allow the employer, through training and supervision, to exercise a degree of control (Hochschild, 1983, p. 147). However, in regard to the third tenet of emotional labour, some writers argue that while the feeling rules for professionals may not be as highly scripted by management, there is nevertheless a pressure for professionals to adhere to the professional ethics, norms, and expectations of their own sphere of public interaction (Anleu and Mack, 2005), and particularly the expectations of direct clients or service users. Such expectations may also place a demand on the professional to perform emotional labour according to ascribed gender roles – demonstrated, for example, in the legal profession (Pierce, 1995); management, social work, and teaching (Bolton and Muzio, 2008); and academia (Bellas, 1999). The performance of gendered emotional labour is discussed further in Chapter 4.

The *reverse* notion that a profession undergoes professional development through the expectations of direct clients (Muzio et al., 2008, cited in Bourne, 2017) is particularly compelling in the case of PR. The unwritten feeling rules governing a PRP's expression of 'passion' for a client's brand are more likely to be learned and internalised through PRPs' multiple interactions within the ambit of the PR firm, than from professional codes, values, and education. As such, there is a similarity between PR and learned emotional expression in management consultancy (Kaiser et al., 2008), which is explored in Chapter 3.

Bolton's typology of workplace emotion

As noted earlier, Bolton (2005) was criticised by Brook (2009) for implying 'a much more benign and de-politicized workplace than in Hochschild's portrayal' (Brook, 2009, p. 18). Bolton asserted that the term 'emotional labour' lacked the 'explanatory power to cover so many different labour processes within so many different sectors', while acknowledging that 'emotional labour remains a useful description for a capitalist labour process that relies heavily on emotion work' (Bolton, 2009, p. 554). What can be concluded from this debate, therefore, is that the term 'emotional labour' is as an ideological construct that was consciously adopted by Hochschild to delineate the 'seriously self-estranging process' of the sale of personality and the 'active emotional labor involved in the selling' found among workers in 'advanced capitalist systems' (Hochschild, 1983, p. ix). However, Bolton does not deem it appropriate to attach the ideological label of emotional labour to all occupations involving emotion work, because, she argues, emotion work is not always experienced as self-estrangement (as in the case of Hochschild's account of the Delta Airlines flight attendants).

According to Bolton, the relative position of the *professional's* emotional labour is perhaps best understood when located within a broader 'typology of workplace emotion', which classifies 'what motivates organisational actors to enact feeling rules in distinct ways' (2005, p. 93). The '4Ps' typology proposed by Bolton places workplace emotion on a continuum:

1   *pecuniary* where emotion work is carried out for material and commercial gain (this, according to Bolton, is where *true* 'emotional labour' belongs as it may be experienced negatively by service workers);
2   *prescriptive* where emotion work is carried out according to professional or organisational feeling rules;
3   *presentational* where emotion work is carried out according to social feeling rules; and
4   *philanthropic*, where emotion work is performed as a sincere 'gift' to others.

First, according to Bolton, *professionals* (see the shaded **'Prescriptive'** column in Table 2.1) actively engage in prescriptive emotion work by willingly internalising professional *feeling rules* in order to meet the 'expectations of their colleagues and the public concerning the "right" image of a professional' (Bolton, 2005, p. 122). Bolton distinguishes between *professional* and *organisational* feeling rules, associating the latter with what is more usually termed 'corporate culture' (Pettigrew, 1979; Deal and Kennedy, 1999). Corporate culture is widely regarded as 'the way we do things around here', referring to the rites and rituals of organisational life, and organisational expectations of workers in displaying correct attitude and behaviours codified through management ideology in policies, mission, and values statements. Professional feeling rules, on the other hand, are associated with codes of conduct set

Table 2.1 Professional emotional labour within the typology of workplace emotion

	Pecuniary	*Prescriptive*	*Presentational*	*Philanthropic*
Feeling rules	Commercial	Professional; organisational	Social	Social
Associated motivations	Instrumental	Altruism Status Instrumental	Ontological Security	Gift
Performance	Cynical compliance	Cynical/sincere	Sincere/ cynical	Sincere
		Consent/ commitment	Commitment/ consent	Commitment
Identity	Imposed/self	Professional/self	Self	Self
Consequences	Alienation	Professional identity	Stability	Stability
	Contradiction Conflict Resistance	Contradiction		Satisfaction

Adapted from Bolton (2005, p. 93)

by the profession and are more concerned with upholding the status of that profession: for example, as an impartial source of expertise. For some professionals, the 'dual demands' (Bolton, 2005, p. 126) of professional feeling rules and organisational feeling rules, especially where the rules are changing to emphasise customer satisfaction (e.g. within the UK public sector, healthcare, and education), may create dilemmas or threats to professional status.

Second, Bolton (2005, p. 93) identifies *associated motivations for feeling rules* as a central feature of the typology because 'it recognises the motivations of organisational actors to enact the feeling rules in distinct ways'. According to Bolton, professionals adhere to feeling rules for instrumental, or material, gain, for reasons of status and sometimes for altruistic reasons. Therefore, it is important not to accept an employee's performance (and, arguably, personal accounts of their own performance) at face value but seek to understand actors' situated motivations for the enactment of feeling rules.

A third element of prescriptive workplace emotion refers to the *performance* itself. For professionals, this includes performance that demonstrates a cynical/sincere attitude to feeling rules, or a consent/commitment attitude. Bolton does not elaborate on this element except to comment that cynical performances are more consistent with motivations to achieve material gain. The cynical/sincere attitude may also be compared with Hochschild's surface acting where the actor knows that they are faking sincerity but realise its instrumental importance in managing the feelings of others to achieve a desired outcome. Consent/commitment refers to the extent that the professional consents and commits to feeling rules. Here, Bolton draws on Goffman (1961) who distinguished between actors' sense of commitment to obligations, which may be enacted with or without enthusiasm, depending upon actors' allegiance to the organisation. Within prescriptive emotion management, sincere performances may arise from professionals' identification with an organisation or professional body in some situations, while distancing themselves in other situations.

A fourth element of the prescriptive emotion management is *identity*. For professionals, identity is both associated with professional identity and self-identity. Identity, according to Bolton (2005, p. 126), is intertwined with the image of a particular profession; thus, emotional effort will be put into conforming to feeling rules to live up to that image, while retaining 'discretion and autonomy in the interpretation of professional feeling rules'.

Fifth, Bolton (2005) discusses the *consequences of emotion management* for some professionals in terms of threats or reinforcements to professional identity, as well as contradictions or conflicts that might arise from the dual demands of both professional and organisational feeling rules.

These five dimensions of prescriptive emotion work may be brought together in work: for example, 'associated motivations for feeling rules' bring together the four related elements of 'feeling rules', 'performance', 'identity', and 'consequences' which help to explain why professionals enact their emotion management in a distinct way. It is also important to recognise that prescriptive emotion management is just one of the 4Ps, and that it is possible that some situations may require professionals to 'slip' into other parts of the typology. As already discussed, Lewis (2005) observed that nurses adhered to professional or prescriptive feeling rules when dealing with clinicians; yet at the same time they felt that personal emotion work ('philanthropic') was part of their identity as carers.

Bolton's emotion management typology can be usefully applied to PR in that it helps to analyse in detail the prescriptive emotion work undertaken by professionals. However, as I have argued, as one of the new, entrepreneurial professions (Muzio et al., 2008), PR does not have a set of professional norms: core values or a code of ethics that are strongly adhered to by practitioners (who may or may not be members of professional associations). Furthermore, those working in PR agencies may more naturally align with market demands than the demands of professional associations. Therefore, I would concur with Bourne (2017) that PR's professional norms are shaped by the expectations of client organisations. Another weakness in the typology is that it does not explicitly bring gender into the analysis. Gender was of key concern for Hochschild in the performance of emotional labour, and is a key focus in this volume given the structural concerns pertaining to women in the PR profession. The statistical over-representation of women in PR firms in the United Kingdom and the phenomenon of gender segregation in the PR industry warrant closer examination. Gender and emotional labour are given specific attention in Chapter 4.

Emotional labour and PR

One of the earliest references to emotional labour, relating to PR as an occupation, can be traced back to Donato (1990, p. 139) who asserted:

> Like flight attendants, an occupation Hochschild studied, public relations specialists engage in emotional labor by managing emotions and by being 'nice' to others. It is exactly these tasks that are important in public relations. To the extent that public relations work increasingly involves emotional labor, employers prefer women.

Although Donato provided a footnote explaining that she did not have the evidence to prove that 'public relations work increasingly involves emotional labor', it would seem that her claim was based on the increasing number of women entering the profession in the United States during the 1980s and an earlier study conducted by Ghiloni (1984) in the public affairs department of a Fortune 500 company. Donato linked the rise in women entering the PR profession to several factors including: affirmative action policies designed to attract female workers and make employers look good; female-intensive industries including professional services firms; women as a 'better-buy' (i.e. women occupied lower-status 'PR technician' roles that attracted lower pay);

and finally gender ideology which 'viewed emotional work as women's work' (p. 139). Donato's emotional labour thesis might have offered a promising line of enquiry for future researchers, but it is important to note that she approached PR from the perspective of an industrial sociologist, not a PR scholar whose main focus was on 'improving practice'. Indeed, as I go on to discuss in Chapter 4, while US PR scholars (e.g. Toth, 2001; Aldoory and Toth, 2002) acknowledge Donato's factors for understanding the numerical feminisation of PR, they do not attend to the concept of emotional labour and its association with 'women's work'. That emotional labour was over-looked by those PR researchers and educators who were interested in 'im-proving practice' may be explained by the fact that they were engaged in the PR professional project: *their* interests, supported by the professional bodies, were to emphasise the acquisition of technical knowledge over personality and interpersonal skills (van Ruler, 2005). This is in contrast, for example, to the nursing literature, where emotional labour is recognised as an important skill that requires understanding through education: it is not simply regarded as part of the nursing professional's role because the emotion work is mainly carried out by women (Smith and Gray, 2000).

Within the PR field, studies that draw on emotional labour theory in-clude Bridgen (2011) who interviewed UK practitioners about their use of social media, and Elmer (2012) in an ethnographic study of UK PRPs' con-structions of PR labour. Bridgen's findings are examined in the discussion of digital emotional labour (Chapter 4), while Elmer's findings are pertinent to discussions of the PR professionalisation project, the client relationship, and the centrality of practitioners' 'personal qualities', including embodied performances in enacting the PR role (Elmer, 2012, p. 288), as discussed in Chapters 6 and 7.

Conclusion

Hochschild's (1983) emotional labour theory has generated a large number of studies of emotional labour in service industries. However, recent stud-ies have challenged the notion that service workers are mere instruments of labour who become self-estranged; rather, they are 'multi-skilled actors' (Bolton and Boyd, 2003) who are able to present different selves to different audiences during their different everyday interactions. Importantly, Bolton's '4Ps' typology of workplace emotion locates prescriptive emotion manage-ment, enacted by professionals, on a continuum that also recognises differ-ent motivations for adhering to feeling rules. Professionals are motivated to adhere to feeling rules for reasons of status as well as material gain. Profes-sionals, it is argued, enjoy more autonomy in their work, in contrast to set-tings in which front-line workers are kept under strict surveillance by their supervisors. However, the problem of accepting Bolton's preference for the term 'emotion management' and the 4Ps typology is that there is no apparent problem of emotional labour outside the commercial domain of front-line workers who are motivated by pecuniary reward. So while agreeing with Bolton that the complete 'transmutation of feeling' from private emotion to managed commodity may not be immediately recognisable in the labour process for PRPs, the emotional demands that professionals face in the pursuit of legitimacy with client organisations, professional status, and recognition are potential sources of conflict and emotional dissonance and therefore worthy of scrutiny, particularly in relation to the demands of 'always on' digital capitalism (Turkle, 2008; Wajcman, 2015).

Furthermore, Hochschild's concern with female workers as the most suitable candidates for emotion work is not made explicit in Bolton's discussion of the 4Ps typology. Given the female majority in PR in some European countries, including the United Kingdom and Germany, as well as in Australia, the United States, and in some Asian countries, it is important that gender is brought into a framework for the analysis of the day-to-day emotion work of PRPs.

Within this volume, I refer to 'emotional labour' primarily, although not exclusively, as an *ideological* construct and 'emotion management' when referring to what practitioners *do* through their everyday interactions, including the strategies that they deploy in managing their own feelings and the feelings of others. Other terms used in this book such as 'relational work' and 'emotion work' may also be used synonymously with 'emotion management'. This is not to undervalue the power of Hochschild's emotional labour thesis, but, like Bolton (2005), to question the agency of PRPs in their ability to exercise control in their professional relationships within different contexts.

References

Aldoory, L. and Toth, E. (2002) Gender discrepancies in a gendered profession: A developing theory for public relations. *Journal of Public Relations Research*, 14 (2), pp. 103–126.

Anleu, S. R. and Mack, K. (2005) Magistrates' everyday work and emotional labour. *Journal of Law and Society*, 32 (4), pp. 590–614.

Bellas, M. (1999) Emotional labor in academia: The case of professors. *The ANNALS of the American Academy of Political and Social Science*, 1, pp. 561–96.

Bolton, S. C. (2005) *Emotion Management in the Workplace*. Houndsmill, Hampshire, Palgrave Macmillan.

Bolton, S. C. (2009) Getting to the heart of the emotional labour process: A reply to Brook. *Work, Employment and Society*, 23 (3), pp. 549–560.

Bolton, S. C. and Boyd, C. (2003) Trolley dolly or skilled emotion manager? Moving on from Hochschild's Managed Heart. *Work, Employment and Society*, 17 (2) pp. 289–308.

Bolton, S. C. and Muzio, D. (2008) The paradoxical processes of feminization in the professions: The case of established aspiring and semi-professions. *Work, Employment and Society*, 22 (2), pp. 281–299.

Bottomore, T. B. and Rubel, M. eds. (1963) *Karl Marx: Selected writings in sociology and social philosophy*. London, Penguin.

Bourne, C. (2017) *Trust, Power and Public Relations in Financial Markets*. Abingdon, Oxon, Routledge.

Bridgen, L. (2011), Emotional labour and the pursuit of the personal brand: Public relations practitioners' use of social media, *Journal of Media Practice*, 12 (1), pp. 61–76.

Brook, P. (2009) In critical defence of 'emotional labour': Refuting Bolton's critique of Hochschild's concept. *Work, Employment and Society*, 23 (3), pp. 531–548.

Brooks, A. and Devasahayam, T. W. (2010) *Gender, Emotions and Labour Markets: Asian and Western perspectives*. London, Routledge.

Brotheridge, C. M. and Grandey, A. A. (2002) Emotional labor and burnout: Comparing two perspectives of 'people work'. *Journal of Vocational Behavior*, 60, pp. 17–39.

Burkitt, I. (2014) *Emotions and Social Relations*. London, Sage.

Cahill, S. E. (1999) Emotional capital and professional socialization: The case of mortuary science students (and me). *Social Psychology Quarterly*, 62, pp. 101–116.

Calhoun, C., Gerteis, J., Moody, J., and Pfaff, S. (2007) *Classical Sociological Theory*, 2nd ed. Wiley-Blackwell.

Collinson, D. L. (1992) *Managing the Shopfloor: Subjectivity, masculinity and workplace culture*. Berlin, Walter de Gruyter.

Deal, T. and Kennedy, A. (1999) *The New Corporate Cultures*. New York, Orion Business.

D'Cruz, P. and Noronha, E. (2008) Doing emotional labour: The experiences of Indian call centre agents. *Global Business Review*, 9 (1), pp. 131–147.

Deuze, M. (2012) *Media Life*. Cambridge, Polity Press.

Dewey, J. (1922) *Human Nature and Conduct: An introduction to social psychology*. New York, Holt.

Donato, K. M. (1990) Keepers of the corporate image: Women in public relations. In B. F. Reskin and P. A. Roos, eds. *Job Queues, Gender Queues: Explaining women's inroads into male occupations*. Philadelphia, Temple University Press, pp. 129–144.

Duffy, E. (2016) The romance of work: Gender and aspirational labour in the digital culture industries. *International Journal of Cultural Studies*, 19 (4), pp. 441–457.

Edwards, L. (2015) *Power, Diversity and Public Relations*. Oxon, Routledge.

Elias, A. S., Gill, R., and Scharff (2017) Aesthetic labour: Beauty politics in neoliberalism. In: A. S. Elias, R. Gill, and C. Scharff, eds. *Aesthetic Labour: Rethinking Beauty Politics in Neoliberalism*. London, Palgrave Macmillan, pp. 3–50.

Elmer, P. (2012) *The Social Construction of Public Relations Labour*. [Ph.D. thesis]. University of Essex.

Frenette, A. (2013) Making the intern economy: Role and career challenges of the music industry intern. *Work and Occupations*, 40 (4), pp. 364–397.

Gallicano, T. D., Curtin, P., and Matthews, Kelli (2012) I love what I do, but... a relationship management survey of millennial generation public relations agency employees. *Journal of Public Relations Research*, 24 (3): 222–242.

du Gay, P. (1996) *Consumption and Identity at Work*. London, Thousand Oaks, CA, and New Delhi, Sage.

Gerth, H. and Mills, C. W. (1964) *Character and Social Structure: The psychology of social institutions*. New York, Harcourt Brace and World.

Ghiloni, B. W. (1984) Women, power and the corporation: Evidence from the Velvet Ghetto. In G. W. Domhoff and T. Dye, eds. *Power and Elites*. Newbury Park, CA, Sage, p. 38.

Goffman, E. (1959) *The Presentation of Self in Everyday Life.* London, Penguin Books.

Goffman, E. (1961) *Asylums.* London, Penguin Books.

Greco, M. and Stenner, P. (2008) Introduction: Emotion and social science. In M. Greco and P. Stenner, eds. *Emotions: A social science reader.* Oxford, Routledge, pp. 1–21.

Guerrier, Y. and Adib, A. (2003) Work at leisure and leisure at work: A study of the emotional labour of tour reps. *Human Relations,* 56 (11), pp. 1399–1417.

Gyimóthy, S. and Rygaard Jonas, L. (2010) Branding on the shop floor. *Culture Unbound: Journal of Current Cultural Research,* 2, pp. 329–345.

Hall, S. and Waddington, S. (2017) *Exploring the Mental Wellbeing of the Public Relations Profession.* London, PRCA.

Hesmondhalgh, D. and Baker. S. (2011) 'A very complicated version of freedom': Conditions and experiences of creative labour in three cultural industries. *Poetics: Journal of Empirical Research on Culture, the Media and the Arts,* 38 (1), pp. 4–20.

Hickman, A. (2018) PR in the grips of 'overtime epidemic' – Professionals work 24 extra days unpaid per year, study finds. *PR Week,* 17 November. Available from: https://www.prweek.com/article/1498817/pr-grips-overtime-epidemic-professionals-work-24-extra-days-unpaid-year-study-finds. Accessed 18 November 2018.

Hirst, A. and Schwabenland, C. (2018) Doing gender in the 'new office'. *Gender, Work and Organization,* 25 (2), pp. 159–176.

Hochschild, A. R. (1983) *The Managed Heart: Commercialization of human feeling.* Berkeley, University of California Press.

Hochschild, A. R. (2003) *The Managed Heart: Commercialization of human feeling,* 2nd ed. Berkeley, University of California Press.

Hochschild, A. R. (2008) Emotion work, feeling rules, and social structure. In M. Greco and P. Stenner, eds. *Emotions: A social science reader.* Abingdon, Oxon, and New York, Routledge, pp. 121–126.

Hughes, J. (2003) Intelligent hearts: Emotional intelligence, emotional labour and informalization, Working paper 43, Centre for Labour Market Studies, Leicester, University of Leicester.

van Iterson, A., Mastenbroek, W., and Soeters, J. (2001) Civilizing and informalizing: Organizations in an Eliasian context. *Organization,* 8 (3) pp. 497–514.

Johansson, C. (2009) On Goffman. In Ø. Ihlen, B. van Ruler, and M. Fredriksson, eds. *Public Relations and Social Theory: Key figures and concepts.* New York and London, Routledge, pp. 119–140.

Kaiser, S., Müller-Seitz, G., and Cruesen, U. (2008) Passion wanted! Socialisation of positive emotions in consulting firms. *International of Work Organisation and Emotion,* 2, (3), pp. 305–320.

Kleinman, S. (2002) Emotions, fieldwork and professional lives. In T. May, ed. *Qualitative Research in Action.* London, Thousand Oaks, CA, and New Delhi, Sage, pp. 375–394.

Korczynski, M. (2003). Communities of coping: Collective emotional labour in service work. *Organization,* 10 (1), pp. 55–79.

Lefebvre, H. (1991) *The Production of Space.* Oxford, Blackwell.

Leidner, R. (1993) *Fast Food, Fast Talk: Service work and the routinization of everyday life.* Berkeley, University of California Press.

Lewis, P. (2005) Suppression or expression: An exploration of emotion management in a special care baby unit. *Work, Employment and Society,* 19 (3), pp. 565–581.

Lewis, P. (2008) Emotion work and emotion space: Using a spatial perspective to explore the challenging of masculine emotion management practices. *British Journal of Management*, 19, pp. S130–S140.

Lively, K. (2006) Emotions in the workplace. In J. H. Turner and J. E. Stets, eds. *The Handbook of the Sociology of Emotions*. New York, Springer Science and Business Media, pp. 569–590.

Lutz, C. A. (2007) Emotion, thought and estrangement: Emotion as a cultural category. In H. Wulff, ed. *The Emotions: A cultural reader*. Oxford and New York, Berg, pp. 19–30.

Mann, S. (2004) People work: Emotion management stress and coping. *British Journal of Guidance and Counselling*, 32 (2), pp. 205–22.

Mastracci, S. H., Newman, M. A., and Guy, M. E. (2006) Appraising emotion work: Determining whether emotional labor is valued in government jobs. *American Review of Public Administration*, 36 (2), 123–138.

Mead, G. H. (1934) *Mind, Self, and Society*. Chicago, IL, University of Chicago Press.

Mészáros, I. [1970] (1986) *Marx's Theory of Alienation*, 4th ed. London, Merlin Press.

Mills, C. W. (1956) *White Collar*. New York, Oxford, Galaxy.

Muzio, D., Ackroyd, S., and Chanlat, J.-F. (2008) Introduction: Lawyers, doctors and business consultants. In D. Muzio, S. Ackroyd, and J.-F. Chanlat, eds. *Redirections in the Study of Expert Labour*. Basingstoke, Palgrave Macmillan, pp. 1–30.

Ogbonna, E. and Harris, L. C. (2004) Work intensification and emotional labour among UK university lecturers: An exploratory study. *Organization Studies*, 25 (7), pp. 1185–1203.

Pettigrew, A. M. (1979) On studying organizational cultures. *Administrative Science Quarterly*, 24, pp. 570–81.

Pierce, J. (1995) *Gender Trials. Emotional lives in contemporary law firms*. Berkeley, University of California Press.

Porter Novelli (2008) Intelligent dialogue: Millennials [White paper]. Retrieved from http://www.porternovelli.com/intelligence/millennials. Accessed 28 October 2018.

Poynter, G. (2002) Emotions in the labour process. *European Journal of Psychotherapy, Counselling and Health*, 5 (3), pp. 247–262.

Public Relations and Communications Association (2018) *PRCA Census 2018*. London, PRCA.

Reskin, B. and Padavic, I. (1994) *Women and Men at Work*. Thousand Oaks, CA, Pine Forge Press.

Rodino-Colocino, M. and Beberick, S. N. (2015) 'You kind of have to bite the bullet and do bitch work': How internships teach students to unthink exploitation in public relations. *Triple-C*, 13 (2), pp. 486–500.

Roy, D. (1973) Banana time: Job satisfaction and informal interaction. In G. Salaman and K. Thompson, eds. *People and Organizations*. London, Longman, pp. 205–222.

van Ruler, B. (2005) Commentary: Professionals are from Venus, scholars are from Mars. *Public Relations Review*, 31 (2), pp. 159–173.

Schweingruber, D. and Berns, N. (2005) Shaping the selves of young salespeople through emotion management. *Journal of Contemporary Ethnography*, 34 (6) pp. 679–706.

Shuler, S. and Davenport Sypher, B. (2000) Seeking emotional labor: When managing the heart enhances the work experience. *Management Communication Quarterly*, 14 (1), pp. 50–89.

Smith, A. C. and Kleinman, S. (1989) Managing emotions in medical school: Students' contacts with the living and the dead. *Social Psychology Quarterly*, 52, pp. 56–69.

Smith, P., and Gray, B. (2000) *The Emotional Labour of Nursing: How students and qualified nurses learn to care*. London, South Bank University.

Toth, E. (2001) How feminist theory advanced the practice of public relations. In R. L. Heath, ed. *Handbook of Public Relations*. Thousand Oaks, CA, London, and New Delhi, Sage, pp. 237–246.

Tse, H. L. T., Chan, L. T. J., Liu, H. Y, and Pierson-Smith, A. (2016) Creative industries in flux – A critical investigation into the challenges, agency and potential of cultural and creative workers in Hong Kong. Presented at British Sociological Association's Work, Employment and Society (WES) Conference, University of Leeds, 6–8 September 2016.

Turkle, S. (2008) Always on/always on you: The tethered self. In J. E. Katz, ed. *Handbook of Mobile Communication Studies*. Boston, MA, MIT University Press, pp. 121–138.

Turner, J. H. and Stets, J. E. (2005) *The Sociology of Emotions*. New York, Cambridge University Press.

Wahl-Jorgensen, K. (2018) *Emotions, Media and Politics*. Cambridge, Polity.

Wajcman, J. (2015) *Pressed for Time: The acceleration of life in digital capitalism*. Chicago, IL, and London, The University of Chicago Press.

Weyher, L. F. (2012) Re-reading sociology via the emotions: Karl Marx's theory of human nature and estrangement. *Sociological Perspectives*, 55 (2), pp. 341–363.

Witz, A., Warhurst, C., and Nixon, S. (2003) The labour of aesthetics and the aesthetics of organization. *Organization*, 10 (1), pp. 33–54.

Wouters, C. (1989) The sociology of emotions and flight attendants: Hochschild's managed heart. *Theory, Culture and Society*, 6 (1) pp. 447–450.

Wulff, H. (2007) *The Emotions: A cultural reader*. Oxford, New York, Berg.

Yeomans, L. (2010) Soft sell? Gendered experience of emotional labour in UK public relations firms, *PRism* [Online], 7 (4). Available from: http://www.prismjournal. org. Accessed 2 October 2018.

Yeomans, L. (2016) Imagining the lives of others: Empathy in public relations. *Public Relations Inquiry*, 5 (1), pp. 71–92.

Yun, H.-A. (2010) Service workers: Governmentality and emotion management. *Culture Unbound: Journal of Current Cultural Research*, 2, pp. 311–327.

3 Promotional culture and the 'market' for emotional labour in public relations

Introduction

The purpose of this chapter is to examine the broader context within which public relations (PR) is embedded. It begins by examining the political, economic, social, and technological conditions that have created the demand for PR as a professional service in the United Kingdom during the past 30 years. It also examines, using Hochschild's concept of a 'market' for emotional labour, the key actors that are involved in this market where PR is provided as a commercial business service: these are the owners of PR firms (agencies/consultancies), PR executives, their clients and actors within the media sphere: primarily journalists and, increasingly, online 'influencers'. The concept of promotional culture, first proposed by Wernick (1991), is explored, as this is particularly relevant to discussing the significance of PR work and its influence on society and culture. This chapter argues that within an era of (digital) promotional culture that seeks to commodify services, products, and ideas, as well as those people engaged in the promotional process, public relations practitioners (PRPs) are immersed in a continuous process of emotional labour to satisfy clients and other stakeholders in generating 'self-interested' (Wernick, 1991) cultural discourses. Further, the emotion work performed in PRP's client relationships may itself represent a key form of expertise or professional knowledge alongside other forms of knowledge.

The growth of the PR industry and the PR agency/consultancy sector

The 'public relations industry' is a term often used to refer to the total number of professionals engaged in PR work in public, private, and third sector (i.e. voluntary) organisations, as well as in PR firms that provide PR expertise to clients. The UK PR industry, according to one industry source, is estimated to contribute £13.8 billion to the UK economy and employs 86,000 practitioners in total (PRCA, 2018a). Fifty-two per cent or 44,720[1] are employed in agencies or consultancy firms (PRCA, 2018a). While estimates of employees working in the PR field in the United Kingdom seem to vary, and may be overstated, industry reports unequivocally point to the continued global growth of PR work (The Holmes Report, 2017a).

PR is widely documented as an early twentieth-century persuasive phenomenon that came to prominence in the United States alongside the growth of mass market consumer goods and the rising influence of the mass media on public opinion and buying habits (Cutlip, 1995; Ewen, 1996). In the United Kingdom, however, PR emerged from the public sector. Moloney (2006) asserts that PR was instrumental in building the modern state through propaganda and mass persuasion techniques in the early twentieth century. He cites L'Etang's history of PR in Britain, noting that both the Institute of Public Administration (founded in 1922) and the local government trade union The National Association of Local Government Officers saw the 'link between PR, service provision and public opinion' in their drive to publicise the state provision of social welfare as well as raise their own status (Moloney, 2006, p. 59).

L'Etang (2004) cites Basil Clarke, a former *Daily Mail* journalist and government director of information, as one of the first PR consultants in the United Kingdom. He founded his own consultancy in 1926 and went on to draft the Institute of Public Relations' (IPR) first code of practice. The main developments in PR as a service industry, however, took place during the 1950s as former journalists began their own consultancies based on editorial services and media liaison, despite a broader definition of communications preferred by the IPR (L'Etang, 2004). In 1969 the Public Relations Consultants Association (PRCA) was set up to maintain professional standards in consultancies and cater for their specific interests. The Chartered Institute of Public Relations (CIPR) and the PRCA (which changed its name to Public Relations and Communications Association in 2016) are the two main membership organisations in the United Kingdom today.

The next phase of development in PR, especially in consultancy practice, was 'driven by commercial interests' (Edwards, 2009, p. 13). The growth in PR agency/consultancy work gained particular momentum in the 1980s and 1990s when expansion rates 'for medium and large British consultancies typically reached 20–40 per cent per annum' (Miller and Dinan, 2000, p. 5). The estimated fee income for the UK PR industry as a whole in 1997 was 3.1 billion US dollars (Miller and Dinan, 2000, p. 9 citing the WPP Group plc.'s estimate (1998) given in US dollars).

In 2005, the CIPR commissioned report *48,000 Professionals; £6.5 Billion Turnover: The Economic Significance of Public Relations* predicted the total UK growth over the next five years in terms of the number of employees (32% growth for consultancies), the levels of spending on PR (2.6%), and the level of turnover in the consultancy sector at 11.6% (CEBR/CIPR, 2005, pp. 23–26). The global financial crisis (GFC) in 2008, followed by a downturn in the economy, led to reports of significant cutbacks in spending on PR in 2009 (Rogers, 2009). Nevertheless, among the 1,940 CIPR members surveyed in 2010, over 60% of those working in PR agencies (22% of respondents) reported that their organisation was likely to recruit within the next 12 months. Members working for PR agencies were reported to be the least worried about being made redundant, compared with their in-house counterparts, many of whom worked in the public sector and were vulnerable to redundancy following the election of a coalition government in May 2010 (CIPR, 2010).

Worldwide growth forecasts among PR consultancy leaders were also reported to be optimistic (ICCO, 2011). The reasons for optimism may be attributed to the industry's leaders' need to generate feelings of confidence, since, according to Stephen Waddington (2015), writing as partner and chief engagement officer of Ketchum, 'Public relations is an anxious, insecure profession'. However, optimism may have also been based on the perceived expansion opportunities into new global markets as well as the rise in digital communications – an area of expertise that largely fell to PR consultancies to advise their clients on. The perceived growth in digital communications in 2006 was described as 'enormous' by the leading PR industry analyst Paul Holmes (Holmes, 2007, p. 22); ten years later, ICCO reported further optimism in a worldwide survey of practitioners, based on predicted growth in digital communications and corporate reputation management (ICCO, 2017). The highest levels of optimism related to the emerging markets of Asia Pacific and Latin America. Thus, while significant changes were taking place in the PR industry, its growth potential, largely fuelled by digital innovations as well as the demand for reputation management advice in emerging markets, appeared to continue unabated.

This chapter is specifically concerned with businesses that provide PR services to organisations, also known as PR *firms, consultancies,* or *agencies.* Therefore, in examining the emotional labour of PRPs, I focus on people who work for these firms, as opposed to PRPs employed by organisations' in-house departments. Verčič (2012) posits that PR *firms* are concerned with providing additional help, or 'arms and legs', supplementing in-house resources, while *agencies* are mainly focused on media relations; and *consultancies* sell expertise. However, in their article discussing collaboration and conflict between agencies and their client organisations in Europe, Verčič et al. (2018) choose the term 'agencies' as a generic descriptor for organisations that provide PR services. In this book I also adopt the term 'agencies' when referring to PR firms generically.

Within the United Kingdom, the vast majority of the top 150 UK PR firms (ranked by fee income) are based in London. Large, often global, publicly traded companies such as Omnicom and WPP are based in London and offer a complete range of communications services, including advertising. Regionally based PR agencies are either small, independent businesses, or regional outposts of London-based firms (McKinley, 2017).

How and why the PR profession has emerged, and has grown so rapidly, I begin with a broad analysis of the context of PR work. While neoliberalism (Harvey, 2005; Eagleton-Pierce, 2016; Risager, 2016) provides the context for discussion on changes in political and economic structures in the United Kingdom, together with the rise of promotional culture (Wernick, 1991; Moor, 2008; Davis, 2013), digital capitalism (Schiller, 2014) has re-configured and accelerated promotional culture, in which PR is structurally enmeshed in perpetuating, together with advertising and other promotional activities.

Moving on from a broad analysis to the individual worker, I then examine what PRPs do at the everyday level and how their work is increasingly impacted by and integrated with rapidly changing information and communications technologies. The key actors in the 'market for emotional labour' (Hochschild, 1983) in PR work are the PR agencies and executives (the *suppliers* of emotional labour), while clients (including government and corporations) and those operating within the media sphere – journalists and online influencers – may be regarded as creating the *demand* for emotional labour. 'PR expertise' (Pieczka, 2002, 2006a) is discussed within the context of the services provided to both clients and the media. Here I argue that this expertise is little understood and that both the concepts of emotion management and emotional labour may help to deconstruct the notion of PR expertise further by focusing on the social transactions that constitute emotional labour (Hochschild, 1983).

Neoliberalism, promotional culture, and the PR industry

Neoliberalism

An understanding of the broader context of contemporary labour and particularly service-orientated work is provided by neoliberalism, both as a set of interrelated concepts and as a process. In this volume, the term 'neoliberalism' refers to the processes of free market capitalism as well as individualisation (Beck and Beck-Gernsheim, 2002) that have impacted society and culture since the 1980s.

According to Harvey (2005, p. 2), in his widely cited book (Risager, 2016), neoliberalism as a 'doctrine' became a 'central guiding principle of economic thought and management' in the United States, the United Kingdom, and post-communist China between 1978 and 1980 and thereafter (Harvey, 2005, p. 2). Neoliberalism is characterised by an institutional framework in which 'strong private property rights, free markets, and free trade' are advocated. Within this framework, human well-being is considered best served by 'liberating individual entrepreneurial freedoms and skills' (Harvey, 2005, p. 2). As I demonstrate later in this chapter, the PR agency sector has benefited considerably from these entrepreneurial freedoms.

Since the 1970s, the widespread 'turn' towards neoliberal political-economic practices in many countries and in international institutions, including the European Union, has been marked by deregulation, privatisation, and withdrawal of the state from many areas of public services, including in the United Kingdom. As a result of this widespread adoption of neoliberal theory, neoliberalism has become 'hegemonic as a mode of discourse' in that it has become taken-for-granted in our way of understanding the world (Harvey, 2005, p. 3). Some of the key concepts associated with neoliberalism worth mentioning here are: freedom, choice, entrepreneurship, and flexibility (Eagleton-Pierce, 2016). Indeed, as Eagleton-Pierce (2016) demonstrates, the lexicon of neoliberalism is so extensive and pervasive that it becomes increasingly difficult to imagine alternative ways of thinking about everyday life, particularly when considering PR as a practice that has developed in tandem with neoliberalism.

Within the United Kingdom, the election of a coalition government in the United Kingdom in 2010 provided renewed vigour to the neoliberal 'project' that began under the years of Margaret Thatcher's premiership (1979–1990) and continued under subsequent political regimes, including New Labour (1997–2010) (Hall, 2003). Indeed, the continued success of the neoliberal project, as Cronin (2018, p. 108) argues, is due to neoliberalism being 'a shifting set of practices [...] best framed as a process'. Writing specifically about PR, Cronin (2018) argues that the process of *neoliberalisation* rearticulates relationships, including organisations' relationships with the public (e.g. as consumer-citizens). In turn, younger generations' relationships to employment are subject to processes of 'individualisation' (Beck and Beck-Gersheim, 2002, p. 202), a term used to denote the 'transformation of social institutions and the relationship of the individual to society'. These processes have, for example, resulted in a mental shift towards 'internalised flexibility' among young people 'across boundaries of class, gender and ethnicity', especially in relation to employment opportunities (Bradley and Devadason, 2008, p. 133).

Neoliberal capitalism has spawned many critiques of its logics and effects, including its relationship to human subjectivities and emotions such as a sense of well-being and happiness. The economist Marc Pilkington (2015) draws attention to how emotions underpinned the 'structural crisis of neoliberalism', following the GFC of 2008, in ways that show how macro-social events link to the micro-social. As the gulf widened, in countries such as the United States, between cooperation and competition, he argues that there were damaging consequences to the individual psyche. Pilkington (2015, p. 269) cites Facebook as 'a flagship of the neoliberal system wherein everyone is obsessed with his branding mission in a process of commodification of the social substrate. The number of friends displayed is a sign of competition rather than individual cooperation'. Facebook, as a social media platform, is arguably the symbol of a contemporary promotional culture, with which the PR industry is deeply enmeshed in perpetuating among the panoply of social media activities designed to engage the consumer.

Promotional culture and the PR industry

The PR industry is significantly larger and established in the United States and the United Kingdom than in other countries (Miller and Dinan, 2000; Holmes, 2007). While recent expansion of the industry is taking place in regions such as Asia Pacific and Latin America, this is facilitated through global outposts of largely US-based PR firms. The growth of the PR industry is integral to the rise in 'promotional culture', a term used by Wernick (1991) to describe a postmodern cultural landscape that is marked by symbolic communications through advertising and other promotional forms.

The promotional industries' persuasive intent and their pervasiveness in culture underpin Wernick's (1991, p. vii) description of promotion as a 'rhetorical form diffused throughout our culture' that shapes 'not only that culture's symbolic and ideological contents, but also its ethos, texture and constitution as a whole'. Moor (2008) notes that promotional culture is associated with neoliberal notions of personalisation, individual consumer choice, and the 'marketisation of everything' – from fast-moving consumer goods through to politics, education, and health services.

Moloney's (2006, p. x) claim that PR 'pours a Niagara of persuasive attitudes, words, visuals and events over liberal democracies such as the UK' was particularly resonant in 2012, the year of the London-based Olympic Games and HM The Queen's Diamond Jubilee. The Jubilee event alone 'resulted in media coverage reaching over one billion people' (UK Parliament, 2014, p. 77). Both events were seen by the UK government as part of a 'soft power' influence strategy to promote national values at home and change perceptions of Britain abroad, constituting major efforts to strengthen relationships and reputation (UK Parliament, 2011, 2014).

While Wernick identified advertising as the most visible rhetorical influence on a society's cultural values, his concerns were linked to a wider phenomenon: the 'pan-promotionalism of contemporary communications' (Wernick, 1991: vii) that characterised late capitalist culture and the 'postmodern turn'. The concept of promotional culture provided a framework for examining what Wernick described as the 'objective side of culture', in other words, promotional outputs in the form of communications. These promotional communications were, in turn, linked to the 'intensive and extensive development of the market as an organizing principle of social life' (Wernick, 1991, p. viii).

Wernick did not explicitly refer to PR promotion. However, in discussing the 'intertextuality of promotional discourse' (1991, p. 94), he described how other, non-advertising promotional processes interrelate in their symbols and messages as part of consumer promotion. He argued that the ties between advertising, commercial media, mass entertainment, and the intertext of the product promotion are 'absorbed into an even wider promotional complex, founded on the commodification, and transformation into advertising, of (produced) culture itself' (1991, p. 95).

While published at a time when the internet was only just beginning to make an impact on business communications and marketing, Wernick's critique is ever more relevant in the twenty-first century. The 'self-interested' promotional processes that he describes and the problems identified can be said to have intensified in an era of digital capitalism and social media as 'emotionally-charged networks' (Beckett and Deuze, 2016, p. 1). These networks, in turn, have been appropriated by corporations for commercial use to generate online 'conversations' with 'digital communities', including in-fluencers and consumers, as well as masquerading as ordinary users. Cronin (2018, p. 110) argues that a new 'commercial democracy' is not only en-hanced by new forms of digital media, but that it is displacing the social con-tract, or promise, between political institutions and the public. Promotional culture, in which PR is embedded, has therefore not only expanded in the twenty-first century but also become 'intensely politicised'.

I now go on to discuss the PR industry's ascent during the latter part of the twentieth century. This, in turn, explains Wernick's oversight of PR in his theorising of promotional culture. PR is a relative latecomer to the broader, so-called 'brandscape' of advertising, marketing, sponsorship, sales promotion, and built environments that are called upon to sell products, services, and ideas to consumers. The reason for relatively late entry of PR to marketing communications may be attributed to several factors. In the early part of the twenty-first century, marketing writers such as Ries and Ries (2002) and Zyman and Brott (2003) argued that advertising was losing its ability to promote brands to consumers effectively. Advertising (or ad-vertisements) had become too self-indulgent as well as expensive, better at winning awards than creating excitement about brands among their target consumers. By contrast, PR services, offered by PR firms, were relatively inexpensive for an organisation's marketing director to purchase. PR, like advertising, also generated publicity for a brand, but this worked through third-party, or editorial, endorsement by a credible news source in the form of a news story or feature article that would be read by target consumers (Bailey, 2009). Increasingly, in terms of 'effectiveness' in building awareness, brand communication campaigns were PR, rather than advertising, driven (Ries and Ries, 2002).

PR agencies have, in turn, benefited in profitability and influence by join-ing established global communications companies such as WPP, which, in 2017, listed on its website a total of 83 PR firms worldwide, including four long-established PR companies, all with head offices in New York City, and operating with offices across five or six continents: Burson-Marsteller, Ogilvy Public Relations Worldwide, Hill+Knowlton Strategies, and Cohn & Wolfe (WPP, 2017). Notable in recent years is the entry by PR firms into non-Western markets including China and countries in the Middle East and North Africa.

In their detailed analysis of the rise of the PR industry in the United Kingdom, Miller and Dinan (2000) attribute the rise in promotional cul-ture in the United States, the United Kingdom, and Japan to the politi-cal and economic factors that led to privatisation and deregulation in these countries during the 1980s. PR expertise was used to support privatisation and deregulation strategies, thus leading to the growth of the PR industry. Wernick (1991), by contrast, does not attribute the rise in promotional cul-ture to any specific political and economic events (although the Reagan-Thatcher alliance is referred to) but rather sees promotional culture as an unbridled expansion of a post-war consumer culture led by advertising, on which much early critique of promotion (for example, emanating from the Frankfurt School of Critical Theory) rests. As mentioned earlier, the least visible and yet the most 'diffusive' aspect of promotional culture, PR, is not explicitly referred to by Wernick, even though he frequently identifies its various manifestations in the forms of publicity stunts and 'newspaper columns' (Wernick, 1991, p. 117). At the turn of the millennium, Miller and Dinan (2000, p. 7) remarked that the 'obvious' political and economic importance of PR and promotional culture more widely were 'markedly under-researched'. These themes are addressed later in this chapter where I discuss more recent contributions to critical PR scholarship.

Miller and Dinan (2000, p. 12) argue that within the United Kingdom, a crucial turning point for PR growth was the 'tilt to the market in government policy' arising from the election of a Conservative government under Margaret Thatcher in 1979. PR expertise of various kinds was required: first to support policies that would privatise the national utilities; second to provide promotional support that would enable the newly privatised companies to compete in national and international markets; and third to support deregulation of city financial institutions and their associated professions such as law and accountancy.

Preparation for deregulation and spending on privatisation by the government (e.g. of national utilities such as British Telecom and British Gas) required skilled promotional strategies that were offered by specialist financial PR firms to sell share ownership both to and through the media and sections of the public and the *idea* of a 'share-owning democracy'. In turn, the newly privatised companies also required PR services to boost their brands and reputations. The deregulation of City financial institutions and the legal and accountancy professions, too, gave rise to a new, competitive business climate in the 1980s which led to mergers and acquisitions – thereby fuelling increased spending on financial PR advice.

Dewe Rogerson, among the top five financial PR firms in the United Kingdom, was reported to have been paid £23 million for the British Petroleum privatisation between 1987 and 1998 (Miller and Dinan, 2000, p. 21). Davis (2000a) observed from his in-depth study of the takeover of Granada by Forte that although PR campaigns within the corporate and financial sphere are directed at other 'corporate elites' within the business and financial pages of national newspapers, these micro-level activities add up to important social changes. He concluded that a 'significant proportion of financial activity, corporate regulation and economic policy-making evolves in a way that is likely to benefit corporate elites and ignore others – and do so out of sight of the general public' (2000a, p. 300). Bourne (2017, pp. 138–139) develops the theme of the hidden work of PR in financial markets, where PR is used to 'enforce silences in financial discourses' where the 'so-called financially illiterate' (i.e. consumer-citizens) are subdued through financial education campaigns. Neoliberal mechanisms are observable where the 'dominant discourse' (p. 138) deployed by governments, regulators, and financial advisers serves the interests of those who profit from financial products.

A further consideration as to why the PR industry has grown worldwide is to 'service mobile capital' (Miller and Dinan, 2000, p. 9) meaning that multinational corporations (MNCs) require the services of global PR firms to support the expansion of MNCs into different countries and cultures, using local knowledge and communication expertise to deal with regulators, local communities, and the media. In the developing economies of India and China, for example, PR firms from the WPP 'family' are established to service the multinational companies that have moved in. Indeed, the competitive landscape in 2017 was such that the top four global public relations brands: Edelman, Weber Shandwick, FleishmanHillard and Ketchum (all US-based) were each reported to earn well above $500 million in global fees (The Holmes Report, 2017b). Miller and Dinan conclude that 'the PR consultancy sector has an elective affinity with market ideology' (2000, p. 28). This suggests that a compatibility between the two exists, in the sense that Protestantism has an 'elective affinity' with capitalism (Swedberg, 2005, p. 83). Market ideology enables the PR agency sector to flourish because it is bound up in the production and distribution of meaning within markets and the wider culture. Thus, a *socio-cultural* reading of PR, recognised as 'a locus of transactions that produce emergent social and cultural meanings', provides an understanding of PR within promotional culture (Edwards and Hodges, 2011, p. 4).

Digital capitalism and promotional culture

Discussing the growth of 'digital capitalism', a term used to foreground information and communication technologies as marking 'dizzying structural change' in the twenty-first century, Schiller (2014, p. 5), similar to Wernick, points to advertising as the most visible and profitable manifestation of brand promotion. While the aftermath of the GFC led to a drop in advertising revenues from traditional newspaper and TV channels, by 2010, the internet was already becoming the 'second largest advertising medium after television' (Schiller, 2014, p. 128). The emergence of social networks and personal mobile devices provided further opportunities for marketing and advertising globally as e-commerce developed rapidly. Through partnerships with successful social media companies such as Facebook, marketing services companies, including WPP and Omnicom, found new ways to reach consumers searching for products online. Indeed, due to advertising's effectiveness in targeting consumers through highly personalised means, based on data obtained from their digital activity, paid-for advertising warrants significant attention in terms of its increasing sophistication in segmenting and the precise targeting of consumers (Schiller, 2014). However, the growing popularity of social networks, and Facebook in particular, provided opportunities not just for the marketing and selling of products but for the stealthy diffusion of political ideologies through paid-for online space.

In the run-up to the date on which the US President Donald Trump was elected in 2016, online users were targeted through 'fake news' stories, or misinformation on websites, apparently initiated by Trump supporters. One large-scale study found that 'Facebook played an important role in directing people to fake news websites' (Guess et al., 2018, p. 11). While the PR associations in the United Kingdom and United States distanced the PR industry from the practice of creating fake news (e.g. PRCA, 2016a; CIPR, 2017a; PRSA, 2017), the lines were becoming ever more blurred between the persuasive techniques of PR and propaganda. If online PR was now recast in terms of 'SEO' (search engine optimisation) '[…] listening to conversations on the web, creating relevant content and building relationships', according to one leading industry expert (Waddington, 2018), then strategically, this is what took place in the US presidential campaign; only 'relevant content' did not have to be factually correct. While practitioners and the PR academy condemn fake news practices as propaganda – not PR – other commentators argue that fake news and PR 'thrive on the same spectrum' (Kelly, 2017). In other words, promoting political ideas is no different from promoting and defending brand reputation for any product given that similar techniques are adopted for both 'good' as well as dubious causes and clients. Furthermore, a digital promotional culture is even more pervasive as citizens and consumers voluntarily embed themselves (and their personal data) within social networks, exposing themselves to any interest group or brand seeking to influence their political opinions and purchasing decisions.

While PR may rhetorically set itself apart from the questionable influencing practices that increasingly take place online, the Bell Pottinger case (Eliseev, 2017; Washbourne, 2017; Segal, 2018) is evidence that highly successful PR firms may partly owe their profitability to defending the reputations of indefensible clients. Furthermore, critics have long argued that 'ethical' PR is difficult to discern from unethical PR, because its success depends on influencing strategies that are generally subtle, if not hidden from public view (Davis, 2000a; Bourne, 2017). As I have already discussed, the practice of third-party endorsement in PR, in which a press release is sent to specific news media outlets to generate media publicity for a brand, is mainly hidden from newspaper and other media audiences. The success of third-party endorsement depends on a credible news source endorsing the message. While audiences have grown used to, for example, celebrities promoting their latest book or film appearance in a variety of media, the mechanisms that enable these publicity opportunities largely take place 'backstage' in PRP offices. They are rarely allowed to become 'frontstage' concerns. I now go on to discuss PR as a profession.

PR as a profession

The normative view of a profession comprises 'traits' that are stabilising mechanisms for society, an idea linked to functionalist sociology (Pieczka and L'Etang, 2001). Up to the 1960s, the traits that described a profession multiplied as different definitions of a profession were developed; however, a typical list of traits might include: foundation on a body of scientific knowledge; an ethical approach; and certification by an occupational organisation. Pieczka and L'Etang (2001) observe that such a 'trait approach' or 'knowledge model' of PR as a profession is one that has been adopted successfully in the United States. However, the situation in the United Kingdom is somewhat different. Although the IPR was established in 1948, and received Chartered status in 2005, its membership of 9,907 (CIPR, 2017b) is still comparatively low against the 86,000 (estimated) professionals (PRCA, 2018a).

The CIPR claims that it is the largest professional body for individual members outside of North America (CIPR, 2017b). Only relatively recently has the PRCA opened up membership to corporate in-house teams and individuals; previously the PRCA was an association of PR agencies. However, from existing figures, it is reasonable to argue that a large number of individual practitioners as well as PR firms are not members of the two professional organisations in the United Kingdom.

In 2006 Pieczka and L'Etang argued that, 'there is no abstract knowledge claimed for the purposes of legitimation or definition of the expertise offered to employers or clients' (Pieczka and L'Etang, 2006, p. 277). While this argument may now seem outdated given the availability of professional certificates and diplomas over a 20-year period, and the establishment of PR degrees[2] over a 30-year period, those professionals equipped with 'abstract knowledge' of PR continue to make up a minority[3] of practitioners (CIPR, 2017c). Less than 46% of those surveyed by the CIPR in 2016 had a relevant professional qualification (e.g. a CIPR certificate or diploma), and only 29.5% had an undergraduate or masters degree in PR or communication.[4] Thus, it is still possible to practise PR with no formal qualifications or membership of the CIPR or the PRCA, providing that practitioners have the appropriate personal skills, qualities, and cultural capital that are suited to interacting with clients (Pieczka and L'Etang, 2006; Edwards, 2008). An alternative argument to professionalisation, however, is one that does not rest on qualifications and professional memberships, but those of jurisdiction and legitimacy.

Drawing on the work of Abbott (1988), Pieczka (2002) examined jurisdiction in PR. Jurisdiction refers to expertise or the 'tasks which the profession has successfully claimed for itself' (p. 301). Pieczka (2002, p. 321) concludes, from a detailed ethnographic study of how consultancy work is routinely carried out, that expertise in PR 'is seen as constituted and transmitted through practice'. Here, the 'professional project' (Larson, 1977) is viewed as an *ideological process* that examines how 'professions win social approval to define and control their work and their relationships with other actors such as clients' (Macdonald, 1995, p. 5, cited in Pieczka and L'Etang, 2001, p. 225). Professions thus position themselves as centres of power, authority, and autonomy that make claims to exclusive expertise by drawing boundaries around themselves (Fournier, 1999).

In an information and communications milieu where expertise in digital communications is highly valued, the PR industry vies with other disciplines in claiming jurisdiction over digital communications expertise. So far, this is a battle that the PR profession is winning when examining the evidence of agency business growth; however, recent studies across Europe reveal increasing shortfalls in knowledge and expertise among practitioners such as the ability to make sense of big data and understand the use of algorithms (Zerfass et al., 2016, 2017). While the majority of practitioners surveyed across Europe agreed that hypermodernity, or 'a growing consumer mentality in all areas of society', was clearly observable in their own country, and saw their organisation as incorporating the features of the hypermodern organisation, only a third followed the debate about social robots and algorithms, and few practitioners planned to use them (Zerfass et al., 2017). The concept of PR expertise is revisited later in this chapter in the discussion of the client–consultancy relationship.

Legitimacy and legitimation 'goes to the core of what the public relations discipline is about: acquiring and preserving [emotional] support from the general public' (Waeraas, 2009, p. 301). Drawing on the legitimacy theories of Max Weber, Waeraas (2009, p. 312) argues that 'charismatic legitimation' is particularly relevant to PR. Charismatic legitimacy is defined by Weber as 'resting on devotion to the exceptional sanctity, heroism, or exemplary character of an individual person' (Weber, 1922/1968, p. 215). Waeraas argues that organisations legitimise their existence by displaying attractive characteristics – e.g. vision, articulacy, and sensitivity to environments and stakeholders, which PR helps them to do. Further, PR seeks approval and support from organisational stakeholders through socially constructed 'myths' or beliefs (what the organisation becomes known for), and the 'strategic influencing of those beliefs' (p. 318).

The ideas of legitimacy and legitimation can be applied to the PR industry and its leaders. To establish beliefs in their right to exist, PR agencies engage in legitimation processes through cultivating personal relationships with client organisations, journalists, and other stakeholders. These processes are supported when an agency is led by people who are perceived as 'charismatic'. As I argue in Chapter 5, legitimation involves a continuous process of reinforcing PR agencies' license to operate through influencing clients' beliefs in PR's expertise, thereby earning their emotional support and trust. The personal, emotional resources of agency leaders and their employees reinforce the legitimation process.

Weber's concepts of legitimacy and legitimation help to explain the purpose of PR as well as PR's professional relationships. However, theorists both within the PR field (e.g. Bourne and Edwards, 2012) and outside it (e.g. Fournier, 1999) have drawn on Foucault's (1978) concept of governmentality to develop compelling interpretations of the ideological process of professionalising and professional conduct within a neoliberal framework. From a Foucauldian perspective, professions are governing mechanisms that discursively control conduct 'at a distance' through the autonomous self-regulation of subjects (Miller and Rose, 1990 cited in Fournier (1999),

p. 282). Importantly, professions are part of a network of accountability: they need to continuously re-negotiate their legitimacy to establish trust with other constituencies, including the state, clients, and the market. While professions are legitimised through their professional competence, competence is more than the acquisition of a body of scientific knowledge: it also about personal professional conduct, or 'conducting or constituting oneself in an appropriate manner' (Fournier, 1999, p. 287). The appeal to this type of professionalism in the new professions (such as PR) 'serves to regulate autonomous conduct in the name of oneself [...] and in the name of the client' (Fournier, 1999, p. 294).

The foregoing discussion would therefore imply that professional competency and conduct in PR agency work are negotiated within a specific situation, according to the client relationship, irrespective of professional associations' codes of conduct, thus ensuring legitimacy and survival as a business. An example of this might be the practice of not paying interns: a PR agency owner may view student interns as valuable, if sometimes unreliable, sources of creative labour who are willing to provide ideas and work on client accounts for free, even though the practice of unpaid internships is formally censured by the professional associations. The client, on the other hand, while demanding a stream of ideas from the PR agency, may (for whatever reason) threaten to withdraw its account, forcing the agency to work for a lower fee. Appropriate conduct in this situation may differ from agency to agency. While 'over-servicing' the client (i.e. working over and above contracted hours) may compel some agency owners to withdraw from the client account, others may feel compromised to undertake lower remunerated work due to obligations in other networks (e.g. as member of a local sports club).

A category of 'entrepreneurial professions', or *expert occupations*, whose purpose is to service the market, was crystallised by organisational scholars (Muzio et al., 2008). While focusing on business consultancy in general, which emerged out of the deregulation and globalisation of markets during the 1980s, there are clear parallels with PR. For example, Muzio et al. (2008, p. 5) cite 'largely open access' to these new occupations and almost exclusive reliance on 'regulation by market mechanisms'. Further, the term 'entrepreneurial profession' captures 'typical motivations' that 'appeal to the rhetoric of entrepreneurship, competition and efficiency to account for the value of what they do'. This is in contrast to other occupations with a broader public service remit (Muzio et al., 2008, pp. 5–6).

I argue then, following from analyses of business consultancy (Muzio et al., 2008) and the growth of PR (Miller and Dinan, 2000), that a compelling structural argument for the expansion of PR agencies is the market itself. As previously discussed, 'reputation management' is a growth area worldwide, while the relatively low financial cost of PR services, compared to that of advertising, further adds to PR's market attractiveness to clients (Moloney, 2006) and enables PR services to be offered to 'resource-poor' organisations such as pressure groups and trade unions (Davis, 2000b). These flexible conditions, on the other hand, also open up PR agencies to providing services that are little more than administrative duties, and for low fees, as illustrated by the practice of 'reverse auction' (Sudhaman, 2015).

The following section moves away from the broader social, political, economic, and cultural contexts in which PR operates. The discussion in this section proposes that there is another market in which PR competes which is not merely about price. Instead, it is about the emotional resources that PRPs are required to use as part of their everyday practice, and how these resources contribute to perceived 'expertise'.

The market for emotional labour: PRPs, clients, and the media

Hochschild (1983, p. 91) proposed the notion of a 'market for emotional labour'. In her study of Delta Airlines, managers, supervisors, advertising personnel, and flight attendants 'set up the sale of emotional labor' for the company to profit from in terms of passenger market share (Hochschild, 1983, p. 91). Emotional labour is sold to the 'flying public' (i.e. the customers) through the airline's expectations of greater market share; advertisers' discourse about reaching the market; in-flight supervisors' discussing the need for 'positive attitude'; and flight attendants who talk about 'handling irates' (p. 91). This focus on 'better service' (p. 91) is linked to competition when airlines are not competing on price. Developing this point, Hochschild argues: 'The more important service becomes as an arena for competition between airlines, the more workers are asked to do *public relations work* [my emphasis] to promote sales' (Hochschild, 1983, p. 92).

In equating 'public relations work' with 'emotion work', Hochschild (1983) provides the link between the structural concepts of neoliberalism and promotional culture previously discussed in this chapter and the daily lives of PR workers. Not only is the PR industry part of promotional culture in sustaining neoliberal economies but also PR workers are themselves subjects of emotional labour whose technical and relational efforts are directed towards securing and maintaining clients and ensuring their clients' success in the marketplace, through the sale of products, ideas, or policies. The next part of this chapter discusses the key actors that comprise the market for PR work, and, in turn, the market for emotional labour in PR. These key actors are: PR agencies; PRPs (i.e. those who *supply* emotional labour); and the clients of PR firms, journalists, and online 'influencers' (i.e. those who *demand* emotional labour).

PRPs working in agencies

In examining the emotional labour performed by PRPs, it is important to establish how labour is organised within PR firms. In most PR agencies, account managers do much of the day-to-day work of liaising with clients and the media. While there may be subtle differences in grade and status according to experience and level of responsibility, most PR firms employ account executives, account managers, and account directors in an ascending hierarchy, all of whom can be considered account handlers. At the top end of PR firms, directors and partners will spend much of their time looking for and winning business for the account handlers to work on.

Research into the roles performed by PRPs falls into two main categories: strategic (e.g. advice-giving and strategic planning) and technical (e.g. crafting press announcements; responding to media enquiries). 'Excellent' or effective PR is more likely to occur when the PRP enacts the 'communication manager' role and participates in strategic decision-making (Dozier, 1992). Within the 'PR roles' literature, the 'technician' role is somewhat denigrated and seen as low status, as Dozier and Broom (2006) acknowledge. The technician role is also gendered, as reported in numerous studies in the United States since 1989 (Toth, 2001).

In the United Kingdom, more than three quarters of PR agency client work involve media relations strategy planning, media relations, and digital and social media duties (PRCA, 2016b). Everyday PR work, therefore, not only involves fostering good relationships with clients in order to win and keep their business but also with journalists, colleagues, and other stakeholders. Although PR is a female intensive profession (64%), only 36% of female PR consultants hold board level positions (PRCA, 2016b). Much of the day-to-day relationship handling is undertaken by White British female practitioners, working in account executive, account director, and associate director roles, a profile which has typified the practice for a number of years (CEBR, 2005; PRCA, 2016b). 'Strategic and 'technical' roles are also reported to be gender-specific: females who mainly occupy executive-level grades are typically consigned to the more 'technical' roles including day-to-day relationship handling, and, as Donato (1990) proposed, doing the emotion work in PR. These gendered aspects of the PR profession in the United Kingdom, including a discussion of how gender segregation in PR may be understood, are explored further in Chapter 4.

PR agency work, as already argued, is both competitive and intensive. Agency employees within the communications industry typically work well beyond the standard 35 full-time hours (Clarke, 2013), with around 40% continuing to work out of hours every single day to pick up emails or phone calls (Wyatt, 2013; PRCA, 2018a). Poor mental health in PR is frequently ignored by the industry or regarded as a performance issue (Hall and Waddington, 2017). Clients of PR firms, especially small firms, have high expectations concerning the level of interaction as well as of who is performing the service (Mart and Jackson, 2005); therefore the practitioner who embodies such expectations is paramount to a good service. A mental health crisis, endemic across a range of institutions and occupations, would suggest that people from all walks of life are required to manage their emotions, both in their personal lives and at work; but when the illusion of being in control is crucial to a profession such as PR, then denial of these pressures may prevail.

PRPs as cultural intermediaries

Critical scholars, such as Miller and Dinan (2000) and Moloney (2006), share a political economy perspective that views PR as intertwined with the rise of neoliberalism 'characterised by unregulated markets, serviced by unfettered, capitalist enterprise in societies that encourage possessive individualism' (Moloney, 2006, p. 32). I have already established that within the framework of neoliberalism, PR has joined the panoply of communications services such as advertising and sales promotion that comprise a promotional culture in support of organisations that compete within different markets.

Analyses of the role of PR by critical PR scholars adopting a socio-cultural perspective (Curtin and Gaither, 2005; Hodges, 2006; Pieczka, 2006a; L'Etang et al., 2007; Edwards and Hodges, 2011; Hodges and Edwards, 2013) posit that within the 'circuit of culture' (du Gay et al., 2013, p. 3), PR seeks to influence meaning at five key moments – identity, production, consumption, regulation, representation. From this analysis the economy is presented as a cultural construct (L'Etang, 2008). PR produces meaning by acting as a cultural intermediary, 'creating symbols, values and language' (p. 216) linking lifestyles with products within neoliberal economies. In doing so, PRPs have been defined as:

> discourse technologists ... involved in the maintenance and transformation of discourse primarily through the *production and distribution of texts* [my italics]. They participate in discursive struggles by shaping texts and by strategically deploying texts which facilitate certain socio-cultural practices and not others.
>
> (Motion and Leitch, 1996, p. 299)

This means that the texts, or discourses, that are in circulation within a promotional culture are by their nature *self-interested* and exist to give voice to self-interested parties – more commonly organisations rather than individuals – within the pluralist notion of a 'marketplace for ideas' (Moloney, 2006). As already discussed in relation to financial markets (Bourne, 2017), the PR practices of corporate and government elites 'function to diminish or silence oppositional voices' (Weaver, 2001, p. 283). Through the 'production and distribution of texts' and 'creation of symbols', PRPs act as brokers or intermediaries between a wide range of stakeholders, primarily clients and the media (e.g. reporters, news editors, feature writers, broadcast producers, etc.). Furthermore, since PRPs would appear to 'exhibit a similar volume, range, and type of cultural capital as dominant social groups' (Edwards, 2008, p. 371), they generate symbolic power that sustains the social and economic status quo – in other words, as Miller and Dinan (2000) argue, practitioners and PR agency practitioners, in particular, support the ideology of the free market that goes hand in hand with neoliberal economies.

While much theorising of cultural intermediaries has shaped PR scholarship, relatively few studies have engaged with practitioners to analyse how relationships with clients, journalists, and others are 'brokered' or mediated in order to influence culture(s). The lens of emotional labour, on the other hand, offers insights into how meanings and identities are constructed through these social interactions, particularly from a phenomenological perspective.

PRPs as 'millennial' employees

Just under 50% of practitioners working for UK PR agencies are aged between 16 and 34 (CIPR, 2018a, p. 14), indicating a particularly youthful profile for this sector, compared to in-house (35%). The generation born between 1982 and 2004 has been labelled as the 'millennial generation' (Meng et al., 2017). So-called millennials include the 16–34 age group and in the CIPR survey report, millennials overlap with an older group aged 35–44 (CIPR, 2018a).

Critical writers in organisation studies, for example, have cautioned against popular discourse and theory that categorises and stereotypes different generations: 'a theory of generations which, when applied in work organizations has been taken to argue that individuals from the same generation have the same attitudes, preferences and orientations to work' (Thomas et al., 2014, p. 1576). And yet a theory of generations is highly appealing. After all, if 'generational insight' produced by management consultants identifies the key attributes of a particular generation, this information potentially helps employers with information that may help to attract and recruit people to specific types of job, as well as to target consumers who also fit a particular age profile. Thomas et al. (2014) argue that generational categories ignore other markers of social identity that intersect with age (e.g. gender, ethnicity, race, sexuality, etc.) as well as understandings of identity that are not fixed but context-specific and evolving. Furthermore, they argue, generational stereotypes run the risk of setting generation against generation. A brief look at the academic research on millennials in the workplace, however, would suggest that a number of researchers and scholars, including PR scholars, have attempted to go beyond industry and popular literature to establish whether intergenerational differences in values and expectations, particularly those of the millennial generation, can be agreed upon and validated.

In their well-cited paper, Myers and Sadaghiani (2010, p. 225) observed that millennials were negatively stereotyped as: the 'Look at me' generation, lacking loyalty and work ethic, as well as being impatient and self-important. On the other hand, millennials from an organisation's perspective are popularly described as being more accepting of diversity than previous generations and more adept at using advanced communication and information technologies, as well as more comfortable working in teams. Beyond the popular press and literature, Myers and Sadaghiani (2010) noted that empirical evidence of millennials' values and expectations in the workplace was relatively limited. However, several US PR scholars have since examined (largely through survey methods) millennials' employment expectations in PR departments or agencies (e.g. Curtin et al., 2011; Gallicano et al., 2012; Gallicano, 2013; Meng et al., 2017). The PR literature suggests that the millennial generation employees have identifiable characteristics such as high self-esteem and expectations of work that provides a personal challenge and gives them responsibility. For example, Meng et al. (2017), in a qualitative study of 39 millennial communication professionals (i.e. defined as those born between 1982 and 2004 in the United States), queried how PR agencies and communication departments could best engage their employees. The study found that millennials were 'a contradictory generation, desiring independence, flexibility, and challenges balanced with clear expectations, regular evaluation, and safety nets in case of failure'. Meng et al.'s (2017) participants as PR professionals all struggled with work-life balance but a workplace culture that was 'friendly, supportive and enjoyable' could make the difference to how they felt about their job.

Finally, it is worth noting Thomas et al.'s (2014) research questions when considering the significance of a generational world view within empirical data. At least one question of relevance to the empirical findings reported in Chapter 6 is: 'what currency do different generational categories have within organizations?' (Thomas et al., 2014, p. 1577).

Clients

Who are the clients of PR agencies? Why do client organisations hire PR agencies and what are their expectations of a PR service? Within the United Kingdom, the PRCA reported the increased importance of the technology and consumer services, media and marketing sectors for agency practitioners and freelancers (PRCA, 2016b). Those who hold the PR budgets and purchase PR services are typically 'in-house' heads of corporate communications and corporate marketing directors within corporations, public sector organisations, and charities. The client contact for a small business may be the managing director, chief executive, director or partner (if the firm is a professional services firm), or a marketing director (if the firm is a large corporation).

Few studies examine PR from the client's perspective, although insights from a European-wide survey (Verčič et al., 2018) are considered later in this review. In their examination of the value of the PR industry in Scotland, Gabbott and Hogg defined PR services from a purchaser's or client's point of view as: '...a business advisory service concerned with the management of reputation or image' (1996, p. 438). From a client's perspective, it is often hard to see what kind of 'product' they are getting in buying PR services. PR, in 'managing reputation', is notoriously intangible and difficult to evaluate 'even after the service has been delivered' (p. 438).

PR therefore has much in common with business advisory services in general. It is characterised by expertise, the cooperation of the purchaser and provider in specifying the service to be provided, a 'perishable' service where the service outcome may serve a purpose for a short period of time, and situation-specific strategies that are not applicable to another situation and may be over-ridden by events outside the control of the PR adviser. From this, Gabbott and Hogg (1996, p. 440) argue that in buying PR services, 'the client is buying ideas, management discipline, market knowledge and personal chemistry'. Gabbott and Hogg's study concludes that PR services are used by clients in three ways: to supplement existing expertise within the organisation, to outsource PR expertise instead of employing their own staff (e.g. to keep control of overheads), and finally to implement already-decided strategies where advisors are used for their technical ability rather than their creative, strategic, and advisory skills.

In a more recent, European-wide survey Verčič et al. (2018) compared findings from agencies and communication departments on the reasons for hiring agencies, with some interesting results. According to communication departments, the top reason for hiring agencies was 'creativity and innovation'. The second reason for hiring agencies was to outsource 'additional arms and legs' and the third reason was 'expertise regarding specific geographies or markets'. However, agencies overestimated the importance of their creativity and innovation as well as their expertise regarding specific geographies or markets. On the other hand, agencies underestimated the 'arms and legs' reason for organisations to hire them. While a mismatch in PR agency–client expectations of hiring may be one potential source of tension, Verčič et al. (2018) also identified the specific sources of conflict between communication departments and agencies. For communication departments, the most important source of conflict was 'lack of knowledge of the client's business and processes' and yet this source of conflict was ranked sixth by agency respondents. Perception gaps emerged on seven further sources of conflict, including 'bad chemistry', further to which the authors concluded that 'it is primarily the agency's responsibility to manage its client's expectations' (Verčič et al., 2018, p. 161). The management of client's expectations is a key tenet of emotional-labour theorising in PR (see Chapters 5 and 6), reflecting the 'anxiety' and 'insecurity' of the PR profession referred to earlier in this chapter (Waddington, 2015).

The importance of agency size and the frequency of professional interactions was highlighted by another study of the PR client/agency relationship. Mart and Jackson (2005) examined clients' perceptions of agency size through four phases of client-agency relationships: agency selection; successful relationships; failing relationships; and agency switching. The study, which involved interviews with ten agencies of different sizes from 'micro' agencies with up to five employees through to 'large' firms with 50 plus employees, concluded that all clients regarded '"client-agency personal chemistry" as a necessary ingredient to a successful C-A relationship' (Mart and Jackson, 2005, p. 7), echoing Gabbott and Hogg's earlier study. However, there were different client expectations of small agencies and large agencies, the key finding being that the client-agency relationship was more important to clients with smaller agencies. Clients of smaller agencies expected higher levels of service and more frequent communication as well as more informal, enjoyable relationships. As such, poor communication would be a possible reason for switching agencies. Mart and Jackson reported that clients' relationships with larger agencies, on the other hand, were perceived as a 'professional business transaction', which was 'reliant upon the standard of work their individual account handler produces' (Mart and Jackson, 2005, p. 11). Conflict was expected to be an 'everyday part' of the relationship (p. 11). In focusing on the emotional labour experienced by account handlers working in relatively small, regional PR firms, it is essential for account handlers and their directors in small agencies to achieve the right 'client-agency personal chemistry' through frequent, intense communication. PRP-client relationships are explored, from an emotion management perspective, in Chapters 5 and 6.

'PR expertise' deconstructed

The highly situational and personal characteristics of PR have attracted a fresh appraisal by scholars of what constitutes 'PR expertise'. While scholars (e.g. Grunig and Hunt, 1984) and university educators have readily advocated the 'management science' approach to the development of PR expertise, emphasising knowledge of strategies and tactics, practitioners such as Mallinson (1996) have argued that personal qualities are more important than strategies.

Van Ruler (2005, p. 161) describes the 'knowledge model' of a profession as 'the development of an organized group of experts who implement scientifically developed knowledge on a cluster of tasks defined by the professional group, in order to deliver a unique contribution to the well-being of the client and the progress of society'. Van Ruler (2005, p. 164) contrasted the 'knowledge' (or rational intelligence) model of professionalism (driven by scholars) with the 'personality' or (or 'emotional intelligence') model of which 'general learning potential and empathy are essential features' for responding to clients' expectations. She argued, from her research among Dutch PRPs (van Ruler, 1996), that 'practitioners seem much more inclined to the emotional-intelligence perspectives, and maybe even to a large extent, to the personality model'. Although she cites Goleman's (1996) work on emotional intelligence (EI) as competence, van Ruler adopts the term rather loosely. Emotional intelligence is presented as the opposite of 'rational intelligence' when analysing models of professionalism. While 'dualism' of the rational/emotional invites critique in itself, which I discuss in the Appendix (p. x), a key criticism is that emotional intelligence is not sufficiently theorised within van Ruler's paper, except as a client orientation that does not utilise scientific knowledge. Nonetheless, from interviews with UK practitioners of all ages, Pieczka and L'Etang (2006, p. 276) drew similar conclusions to van Ruler: 'practitioners do not identify specific knowledge [to be a successful practitioner] but rather focus on personal qualities such as creativity, lateral thinking, flexibility, articulateness, persuasiveness, common sense, and integrity'.

Interestingly, in deconstructing PR expertise within the context of a client pitch presentation (the selling of PR services), Pieczka (2006b, p. 306) found that for clients, 'chemistry' 'functions as a guarantee that an appropriate service will be obtained' whereas for consultants, 'chemistry' may partly act as a 'substitute for detailed expert advice'. Such 'chemistry' can make the crucial difference to a client choosing a consultancy in a competitive pitch where different consultants' credentials and ideas are 'evenly matched' (p. 306). One particularly angry story of 'overservicing' (p. 309) a client (in other words, working long hours to deliver on ambitious targets) is an example of the intense pressure felt by staff within the PR consultancy environment. Further discussion of chemistry as the performance of personal qualities in the process of agency-client matching is in Chapter 6.

Pieczka (2000, 2002) argued that the critical question of knowledge base of PR and claims to professional status warranted further analysis. She argued that PR should be subjected to similar sociological analysis as other professions. Drawing on different typologies used in management, Pieczka observed that there was a 'striking similarity' (2000, p. 218) between the management and PR consultancy industries. Not only did they share similar structural features such as low barriers to entry and a 'heterogeneity' of service providers, but crucially, both occupations relied on rhetorical strategies (Alvesson, 1993) that involved convincing the client of their worth during client-consultant interactions. These rhetorical strategies can be viewed as 'charismatic' legitimation strategies (Waeraas, 2009), in which the PRP uses their emotional resources. The discourses and meanings, therefore, that establish PR 'expertise' warrant further examination. These are discussed in Chapter 5.

The social and cultural practice of PR is therefore open to theory-building using disciplinary frameworks that focus attention on the micro-level interactions of PRPs – and how these interactions construct knowledge within the field. Both Edwards (2008) and Elmer (2012) have provided alternative frameworks based on Bourdieu's notion of power deriving from different forms of capital, including cultural capital (Bourdieu, 1997). From exploratory research into the patterns and volume of cultural capital belonging to 178 PRPs in the United Kingdom, Edwards argued that PRPs have high levels of cultural capital, 'exhibiting a similar volume, range, and type of cultural capital as dominant social groups' (2008, p. 371). Edwards characterises this occupational group as 'cultural omnivores' whose cultural capital attracts symbolic value, which is transformed into symbolic capital. Symbolic capital, in turn, assures their future status and symbolic power. She argues: 'For practitioners at any level, cultural omnivorousness is likely to generate tangible benefits in the ability to mix with a variety of people, securing extensive social networks that could lead to better results or new clients' (2008, p. 371). Elmer's (2012) ethnographic study of 39 UK PRPs focused on the concept of embodied cultural capital. His in-depth observations and interviews with UK practitioners complement that of Edwards, arguing that while

> normative *[professional]* barriers and standards may be weak, the rules that govern acceptance as a 'public relations person' for example, are enacted on terms that are relational and performative, they enact a commercial culture that is also gendered, classed and generational.
>
> (Elmer, 2012, pp. 292–293, my italics)

The notion of the exchange of social and cultural capitals providing legitimacy for PRPs in their client work is an important turning point in understanding PR as a relational practice: these ideas will be returned to later in this volume. However, I have previously argued (e.g. Yeomans, 2007, 2016) that the concept of emotional labour offers a compelling vantage point for analysing PR as a service industry. Within the concept of emotional labour is the idea of a 'social exchange' of feeling where the emphasis is on the service relationship itself and how that is understood to work – implicit in this is the notion of 'personal chemistry' between the practitioner and client. While Elmer (2012) acknowledges the necessity for emotional labour in his account of PR workers' labour, I explore it in depth. My aim is to understand the micro-level day-to-day practice and interactions of PR executives in agencies, using emotional labour theory (Hochschild, 1983) and extensions of this theory (e.g. Bolton, 2005) as an analytic framework.

The media

The pervasive influence of PR on contemporary media – the 'PR-isation' of news (Moloney, 2006; Moloney et al., 2013) – can be explained by waves of political, economic, and technological developments, viewed simply as fundamental changes to the demand and supply of news. The demand for news is greater than ever owing to the commercialisation, expansion, and proliferation of media, including satellite channels and online media; however editorial resources have not grown to cope with the demand. The worldwide decrease in editorial resources, including further decline in the print media industry in many countries, has put pressure on journalists to do more with less time. Washbourne (2009) cites further pressures on journalists that are conversely opportunities for PRPs. These include the extension of the media cycle to 24 hours providing more editorial space to fill, as well as increased competition among organisations of different kinds for reaching specific, niche audiences (perhaps typically, youth markets). Such changes may be understood as part of the rise of promotional culture as a process of neoliberal capitalism (Davis, 2013), already discussed in this chapter. Here, though, it is worth noting again that in a 40-year period which has seen a growth in the influence of 'promotional intermediaries' (Davis, 2013, p. 92) which includes the advertising, PR, and market research industries, it is PR that has expanded, flourished, and become institutionalised. PR operates as a major news subsidy as well as a means to influence news production. One of the consequences of PR dominance of the media agenda is the threat to, even loss of, the professional identity of the journalist (Fredriksson and Johanssen, 2014; Grubenmann and Meckel, 2017). As I have argued in this chapter, identities are relevant to professional relationships and the performance of emotional labour; therefore the professional identity of the journalist is of central concern in this part of the chapter.

Journalism functions, it is argued, as an ideology comprising five ideal-typical core values that give meaning to what journalists do: public service, objectivity,[5] autonomy, immediacy, and ethics (Deuze, 2005). The journalist's professional identity is one that has to be preserved and protected for news reporters to operate autonomously. While each of the five core values may be critiqued – for example, pure 'objectivity' is recognised as impossible among journalists – it is nevertheless held as an embodied ideal (Richards and Rees, 2011). Therefore, the oft-reported 'antagonistic' relationship between PR and journalism is partly shaped by journalists' efforts to preserve an independent status, in spite of commercial constraints and other realities that mitigate this status, including the changing relationship between the media and the public. There is a common acceptance among journalists that PR is a 'necessary evil' (Obermaier et al., 2015, p. 4); therefore it is unsurprising that journalists 'have very mixed emotions [...] about public relations professionals' as one of their major suppliers (Jackson and Moloney, 2016, p. 763).

'PR-isation' of news, consumer trends, and threats to reporter autonomy

PR is acknowledged as a major supplier of news. While measures of personnel employed directly in PR and journalism are subject to annual fluctuations and contradictory claims about PRP and journalist 'bodies' within the workforce,[6] the UK Labour Force Survey in 2018 found 53,000 describing themselves employed as PR professionals (excluding directors) and 90,000 employed as journalists, newspaper and periodical editors (ONS, 2018). Interestingly, while an additional 28,000 identify as self-employed journalists (full-time and part-time), a 'journalist' could well be writing copy for a variety of outlets, including social media and customer publishing (Cox, 2016). Regardless of the arbitrariness of job titles and how people identify with them within a dynamic media environment, it is clear that the media industries are changing rapidly in response to a range of factors, including how people perceive and consume news. Among a broad range of consumer trends affecting journalism across more than 30 countries and five continents, the Reuters Institute found that TV and online news are the most popular and frequently accessed news sources; there is an increasing use of smartphones for online news consumption, and there is a significant decline in printed newspapers (Newman et al., 2017). Predictions in journalism, media, and technology include 'further job cuts and losses across the news industry. More papers in the US and Europe go out of business, slim down or become online-only' (Newman, 2017, p. 2). Of the factors cited as having led to the 'PR-isation' of news, arguably the most significant and detrimental is the decline in editorial resources and increased dependence on ready-made news as more journalists are required to do more with less time. Lewis et al.'s insightful study (2008) revealed the following experiences reported by journalists:

> 'Today it's not uncommon to be knocking out 5 or 6 [stories] in a day – and when you're doing that you rely more on the wires and on PR than you did before'. A correspondent at the Press Association agency elaborated further: 'I average about 10 a day…The main difference has been the growth in 24-hour news stations which need stories all day and night, so there is no peace for an agency journalist […] I don't usually spend more than an hour on a story, otherwise I wouldn't be able to write so many.'
>
> (Lewis et al., 2008, p. 49)

Davies (2008), writing as a journalist for a popular readership, drew on Lewis et al.'s study to argue that the many commercial pressures on news organisations from the late 1980s to the present day had led to a concentration of media ownership into fewer hands; a loss of thousands of jobs within local and national newspapers as well as broadcast media (including the BBC which had their own internal markets to consider); and a reliance on all too few 'supply lines' of news from local to national level. The outcome of this reduction or removal of news supply is: '…only 12% of their [journalists'] stories turn out to be their own work; and only 12% of their key facts are effectively checked' (Davies, 2008, p. 69). It would seem that for journalists to uphold standards of impartiality, accuracy, and balance in keeping with the BBC's official guide (for example) would be contradictory to its requirement for breaking news within five minutes of receiving it: the result being that reporters are 'reduced to churnalism, to the passive processing of material…supplied for them by outsiders, particularly wire agencies and PR' (2008, p. 73).

A further, multifaceted study, which measured the impact of PR on published news in Israel, concluded that

> items totally free of PR involvement are an exceptionally rare phenomenon: only 40 percent of the items involve no direct input of information and no more than quarter of them are totally free of any kind of PR involvement, as far as reporters can tell.
>
> (Reich, 2010, p. 810)

Thus, for journalists to produce a reliable account of events, they are to a great extent reliant on the accuracy of information supplied by PR professionals. Furthermore, the phenomenon of 'media catching' (Waters et al., 2010, p. 241) suggests that reporters are increasingly using websites such as

Help a Reporter (HARO) as well as social media sites such as Twitter to specifically 'target large numbers of public relations practitioners for specific content for story ideas'.

Moloney (2006, p. 151) argues that the media is being 'colonised' by PR. This 'PR-isation' has led to the 'disablement of their [journalists'] critical faculties'. Journalism's role as scrutiny, he argues, is compromised by journalism's own complicity in manufacturing news through editors' 'deals' with PR personnel; an increased reliance on secondary sources due to the speeding up of news cycles and fewer staff; the recruitment of more 'young, inexperienced and low-cost staff' (p. 155); and the dominance of a marketing culture that is focused on repetitively promoting the 'superficially new and that which produces more revenue' (p. 156). More than ever, journalists rely on their PRP contacts for a steady supply of 'information subsidies' (Gandy, 1982), or news stories and research. PRPs rely on journalists to promote their clients' interests, thus increasing their clients' legitimacy and authority which, in turn, enables them to accumulate cultural capital within the public sphere (Davis, 2000b).

The 'emotionally-charged networked environment' and journalists' (unacknowledged) emotional labour

The emotional news environment and the emotional labour of journalism have attracted relatively little attention from scholars. However, in their essay on the role of emotion in the future of journalism, Beckett and Deuze (2016, pp. 1–6) present several compelling arguments for a greater understanding of emotion due to the 'emotionally charged networked environment' of media and the public's intimate engagement with it, both in how it is produced and consumed. For journalism to remain valued, they argue, it should empower the public to pay critical attention to news and put human interest at the centre. Such an approach forces traditional news values to be questioned:

> the old idea of 'hard' news' that shocks, frightens, disturbs, and alarms can leave the audience feeling alienated, disempowered, helpless and, worst of all, apathetic, insensitive, and even hostile to learning about our world. Taking 'vacations' from the news or otherwise instituting newsbreaks are understandable tactics to deal with the onslaught of news.
> (Beckett and Deuze, 2016, p. 2)

In other words, they argue that whole gamut of emotions should be reflected in stories, as they are currently in the popular internet media site *Buzzfeed*. Beckett and Deuze argue that the 'problematic and gendered false dichotomy between "quality" and "popular" journalism' should be abandoned and that instead, emotions and everyday life should be integrated with the news 'using notions of public quality' (Beckett and Deuze, 2016, p. 4).

Up to a third of global news consumers actively avoid the news due to its negative effect on mood or its unreliability (Newman et al., 2017). Such a shift in audience tastes can be seen in the introduction of a new editorial policy at BBC Radio 4's 'flagship' *Today* breakfast programme. In response to charges of 'dumbing down', the editor Sarah Sands defended her decision to include more in-depth magazine-type content on the arts and fashion by explaining that she wanted to broaden the listening audience (Dixon, 2017; Martinson, 2017). However, while a young or female audience might be more inclined to listen to human interest stories, stepping into these waters brings challenges for the presenter more comfortable with interrogating politicians (Sturges, 2017). The veteran *Today* presenter John Humphrys came under particular criticism on Twitter for an in-depth item on transgender issues. One listener tweeted 'I listened, despite Humphrys. I think someone else would have presented it better. With empathy. Too much focus on one person who "made a mistake"' (Nissim, 2017).

Journalism, as illustrated, is therefore 'less hospitable to emotional literacy than some other professions' according to one study (Richards and Rees, 2011, p. 865), while other research found that the 'suppression of personal, emotional identity for the sake of an ideologically driven, detached professional self' meant that acute emotion experienced by news reporters was deferred and often not fully dealt with, leading to negative feelings including self-hate or guilt (Hopper and Huxford, 2015, p. 38). The authors of these studies, along with Beckett and Deuze (2016), argue for greater emotional literacy for journalists, offered through standard training and education, and not just for those who have to deal with post-traumatic stress following disaster reporting.

While the studies on journalists' emotional literacy (or the lack of) are not concerned with journalist-PR interactions, they nevertheless provide insights into the professional values and norms of journalism and how they are learned and performed, often through emotionally stressful routines and rituals as part of occupational socialisation. Although Moloney (2006, p. 164) advocates a greater separation between journalism and PR, and for journalists to adopt (a traditional) attitude of 'scepticism, bordering on polite hostility' towards PR people, such an attitude would be counterproductive to the interests of the networked journalist in the twenty-first century, characterised as follows:

> their work is insecure, their pay limited, the people's trust precarious, and their working time stretches beyond the boundaries of a print deadline or broadcast schedule — and more often than not today necessarily includes a fair amount of personal branding along with constant re-skilling and multi-skilling demanded by the ever-changing technological context of media work.
>
> (Beckett and Deuze, 2016, p. 5)

Some researchers argue that there is a gap between journalists' attitudes towards PR as a *profession* and individual PRPs, who many find helpful on a personal level, particularly where there is a close working relationship (Sallot and Johnson, 2006). Nonetheless, threats to journalists' professional identity arising from changing work practices mean that experienced journalists are more likely to emphasise professional ideology as a form of resistance. Resistance includes a critical view of PR, particularly demonstrated through hostile attitudes towards fellow journalists who start working as PRPs (Fredriksson and Johansson, 2014).

Other journalists' criticisms are levelled at PRPs inadequate media relations skills. Sallot and Johnson (2006) found that 74% of journalists in the US reported that PRPs lacked news sense, values, accuracy, timeliness, and presentation style. In the United Kingdom, similar issues about PR have appeared in the professional journals and trade magazines, such as *PR Week*, highlighting editors' complaints about PRPs as: being unaware of their publication's news deadlines; time-wasting while attempting to 'pitch' or sell-in irrelevant stories; sending 'blanket' press releases and inability to write literate news copy. Conferences targeted at PRPs encourage them to learn 'what the media wants from PR' with the emphasis being on meeting editors and news editors face-to-face, while regular training sessions organised by professional associations continue to offer advice to practitioners on effective media relations (e.g. CIPR, 2018b; PRCA, 2018b). These activities continue, despite a perception that the mainstream media has surrendered its potency as a news source to social media influencers (SMIs) in many consumer sectors.

SMIs ('bloggers'): compensations, identity, and emotional labour

The 'blogosphere', comprising social media networks, blog-hosting websites, as well as other internet sites, has become a 'legitimate platform for PR activity' (Smith, 2010; Lahav and Roth-Cohen, 2016), opening up a myriad of opportunities for PRPs to influence consumers online. Whereas journalists employed by the mainstream media were once the main focus of PR attention, PRPs are now required to navigate relationships with bloggers, or SMIs, within a new media ecology. Indeed, some practitioners bypass the mainstream media all together for some clients (typically, youth orientated clients), choosing instead to build direct, interpersonal relationships with highly influential bloggers who are provided incentives to write about their client's brand and, in turn, influence a large number of followers on social media sites such as Instagram (for further discussion, see Chapter 6).

Although some clients in some market sectors might view bloggers as 'unprofessional micro opinion leaders' (Lahav and Roth-Cohen, 2016, p. 930), lacking the credibility and influence of high profile journalists, there has been a shift in recent years towards PR strategies that are based around influencing consumers online due to an increasing regard for and use of social networking platforms among younger generations. Instagram, for example, is one of the most popular social media networks for mobile photo-sharing worldwide, with a reported 800 million monthly active users, and is 'most popular among teens and Young Millennials' (Statista, 2018). In 2016, 98% of fashion brands were reported to have an Instagram profile, thus allowing fashion bloggers to easily share visual content from fashion brands and vice versa (Statista, 2018).

Bloggers operate, according to an Australian study, 'on a grey shaded scale between hobbyist and professional', and represent a new class of 'precariat' with unreliable sources of income (Archer and Harrigan, 2016, p. 75). Influential bloggers have increasingly adopted a business-like approach to their labour, including expectations of compensation or payment in-kind for brand mentions (Yeomans and Baxter, 2014; Archer and Harrigan, 2016; Lahav and Roth-Cohen, 2016). Lavishing 'freebies', or other benefits, on bloggers to encourage positive reviews of a client's brand has proven particularly effective from a PR perspective. The result of these interactions, according to another study conducted in Israel, is 'the intensification of PR practitioner control over bloggers content: from the independent blogger on to the current blogger type, who works under a regulated, prearranged, and organized system managed by PR experts' (Lahav and Roth-Cohen, 2016, p. 931).

The long-established practice of offering 'free' products and press 'junkets' (i.e. paid-for travel and accommodation) to journalists in exchange for a favourable review continues in PR. However, for some bloggers, the expectation of compensation for a brand mention is particularly acute when assessing the benefits to their readership, their personal autonomy, society, and the greater good (Archer and Harrigan, 2016, p. 75). Yet the motivations for blogging are complex: while some bloggers may prefer to carve out identities that stay true to their community of loyal followers – e.g. when writing about a sensitive topic such as health – and may feel compromised by approaches from PRPs, others may seek 'micro celebrity' status within the digital sphere through a process of strategic self-branding (Khamis et al., 2017).

Within the fashion sector, for example, Duffy and Hund (2015, p. 3) argue that bloggers' self-branding, which they conceptualise as 'entrepreneurial femininity', is contextualised by neoliberal narratives of individualism and creative autonomy. The authors contend that self-branding relies on emotional labour, since, for fashion bloggers, making a living requires working on the self to share their 'passions' with their readers, rendering themselves *simultaneously* as 'authentic' and as equals with famous models and brands within the fashion industry. Based on their study, which included an analysis of fashion bloggers' Instagram accounts, Duffy and Hund (2015) argue:

> The practice of 'tagging,' or linking to a branded product in one's blog or Instagram feed, stands as public recognition of a commercial gift [...]
> Comments such as these tended to generate substantial feedback, an indicator of the gendering of the 'social media audience commodity'

whereby (female) consumer-audiences provide valuable data that can be harnessed by marketing institutions.

(Shepherd, 2014)

For some bloggers, therefore, referring to their gifts or compensations in their blogs serves to raise their personal status with their followers. As part of the self-branding process, bloggers may scale up their requests for compensation, for example, ask to be given the opportunity to 'curate' their own designer collections. This, in turn, creates a demand for emotional labour from PRPs themselves, whose work is to negotiate the 'deal' with their client, fulfil the blogger's requirements, and manage expectations with all parties. However, as previously discussed, bloggers have to tread a fine line between seeing to be 'doing it just for the money' and maintaining their own brand, in particular, doing 'work that doesn't seem like work' (Duffy and Hund, 2015, p. 9).

PRPs occupational identities

Studies of professional identity formation disrupt modernist notions of stable identities, particularly when concerning new professions, such as PR, that are not characterised by the same levels of credentialism as, say, law or medicine. Reed's poststructuralist examination of UK PRPs professional identities draws attention to the importance of the 'shapeshifter' identity in the negotiation of ambiguity in PR work (Reed, 2013). PR identities, rather than being fixed to a particular set of professional values (as seems to be the case for journalism up to the present), are in a state of becoming: 'at the heart of the shapeshifter identity is relationships with others and how they conceive of you as an expert' (Reed, 2013, p. 245). These findings echo Bourne's (2017) assertion that the PR profession undergoes professional development through the expectations of direct clients.

PRPs have generally positive views towards journalists, sharing similar values and regarding them as part of the same media community, especially when practising media relations (Mellado and Hanusch, 2011). The frustrations that PRPs have with their journalist contacts are less well-documented, possibly because within a service environment, PRPs, particularly those working in PR firms, are continually engaged in a process of gaining acceptance of their story idea or information through persuasion and negotiation with journalists: there is a dependency relationship. And as principal actors in the sale of emotional labour, practitioners may well learn to manage their feelings by focusing on 'what the other person might be thinking and feeling: imagine a reason that excuses his or her behaviour' (Hochschild, 1983, p. 113).

Thus the market for emotional labour in PR is characterised by the need for PRPs, on the one hand, to forge a continuous dialogue with clients to establish legitimacy: demonstrating their professional expertise, maintaining the client's confidence and trust, and achieving results in the form of media coverage; and on the other hand, to negotiate trusting relationships with journalists that shift back and forth according to the PRP's clients' requirements for media publicity, and the journalist's demand for news from their PR sources. These relationships are set within the context of high-pressured, fast-paced 24 hour news across a proliferation of commercial media outlets that, in turn, feed and sustain promotional culture (Davis, 2013). While journalists' pressures for news supply are conversely opportunities for PRPs, the negotiation of news values and professional identities between the two parties evokes and involves a site for emotional struggles, a site now shared with online actors in the form of SMIs. SMIs not only represent potential sources of information and gossip for the mainstream media, but also potent channels for PRPs to directly endorse their clients' messages. For some PRPs, operating in some markets, the content demands from online influencers are equally, if not more, important than those of the mainstream news media.

Conclusion

In this chapter, neoliberalism and promotional culture are presented as important explanatory frameworks for the expansion of the PR industry during the past 40 years. Promotional culture is linked to neoliberal economies and the rise of the market in every sphere of life – the commoditisation and 'marketisation of everything' from fast-moving consumer goods through to politics, education, and health services. An understanding of the social, cultural, and political trends arising from neoliberal ideas, and in the United Kingdom, the Conservative free market policies of the 1980s and 1990s, is fundamental to understanding PR as a 'self-interested' process of promotional culture which both produces and sustains discourses of culture that shape the public's relationship with institutions, increasingly through emotionalised digital networks. Furthermore, the promotional services that drive neoliberal economies are in increasing demand across the developing markets of Asia Pacific and Latin America.

I have also examined the key actors that 'set up the sale' (Hochschild, 1983, p. 91) of emotional labour in PR. These are the directors of PR firms and PR executives (also referred to as PRPs) and those who are behind the *demand* for emotional labour in PR: their clients, journalists, and, increasingly, online 'influencers'. PR here is characterised as an entrepreneurial, 'new' profession and PRPs as cultural intermediaries. PR draws its power from the market in providing services that protect and enhance organisational or brand reputation by influencing public perceptions through discourse. The value of the PR service to the client is in expertise, but this expertise is often fragile, based on situational and personal characteristics, rather than an established body of scientific knowledge, despite advances in professional certification. While the knowledge base required to practise PR successfully is changing rapidly as a consequence of digital capitalism and associated technological developments, PRPs within agencies continue to work performatively, drawing on personal and emotional resources to convince clients of their worth through building strong relationships and managing their expectations. Journalists, meanwhile, rely on PR sources for the supply of news stories, ideas, and research. Journalists' ever-increasing dependency on PR sources, at the same time, presents a threat to journalists' professional identities as independent reporters of facts and upholders of standards. This is particularly true at a time when journalism itself is undergoing a crisis of public trust and identity within a dynamic and 'emotionally-charged networked environment' populated by media actors who are better able to tune into audience tastes (Beckett and Deuze, 2016). Because of journalists' conflict of self-identity between 'churnalism' and upholders of standards, PRPs are the focus of criticism and, to a certain extent, media contempt.

Finally, while PRPs need to work on their emotions to ensure they are trusted by their journalist contacts, in some client sectors, emotional effort has been diverted to the demands of bloggers or SMIs as more powerful endorsers of PR messages, thus disrupting established media ecologies. From this depiction of the market for emotional labour in PR, I argue that PRPs are immersed in a continuous process of emotional labour to fulfil the demands of their management, their clients, and multiple media actors.

Notes

1 Based on 2018 survey data (personal communication, PRCA, 12.10.18).
2 In 2018, the CIPR listed around 50 masters and bachelors degrees in the United Kingdom. Two institutions, Bournemouth University and Wolverhampton University, announced official closure of their PR degrees in the same year.
3 45.9% in total reported to having a professional qualification in PR, including a foundation award, Advanced Certificate, or Diploma; 15.7% reported as having an 'undergraduate degree in PR or communications'; and 13.8% reported as having a 'masters degree in PR or communications' in the CIPR State of the Profession Survey 2016/2017.
4 There is likely to be some doubling-up of qualifications in the responses.
5 'Objectivity' is translated into broadcasting editorial guidelines in the United Kingdom as 'impartiality' (BBC) or 'due impartiality' (Channel 4 News). However, the National Union of Journalists code of conduct in the United Kingdom does not mention impartiality or objectivity, only that a journalist should 'differentiate between fact and opinion'.
6 The UK's Public Relations and Communications Association (PRCA) Census 2018 claimed that 86,000 practitioners were employed within the PR industry.

References

Abbott, A. (1988) *The System of Professions*. London, University of Chicago Press.
Alvesson, M. (1993) Organizations as rhetoric: Knowledge-intensive firms and the struggle with ambiguity. *Journal of Management Studies*, 30 (6), pp. 997–1015.
Archer, C. and Harrigan, P. (2016) Show me the money: How bloggers as stakeholders are challenging theories of relationship-building in public relations. *Media International Australia*, 160 (1) 67–77.
Bailey, R. (2009) Media relations. In R. Tench and L. Yeomans, eds. *Exploring Public Relations*, 2nd ed. Harlow, Pearson Education, pp. 295–315.

Beck, U. and Beck-Gernsheim, E. (2002) *Individualization*. London, Sage.

Beckett, C. and Deuze, M. (2016, July–September) On the role of emotion in the future of journalism. *Social Media + Society*, 2 (3), pp. 1–6.

Bolton, S. C. (2005) *Emotion Management in the Workplace*. Houndsmill, Hampshire, Palgrave Macmillan.

Bourdieu, P. (1997) The forms of capital. In A. H. Halsey, H. Lauder, P. Brown, and A. Stuart Wells, eds. *Education, Culture, Economy, Society*. Oxford, Oxford University Press, pp. 46–59.

Bourne, C. (2017) *Trust, Power and Public Relations in Financial Markets*. Abingdon, Oxon, Routledge.

Bourne, C. and Edwards, L. (2012) Producing trust, knowledge and expertise in financial markets: The global hedge fund industry 're-presents' itself. *Culture and Organization*, 18 (2), 107–122.

Bradley, H. and Devadason, R. (2008) Fractured transitions: young adults' pathways into contemporary labour markets. *Sociology*, 42 (1), pp. 119–136.

CEBR: Centre for Business and Economic Research/Chartered Institute of Public Relations (2005) *48,000 Professionals; £6.5 Billion Turnover: The economic significance of public relations*. London, Centre for Business and Economic Research.

Chartered Institute of Public Relations (2010) *2010 CIPR membership survey: The state of the PR profession: Benchmarking survey*. London, CIPR/ComRes.

Chartered Institute of Public Relations (2017a) 'We must elevate the importance of ethics' – CIPR welcomes fake news inquiry. Available from: http://newsroom. cipr.co.uk/pr-must-elevate-the-importance-of-ethics---cipr-welcomes-fake-news-inquiry/. Accessed 6 April 2018.

Chartered Institute of Public Relations (2017b) Integrated report 2016. Available from: https://www.cipr.co.uk/sites/default/files/CIPR_Integrated%20Report% 202016%20%28final%29...pdf. Accessed 12 April 2018.

Chartered Institute of Public Relations (2017c) State of PR survey 2016 [data tables]. Available from: https://survation.com/wp-content/uploads/2017/02/Final-CIPR-State-of-PR-Survey-1617-111016PMCH-1c5d7h8.pdf. Accessed 12 April 2018.

Chartered Institute of Public Relations (2018a) State of the profession survey. Available from: https://www.slideshare.net/CIPRPaul/cipr-state-of-the-profession-2018. Accessed 14 May 2018.

Chartered Institute of Public Relations (2018b) Effective media relations. Available from: https://www.cipr.co.uk/training/effective-media-relations. Accessed 14 April 2018.

Chartered Institute of Public Relations (2018c) Our organisation. Available from: https://www.cipr.co.uk/content/our-organisation. Accessed 12 April 2018.

Clarke, C. (2013) 70% of marketing and communications agency employees say work affects their health. *The Drum*, 22 May. Available from: http://www.thedrum. com/news/2013/05/22/70-marketing-and-communications-agency-employees-say-work-affects-their-health. Accessed 28 October 2018.

Cox, J. (2016) Record 84,000 journalists in the UK in 2016 according to Labour Force Survey (up 20,000 in a year). *Press Gazette*, 12 December. Available from: http://www.pressgazette.co.uk/record-84000-journalists-in-the-uk-in-2016-according-to-labour-force-survey-up-20000-in-a-year/?page=2. Accessed 28 October 2018.

Cronin, A. M. (2018) *Public Relations Capitalism: Promotional culture, publics and commercial democracy*. Cham, Switzerland, Palgrave Macmillan.

Curtin, P. and Gaither, T. K. (2005) Privileging identity, difference and power: The circuit of culture as a basis for public relations theory. *Journal of Public Relations Research*, 17 (2), pp. 91–115.

Curtin, P. A., Gallicano. T. D., and Matthews, K. (2011) Millennials' approaches to ethical decision making. *Public Relations Journal*, 5 (2), pp. 1–22.

Cutlip, S. M. (1995) *Public Relations History: From the 17th to the 20th century: The antecedents.* Mahwah, NJ: Lawrence Erlbaum.

Davies, N. (2008) *Flat Earth News: An award-winning reporter exposes falsehood, distortion and propaganda in the global media.* London, Vintage Books.

Davis, A. (2000a) Public relations, business news and the reproduction of corporate elite power. *Journalism*, 1 (3), pp. 282–304.

Davis, A. (2000b) Public relations, news production and changing patterns of source access in the British national media. *Media, Culture and Society*, 22 (1), pp. 39–59.

Davis, A. (2013) *Promotional Cultures.* Cambridge, Polity.

Deuze, M. (2005) What is journalism? Professional identity and ideology of journalists reconsidered. *Journalism*, 6 (4), pp. 442–464.

Dixon, H. (2017) Radio 4's Today editor hits back at dumbing down accusations. *The Telegraph*, 9 October. Available from: http://www.telegraph.co.uk/news/2017/10/09/radio-4s-today-editor-hits-back-dumbing-accusations/. Accessed 28 October 2018.

Donato, K. M. (1990) Keepers of the corporate image: Women in public relations. In B. F. Reskin and P. A. Roos, eds. *Job Queues, Gender Queues: Explaining women's inroads into male occupations.* Philadelphia, Temple University Press, pp. 129–144.

Dozier, D. M. (1992) The organizational roles of communications and public relations practitioners. In J. E. Grunig, ed. *Excellence in Public Relations and Communication Management.* Mahwah, NJ, and Hillsdale, MI, Lawrence Erlbaum Associates, pp. 327–355.

Dozier, D. M. and Broom, G. M. (2006) The centrality of practitioner roles to public relations theory. In C. H. Botan and V. Hazleton, eds. *Public Relations Theory II,* Mahwah, NJ, Routledge, pp. 120–148.

Duffy, E. and Hund, E. (2015, July–December) 'Having it all' on social media: Entrepreneurial femininity and self-branding among fashion bloggers. *Social Media + Society*, 1 (2), pp. 1–11.

Eagleton-Pierce, M. (2016) *Neoliberalism: The key concepts.* Abingdon, Oxon, Routledge.

Edwards, L. (2008) PR practitioners' cultural capital: An initial study and implications for research and practice. *Public Relations Review*, 34 (4), pp. 367–372.

Edwards, L. (2009) Public relations origins: Definitions and history. In R. Tench and L. Yeomans, eds. *Exploring Public Relations.* Harlow, Pearson Education, pp. 3–18.

Edwards. L. and Hodges, C. E. M. (2011) *Public Relations, Society and Culture: Theoretical and empirical explorations.* London and New York, Routledge.

Eliseev, A. (2017) The Gupta scandal: How a British PR firm came unstuck in South Africa. *New Statesman*, 20 July. Available from: https://www.newstatesman.com/culture/observations/2017/07/gupta-scandal-how-british-pr-firm-came-unstuck-south-africa. Accessed 3 April 2018.

Elmer, P. (2012) *The Social Construction of Public Relations Labour.* [Ph.D. thesis]. University of Essex.

Ewen, S. (1996) *PR! A Social History of Spin.* New York: Basic Books.

Foucault, M. (1978) Lecture, 29 March 1978.

Fournier, V. (1999) The appeal to professionalism as a disciplinary mechanism. *Sociological Review*, 47 (2), pp. 280–307.

Fredriksson, M. and Johansson, B. (2014) The dynamics of professional identity. *Journalism Practice*, 8 (5), pp. 585–595.

Gabbott, M. and Hogg, G. (1996) Purchasing public relations: The case of the public relations industry in Scotland. *Journal of Marketing Management*, 12, pp. 437–453.

Gallicano, T. D. (2013) Relationship management with the millennial generation of public relations agency employees. *Public Relations Review*, 39 (3), pp. 222–225.

Gallicano, T. D., Curtin, P., and Matthews, K. (2012) I love what I do, But... A relationship management survey of Millennial generation public relations agency employees. *Journal of Public Relations Research*, 24 (3), pp. 222–242.

Gandy, O. (1982) *Beyond Agenda Setting: Information subsidies and public policy*. Norwood, USAL Ablex.

du Gay, P., Hall, S., Janes, L., Madsen, A. K., Mackay, H., and Negus, K. (2013) *Doing Cultural Studies: The story of the Sony Walkman*, 2nd ed. London, Sage Publications in association with the Open University.

Goleman, D. (1996) *Emotionele intelligentie als sleutel tot succes [Emotional Intelligence as Key to Success]*. Amsterdam, Contact.

Grubenmann, S. and Meckel, M. (2017) Journalists' professional identity, *Journalism Studies*, 18 (6), pp. 732–748.

Grunig, J. E. and Hunt, T. (1984) *Managing Public Relations*. New York, Holt, Rinehart and Winston.

Guess A., Nyhan B., and Reifler J. (2018) Selective exposure to misinformation: evidence from the consumption of fake news during the 2016 US presidential campaign. *Working Paper. European Research Council*. Available from: https://www.dartmouth.edu/~nyhan/fake-news-2016.pdf. Accessed 23 April, 2018.

Hall, S. (2003) New Labour's double shuffle. *Soundings*, 24, pp. 10–24.

Hall, S. and Waddington, S. (2017) Exploring the mental wellbeing of the public relations profession, 21 February. Available from: http://www.futureproofingcomms.co.uk/thelatest/2017/2/21/gd41ooq0nru1rsr57thsm6e5qpcx8t. Accessed 28 October 2018.

Harvey, D. (2005) *A Brief History of Neoliberalism*. Oxford, Oxford University Press.

Hochschild, A. R. (1983) *The Managed Heart: Commercialization of human feeling*. Berkeley, CA, University of Berkeley.

Hodges, C. (2006) 'PRP culture': A framework for exploring public relations practitioners as cultural intermediaries. *Journal of Communication Management*, 10 (1), pp. 80–93.

Hodges, C. M. and Edwards, L. (2014) Public relations practitioners. In J. Smith Maguire and J. Matthews, eds. *The Cultural Intermediaries Reader*. London, Sage, pp. 89–99.

Holmes, P. A. (2007) *The state of the public relations industry: Preliminary report: June 2007, for Huntsworth plc*. Available from: http://www.huntsworth.com/docs/Paul%20Holmes%20Report%20-%20The%20State%20of%20the%20PR%20Industry.pdf. Accessed 5 February 2009.

Hopper, M. K. and Huxford, J. E. (2015) Gathering emotion: Examining newspaper journalists' engagement in emotional labour. *Journal of Media Practice*, 16 (1), pp. 25–41.

International Communications Consultancy Organisation (2011) International Communications Consultancy Organisation's (ICCO) first quarterly trends barometer survey. Available from: http://www.iccopr.com/#. Accessed 27 April 2011.

International Communications Consultancy Organisation (2017) World PR report 2017. Available from: https://iccopr.com/wp-content/uploads/2015/01/World-PR-Report-2017.pdf. Accessed 28 October 2017.

Jackson, D. and Moloney (2016) Inside churnalism. *Journalism Studies*, 17 (6), pp. 763–780.

Kelly, A. (2017) Fake news: PR's little monster. *Huffpost*, 25 February. Available from: https://www.huffingtonpost.com/entry/fake-news-prs-little-monster_us_ 58a777e0e4b026a89a7a2afb. Accessed 3 April 2018.

Khamis, S., Ang, L., and Welling, R. (2017) Self-branding, 'micro-celebrity' and the rise of social media influencers. *Celebrity Studies*, 8 (2), pp. 191–208.

Lahav, T. and Roth-Cohen, O. (2016) The changing blogosphere and its impact on public relations practice and professional ethics: The Israeli case. *Public Relations Review*, 42, pp. 929–931.

Larson, M. S. (1977) *The Rise of Professionalism: A sociological analysis*. Berkeley, CA, University of California Press.

L'Etang, J. (2004) *Public Relations in Britain: A history of professional practice in the 20th century*. Mahwah, NJ, Lawrence Erlbaum Associates.

L'Etang, J. (2008) *Public Relations: Concepts, practice and critique*. Sage, London.

L'Etang, J., Falkheimer, J., and Lugo, J. (2007) Public relations and tourism: Critical reflections and a research agenda. *Public Relations Review*, 33 (1), pp. 68–76.

Lewis, J., Williams, A., Franklin, B. Thomas, J., and Mosdell, N. (2008) The quality and independence of British journalism. Cardiff School of Journalism, Media and Cultural Studies Report. Available from: https://orca.cf.ac.uk/18439/1/ Quality%20%26%20Independence%20of%20British%20Journalism.pdf. Accessed 28 October 2018.

Macdonald, K. M. (1995) *The Sociology of the Professions*. London, Sage.

Mallinson, B. (1996) *Public Lies and Private Truths: An anatomy of public relations*. London, Cassell.

Martinson, J. (2017) Today editor Sarah Sands: 'How can you say it's not worth talking about a £30bn industry because it's to do with women?' *The Guardian*, 28 October. Available from: https://www.theguardian.com/media/2017/oct/28/ radio-4-todays-editor-sarah-sands-interview. Accessed 6 April 2018.

Mart, L. and Jackson, N. (2005) Public relations agencies in the UK travel industry: Does size matter? *PRism*, 3 (1). Available from: http://www.prismjournal.org/ vol_3_iss_1.html. Accessed 2 May 2018.

McKinley, R. (2017) PR Week reveals the top 150 UK PR consultancies in 2017. *PR Week*, 2 May. Available from: https://www.prweek.com/article/ 1431857/prweek-reveals-top-150-uk-pr-consultancies-2017. Accessed 28 October 2018.

Mellado, C. and Hanusch, F. (2011) Comparing professional identities, attitudes, and views in public communication: A study of Chilean journalists and public relations practitioners. *Public Relations Review*, 37, pp. 384–391.

Meng, J., Berger, B. H., and Rogers, H. (2017) Managing millennial communication professionals: Connecting generation attributes, leadership development, and employee engagement. *Acta Prosperitatis*, 8, pp. 68–83. Riga, Turiba University. Available from: http://www.turiba.lv/f/Izdevnieciba/AP8-internetam.pdf. Accessed 28 October 2018.

Miller, D. and Dinan, W. (2000) The rise of the PR industry in Britain, 1979–98. *"European Journal of Communication"*, 15 (1), pp. 5–35.

Miller, P. and Rose, N. (1990) Governing economic life. *Economy and Society*, 19 (1), pp. 1–31.

Moloney, K. (2006) *Rethinking PR: PR propaganda and democracy.* London, Routledge.

Moloney, K., Jackson, D., and McQueen, D. (2013) News journalism and public relations: A dangerous relationship. In S. Allan and K. Fowler Watt, eds. *Journalism: New challenges.* Bournemouth, Centre for Journalism and Communication Research, Bournemouth University, pp. 259–281.

Moor, L. (2008) Neo-liberalism and promotional culture. *Soundings*, 38. Available from: http://www.lwbooks.co.uk/journals/soundings/cultures_capitalism/cultures_capitalism10.html. Accessed 3 April 2008.

Motion, J. and Leitch, S. (1996) A discursive perspective from New Zealand: Another world view. *Public Relations Review*, 22 (3), pp. 297–309.

Muzio, D., Ackroyd, S., and Chanlat, J.-F. (2008) Introduction: Lawyers, doctors and business consultants. In D. Muzio, S. Ackroyd, and J.-F. Chanlat, eds. *Redirections in the Study of Expert Labour.* Basingstoke, Palgrave Macmillan, pp. 1–30.

Myers, K. M. and Sadaghiani, K. (2010) Millennials in the workplace: A communication perspective on millennials' organizational relationships and performance. *Journal of Business Psychology*, 25, pp. 225–238.

Newman, N. (2017) *Digital news project: Journalism, media and technology trends and predictions 2017.* Oxford, Reuters Institute.

Newman, N. with Fletcher, R., Kalogeropoulos, A., Levy, D. A. L., and Nielsen, R. K. (2017) *Digital news report 2017.* Oxford, Reuters Institute.

Nissim, M. (2017) BBC's John Humphrys criticised for suggesting trans women are 'men who think they are women'. *Pink News*, 18 October. Available from: http://www.pinknews.co.uk/2017/10/18/bbcs-john-humphrys-criticised-for-suggesting-trans-women-are-men-who-think-they-are-women/. Accessed 6 November 2017.

Obermaier, M. Koch, T., and Riesmeyer, C. (2015) Deep impact? How journalists perceive the influence of public relations on their news coverage and which variables determine this impact. *Communication Research*, 45 (7), pp. 1031–1053.

Office for National Statistics (2018) Employment by occupation (dataset). Available from: https://www.ons.gov.uk/employmentandlabourmarket/peopleinwork/employmentandemployeetypes/datasets/employmentbyoccupationemp04. Accessed 28 October 2018.

Pieczka, M. (2000) Objectives and evaluation in public relations work: What do they tell us about expertise and professionalism? *Journal of Public Relations Research*, 12 (3) pp. 211–233.

Pieczka, M. (2002) Public relations expertise deconstructed. *Media Culture and Society*, 24 (3), pp. 301–323.

Pieczka, M. (2006a) 'Chemistry' and the public relations industry: An exploration of the concept of jurisdiction and issues arising. In J. L'Etang and M. Pieczka, eds. *Public Relations: Critical debates and contemporary practice.* Mahwah, NJ, and London, Lawrence Erlbaum Associates, pp. 303–327.

Pieczka, M. (2006b) Promotional work: The case of PR consultancy in the UK 1995–2000. [Ph.D. thesis]. University of Stirling.

Pieczka, M. and L'Etang, J. (2001) Public relations and the question of professionalism. In R. L. Heath, ed. *Handbook of Public Relations.* Thousand Oaks, CA, London, and New Delhi, Sage, pp. 223–235.

Pieczka, M. and L'Etang, J. (2006) Public relations and the question of professionalism. In J. L'Etang and M. Pieczka, eds. *Public Relations: Critical debates and contemporary practice*. Mahwah, NJ, and London, Lawrence Erlbaum Associates, pp. 265–278.

Pilkington, M. (2015) Well-being, happiness and the structural crisis of neoliberalism: An interdisciplinary analysis through the lenses of emotions. *Mind & Society*, 15, (2) pp. 265–280.

Public Relations and Communications Association (2016a) Public Relations and Communications Association (PRCA) response to the Culture, Media and Sports Committee's 'Fake News' Inquiry. Available from: https://www.prca.org.uk/sites/default/files/PRCA%20Response%20to%20Fake%20News%20Inquiry.pdf. Accessed 28 October 2018.

Public Relations and Communications Association (2016b) *The PRCA Census 2016*. London, PRCA.

Public Relations and Communications Association (2018a) *The PRCA Census 2018*. London, PRCA. Available from: https://www.prca.org.uk/sites/default/files/PR%20and%20Communications%20Census%202018.pdf. Accessed 28 October 2018.

Public Relations and Communications Association (2018b) Good media relations. Available from: https://www.prca.org.uk/course/good-media-relations. Accessed 14 April 2018.

Public Relations Society of America (2017) PRSA statement on 'alternative facts'. Available from: https://www.prsa.org/prsa-statement-alternative-facts/. Accessed 14 April 2018.

Reed, C. (2013) Becoming a profession: Crafting professional identities in public relations. [Ph.D thesis]. Cardiff University.

Reich, Z. (2010) Measuring the impact of PR on published news in increasingly fragmented news environments. A multifaceted approach. *Journalism Studies*, 11, pp. 799–816.

Richards, B. and Rees, G. (2011) The management of emotion in British journalism. *Media, Culture & Society*, 33 (6), pp. 851–867.

Ries, A. and Ries, L. (2002) *The Fall of Advertising and the Rise of PR*. New York, Harper Collins.

Risager, B. S. (2016) Neoliberalism is a political project: An interview with David Harvey. *Jacobin*. 23 July, 2016. Available from: https://www.jacobinmag.com/2016/07/david-harvey-neoliberalism-capitalism-labor-crisis-resistance/. Accessed 6 October 2018.

Rogers, D. (2009) We find PR enterprise in times of hardship. *PR Week*, 10 July, pp. 24–25.

van Ruler, B. (1996) *Communicatiemanagement in Nederland [Communication Management in The Netherlands]*. Houten, Bohn Stafleu Van Loghum.

van Ruler, B. (2005) Commentary: Professionals are from Venus, scholars are from Mars. *Public Relations Review*, 31 (2), pp. 159–173.

Sallot, L. M. and Johnson, E. A. (2006) Investigating relationships between journalists and public relations practitioners: Working together to set, frame and build the public agenda, 1991–2004. *Public Relations Review*, 32, pp. 151–159.

Schiller, D. (2014) *Digital Depression: Information technology and economic crisis*. Urbana, IL, Chicago, IL, and Springfield, MA, University of Illinois Press.

Segal, D. (2018) How Bell Pottinger, PR firm for despots and rogues, met its end in South Africa. *New York Times*, 4 February. Available from: https://www.nytimes. com/2018/02/04/business/bell-pottinger-guptas-zuma-south-africa.html Accessed 3 April 2018.

Shepherd, T. (2014) Gendering the commodity audience in social media. In C. Carter, L. Steiner, and L. McLaughlin, eds. *The Routledge Companion to Media and Gender* New York, Routledge, pp. 157–167.

Smith, B. (2010). The evolution of the blogger: Blogger considerations of public relations sponsored content in the blogosphere. *Public Relations Review*, 36, pp. 175–177.

Statista (2018) Number of monthly active Instagram users from January 2013 to September 2017 (in millions). Available from: https://www.statista.com/statistics/ 253577/number-of-monthly-active-instagram-users/. Accessed 14 April 2018.

Sturges, F. (2017) The Today programme needs more than a harrumphing John Humphrys. *The Guardian*, 25 September. Available from: https://www.theguardian. com/commentisfree/2017/sep/25/today-programme-john-humphrys-editor-sarah-sands. Accessed 14 April 2018.

Swedberg, R. (2005) *The Max Weber Dictionary: Key words and central concepts*. Stanford, CA, Stanford University Press.

Sudhaman, A. (2015) Pepsico points the way for PR industry's procurement puzzle. 10 December. Available from: https://www.holmesreport.com/latest/article/pepsico-points-the-way-for-pr-industry's-procurement-puzzle. Accessed 2 October 2018.

The Holmes Report (2017a) The Global Communications Report 2017. Available at: http://annenberg.usc.edu/sites/default/files/KOS_2017_GCP_April6.pdf. Accessed 14 December 2017.

The Holmes Report (2017b) Available at: https://www.holmesreport.com/ranking-and-data/global-pr-agency-rankings/2017-pr-agency-rankings/top-250. Accessed 14 December 2017.

Thomas, R., Hardy, C., Cutcher, L., and Ainsworth, S. (2014) What's age got to do with it? On the critical analysis of age and organizations. *Organization Studies*, 35 (11), pp. 1569–1584.

Toth, E. (2001) How feminist theory advanced the practice of public relations. In R. L. Heath, ed. *Handbook of Public Relations*. Thousand Oaks, CA, London, and New Delhi, Sage, pp. 237–246.

UK Parliament (2011) Foreign Affairs Committee – second report. FCO public diplomacy: The Olympic and Paralympic Games 2012. Available at: https:// publications.parliament.uk/pa/cm201011/cmselect/cmfaff/581/58107.htm. Accessed 14 December 2017.

UK Parliament (2014) *House of Lords Select Committee on soft power and the UK's influence: Persuasion and power in the modern world*. London: The Stationary Office.

Verčič, D. (2012) Public relations firms and their three occupational cultures. In K. Sriramesh, and D. Verčič. eds. *Culture and Public Relations: Links and implications* New York, Routledge, pp. 243–257.

Verčič, D., Tench, R., and A. T. Verčič (2018) Collaboration and conflict between agencies and clients. *Public Relations Review*, 44 (1), pp. 156–164.

Waddington, S. (2015) 10 opportunities in the UK's £10 billion public relations market. Available at: http://influence.cipr.co.uk/2015/10/23/10-opportunities-uks-10-billion-public-relations-market/. Accessed 14 December 2017.

Waddington. S. (2018) A SEO PR primer. *Influence*, 20 March. Available at: https://influenceonline.co.uk/2018/03/20/seo-pr-primer/. Accessed 2 April 2018.

Waeraas, A. (2009) On Weber: Legitimacy and legitimation in public relations. In Ø. Ihlen, B. van Ruler, and M. Fredriksson, eds. *Public Relations and Social Theory*. New York and London, Routledge, pp. 301–322.

Washbourne, N. (2009) Media context of contemporary public relations and journalism. In R. Tench and L. Yeomans, eds. *Exploring Public Relations*, 2nd ed. Harlow, Pearson Education, pp. 68–81.

Washbourne, N. (2017) Public relations and democracy. In R. Tench and L. Yeomans, eds. *Exploring Public Relations*, 4th ed. Harlow, Pearson Education, pp. 60–73.

Waters, R., D., Tindall, N. T. S., and Morton, T. S. (2010) Dropping the ball on media inquiries: The role of deadlines in media catching. *Public Relations Review*, 37, pp. 151–156.

Weaver, C. K. (2001) Dressing for battle in the new global economy: Putting power, identity, and discourse into public relations theory. *Management Communication Quarterly*, 15 (2), pp. 279–288.

Weber, M. (1968) *Economy and Society*. New York, Bedminster. (Original work published 1922)

Wernick, A. (1991) *Promotional culture*. London, Sage.

WPP (2017) Our companies. Available from: http://www.wpp.com/wpp/companies/?PageIndex=0&SortBy=Name&PageSize%5B15%5D=15&SortReverse%5Bfalse%5D=A-Z&Mode=company. Accessed 10 July 2017.

Wyatt, R. (2013) The PR census 2013. *PR Week*, 18 December. Available from: https://www.prweek.com/article/1225129/pr-census-2013. Accessed 28 October 2018.

Yeomans, L. (2007) Emotion in public relations: A neglected phenomenon. *Journal of Communication Management*, 11 (3), pp. 212–221.

Yeomans, L. (2016) Imagining the lives of others: Empathy in public relations. *Public Relations Inquiry*, 5 (1), pp. 71–92.

Yeomans, L. and Baxter, H. (2014) How do food bloggers and PR practitioners in the hospitality sector view their relationships? A UK perspective. *Revista Internacional Relaciones Públicas*, 4 (8), pp. 221–244. Available from: http://revistarelacionespublicas.uma.es/index.php/revrrpp/issue/view/8. Accessed 28 October 2018.

Zerfass, A., Verhoeven, P., Moreno, A., Tench, R., and Verčič, D. (2016) *European communication monitor 2016. Exploring trends in big data, stakeholder engagement and strategic communication. Results of a survey in 43 countries*. Brussels, EACD/EUPRERA, Quadriga Media Berlin.

Zerfass, A., Moreno, Á., Tench, R., Verčič, D., and Verhoeven, P. (2017) *European communication monitor 2017. How strategic communication deals with the challenges of visualisation, social bots and hypermodernity. Results of a survey in 50 countries*. Brussels, EACD/EUPRERA, Quadriga Media Berlin.

Zyman, S. and Brott, A. (2003) *The End of Advertising as We Know It*. Hoboken, New Jersey, John Wiley and Sons.

4 Interrogating the 'pink ghetto'

Gender and public relations

Introduction

A gender perspective is essential to understanding relationships between public relations practitioners (PRPs) and their professional contacts from an emotional labour perspective, particularly in the light of the 'feminisation' of the profession over the past 30 years, and Hochschild's (1983) contention that emotion work largely falls to women working in service occupations. Gendered interactions are a key focus of this chapter, in which I extend Hochschild's perspective of gendered emotional labour, as well as examine public relations (PR) as a gendered occupation.

I start by discussing normative (i.e. relatively fixed) and performative (fluid and changing) concepts of gender in social theory. I go on to outline, discuss, and critique Hochschild's position on the relationship between gender and emotional labour. I then examine feminist literature relating to gender and occupations, extending and building on Hochschild's model. The (predominantly) liberal feminist PR literature is then critiqued, especially concerning how the concepts of emotional labour, gender identity, and performativity are underexplored within mainstream PR scholarship. I argue that postfeminist theory has utility as a critical lens to generate a more nuanced understanding of PR – for example, as performative emotional labour within a neoliberal context. Finally, I briefly consider emotional labour as linked to the notion of digital labour, reflecting an increasing requirement for PRPs to simulate intimacies online through social media platforms such as Facebook, Twitter, and LinkedIn. I argue that emotional labour for PRPs working in the 'pink ghetto' of PR agencies can be viewed as gendered struggles for professional identity and legitimacy in day-to-day relations with clients, journalists, colleagues, and online influencers.

Gender in social theory: choice, identity, and performativity

The term 'gender' is widely understood as relating to the biological category of male or female. Scott observes that 'in popular conversation, the terms *sex* and *gender* are as often used synonymously as oppositionally; indeed sometimes it seems that gender is simply a polite euphemism for *sex*' (Scott, 1999, p. 71). However, its meaning in social theory has developed otherwise since the term was first used in the 1970s (Acker, 1988; Howard et al., 1999; Dow and Wood, 2006). Evans (2003, p. 7) notes that feminists 'used the word as the starting point for the study of women and their social subordination'. The 1990s, however, saw a re-conceptualisation of gender, which now recognises 'the impact of the social world on constructions of both masculinity and femininity' (p. 8).

The problematisation of gender, or gender as choice, is widely attributed to the work of Judith Butler (e.g. Walters, 1999, p. 250; Evans, 2003, p. 58; Wood, 2006, p. 4) who, in her pioneering work, *Gender Trouble* (1990) conceived gender as an aspect of identity which is performative: it is repeatedly performed and embodied; gender is what people *do*, not what they *have*. The notion of gender as choice is not new. Simone de Beauvoir's frequently quoted dictum: 'one is not born, but rather becomes a woman' provided inspiration for Butler (1986) in distinguishing sex from the acquisition of gender. However, Butler subsequently stretched the concept of gender to a postmodern notion of identity, something that is fluid, unstable, and deeply dependent upon social context. Butler's notion of performativity is not exclusive, however. Golombisky (2015, p. 402), writing on feminist theory development in PR, contends that Lara Rakow (1986, 1989) pre-dated Butler in her conception of gendered performativity; furthermore, it is Rakow's work that PR feminist scholars should look to for inspiration. I return to Golombisky's discussion of performativity later in this chapter.

Dow and Wood (2006) comment that performative theory, proposed by Butler and others, who talk of 'doing gender' (gender as a verb instead of a noun), has a central role in contemporary research on gender and communication. Here, discourses 'frame performances of gender as either masculine or feminine, place the masculine above the feminine, and use that *hierarchical binary* [my italics] to justify inequalities in the social, political and material conditions of people's lives' (Dow and Wood, 2006, p. xvii). Importantly, Butler's performativity is not a conscious, voluntary act but is a result of discursive repetitions and past citations from which performativities derive their power; therefore 'certain announcements of gender, and certain performances of gender, produce the status and fixity of gender through the forced reiteration of norms' (Brady and Schirato, 2011, p. 46). While Butler acknowledges that it is not possible to remain detached from one's gender, it is possible to subvert repeated gender norms to 'expose the illusion of fixed gender identity' (Fallaize, 1998, p. 30).

Questions concerning gender as fixed/fluid have been taken up elsewhere. Sociologists writing about late (or 'second') modernity such as Beck (1992) and Beck and Beck-Gernsheim (2002, pp. 202–203) argue that the dynamic processes of individualisation and the de-traditionalisation of gender, class, race, the family, and other structural features mean that individuals have to re-negotiate their identities in the workplace and at home. De-traditionalisation, as conceived by Beck and Beck-Gernsheim (2002, p. 26), involves living a life where traditions are chosen or invented rather than imposed, and often this involves living 'in conflict between different cultures; the invention of hybrid traditions'. The vision of individuals negotiating the dynamic conditions of late modernity is therefore done so in relation to historical constructions of gender roles. While young, female PRPs, for example, may be educated to a high level and actively construct their individual 'life projects' that may involve having both a career and a family (Beck and Beck-Gernsheim, 2002), historical constructions of gender around hierarchical binaries are likely to continue to pervade some client organisations as well as their employing PR firms.

Gendered assumptions of the 'universal worker' as a man, images of men's bodies, and masculinity infuse organisational processes. Such processes serve to marginalise women, contributing to sex segregation in the workplace (Acker, 1990). In advancing the theory of gender as an organising principle, Acker (1992, p. 568) proposes that the key question to ask is to what extent has 'the overall institutional structure and the character of particular institutional areas been formed by and through gender?' Gendered processes, according to Acker (1992), operate on four levels. The first is a process of exclusion in the form of overt decisions and procedures that may place people in gendered roles; second, are the creation of 'images, symbols and ideologies' that give legitimacy to institutions: this argument posits that even in apparently 'gender neutral' institutions, the discourse adopted communicates the gendered reality of 'hegemonic masculinity', which is a more subtle process. A third process of gender is through social interaction, in which people 'do gender' (West and Zimmerman, 1987). A fourth process is adopting a gendered 'persona', or gender identity, expressed through demeanour and behaviour, that is appropriate to the situation (Acker, 1992).

In reference to gender pay gaps across the professions, the term 'unconscious bias' became popular in 2017/2018. Research undertaken by the PR industry in the United Kingdom, in an attempt to find the causes behind the industry's own pay gap, uncovered continuing disparities and biases in the way that men and women were hired and promoted to senior levels, particularly in PR agencies that operated with very little transparency (CIPR, 2017a). The findings revealed that 'people tend to gravitate towards and sponsor people who mirror them; meaning male leadership could be reproduced in senior management' (CIPR, 2017a, p. 11). Reskin (2000), according to Rhode (2017, p. 104), theorised that people automatically categorise others based upon 'ascribed characteristics such as gender' involving 'quick cognitive assessments', including gender stereotyping, that may not reflect consciously held values and beliefs. The implication of 'hegemonic masculinity' operating within contemporary PR practice is not new. Earlier research in the United States found that the male is valued by some agency clients who want 'a senior male point of view' (Aldoory and Toth, 2002, pp. 117–125).

Men were favoured over women because of their scarcity and the perceived (different) attributes.

Skeggs (2004), writing from a feminist perspective, and citing the work of Adkins (2000) and Cronin (2000) in particular, rejects what she describes as the middle-class, rhetorical claims of Beck (1992) and others that individualisation and, in particular, 'reflexive modernity' displace traditional notions of class, gender, and race. Women workers, as a social category, for example, have difficulty getting beyond the identity of 'woman worker' because 'certain gendered and sexed identity practices are rendered intrinsic to women workers' and therefore they cannot be free to exchange them as resources in 'the making of the enterprising self' (Skeggs, 2004, p. 74). Thus, the deployment of aspects of femininity by men (i.e. as caring managers) in the workplace is rewarded, whereas women who perform femininity are doing what is expected of them (p. 55) and indeed may be dismissed as being 'too feminine'.

To throw light on the discussions of gender in this chapter, it is important to keep the different conceptualisations of gender in mind; namely, that gender is, on the one hand, interpreted as 'fixed' and linked to the biological category of male or female (including understandings of attributes historically associated with being male and female and the roles of men and women in society); and on the other hand, gender is fluid: it is an aspect of identity that is performed and produced through social interaction. A fluid identity perspective also suggests that gender is agentically used as a resource (or not) in the making of the self within an individualised and detraditionalised society; conversely, these ideas raise questions about who truly has the flexibility to do so and whether PRPs, rather, perform the gender roles that are expected of them in different social contexts.

Gendered emotional labour: status, power, and identity

Hochschild's analysis primarily acknowledges the 'hierarchical binary' (Dow and Wood, 2006) of men and women within American society that compels actors to perform 'gender displays' (Reskin and Padavic, 1994) according to cultural norms both within the workplace and society. She argues that emotion work is gendered: it is more important for women than it is for men in jobs that involve public contact, because women *in general* have 'far less independent access to money, power, authority, or status in society' (Hochschild, 1983, p. 163). With fewer resources to draw on (i.e. money, power, authority, and status), women have to draw on the resources that they *do* have, including their 'capacity to manage feeling and to do 'relational' work' (p. 163). Further, gender differentially influences the emotional tasks required in managing interactions with others: for example, she asserted that women manage other people's anger and aggressive behaviour by 'being nice' whereas for men 'the socially-assigned task of aggressing against those that break rules of various sorts creates the private task of mastering fear and vulnerability' (Hochschild, 1983, p. 163).

Hochschild's performative metaphor likens emotion work to the processes of acting, so that 'being nice', a gender display most often associated with women, often involves what Hochschild refers to as 'evocative emotion work' (Hochschild, 2008, p. 122) or consciously working-up a feeling that is initially absent, whereas suppressing a feeling that is already present requires the cognitive focus of control. Evocative emotion work requires 'deep acting' (Hochschild, 1983, p. 38) which requires framing an actor's feelings in accordance with the approved 'feeling rules' (pp. 57–59) or expectations set by a particular social context or work setting.

Within the Delta Airlines study, Hochschild (1983, p. 175) observed that the women flight attendants were not just women, but represented an American middle-class notion of Woman who is expected, by passengers and the airline company, to

> enact two leading roles of Womanhood: the loving wife and mother (serving food, tending to the needs of others) and the glamorous 'career woman' (dressed to be seen, in contact with strange men, professional and controlled in manner; and literally very far from home).

To fit with cultural expectations of male and female gender roles, a 'fictional redistribution of authority' (Hochschild, 1983, p. 178) led to a complex interplay of gendered performance within Delta Airlines. Male flight attendants were assumed by passengers to hold more seniority (by virtue of their maleness) even though male flight attendants at the time of the study were relatively newcomers to the industry and less likely to hold senior positions. In turn, male flight attendants reacted to passengers as if they *did* hold more authority than in reality, while female flight attendants complied with this gender display by getting their male colleagues to throw warning glances to troublemaking passengers. The assumption by female flight attendants that passengers would be less respectful of their authority led them to use deference and tact in dealing with abuse, even though this approach did not always prevent its escalation. Deferential displays by the female flight attendants, in turn, reinforced the expectations of male workers that female colleagues owed them deference. Thus, terms of address became indicators of status; so that while the women flight attendants referred to themselves as 'girls', its use by male colleagues and passengers was seen as a term of subordination.

The struggle with power, status, and identity that women flight attendants faced, as negotiated through emotional labour, meant that the only defences or 'status shields' that could be enacted to improve their position were the traditionally feminine qualities of supportive 'mother' or 'sexually desirable mate' (Hochschild, 1983, p. 182). These qualities, in turn, became the property of company management. The niceness associated with feminine qualities of enhancing the well-being and status of others (e.g. laughing at the jokes of male passengers and offering compliments) became part of the service. Emotion, then, became a resource for the organisation to demand and exploit.

Hochschild's Marx-inspired theorising of emotional labour centres around the experiences of flight attendants in the 1980s, where the commercial exploitation of their 'feminine' qualities of both mother and 'sexual mate' (Hochschild, 1983, p. 182) led to actors' estrangement, or alienation, from authentic feelings, where their own sense of self, or identity, had yet to be discovered. Within *The Managed Heart*, the emotion work of male flight attendants is underexplored, save for an acknowledgement that the job of maintaining a male identity in a woman's occupation is the 'principal hidden task' (p. 171) of male flight attendants. Male identity is asserted when male flight attendants are called upon to assist female flight attendants who are on the receiving end of verbal abuse from passengers. However, for the men to wield anger and make threats would be stepping beyond the expectations of the role; therefore, argues Hochschild, it is this constraint in identity-expression from which male flight attendants are more likely to feel estranged.

Gendered emotional labour revisited: relational practice in the workplace

Studies of masculinity (e.g. Roper, 1996) argue that Hochschild's work, in presenting a gender hierarchy where women are the main subjects of the commercialisation of feeling, limits representations of 'being masculine' to expressions of aggression or denial of vulnerability. Such depictions ignore the self-presentations by men that include behaviour often associated with *both* masculinity and femininity (Cornwall and Lindisfarne, 1994, cited in Collinson and Hearn, 1996). Gendered self-presentations are particularly relevant to the study of male and female PRPs in a profession that is female-dominated at the middle and lower levels of agency work (PRCA, 2016; CIPR, 2017b). Indeed, the processes of everyday PRP-client relations, which have an emphasis on building rapport and empathy, suggest that a feminine relational approach is performed by both male and female PRPs (Yeomans, 2013). The concept of relational work is referred to only briefly in *The Managed Heart* but Hochschild (1983, p. 163) clearly associates this work with women using feeling as an important resource offered as a gift to men in 'in return for the more material resources they lack', referring to the women's economic subordination. However, Hochschild's interpretation of relational work in service occupations limits the scope for nuanced exploration of gender in PR. In a postmodern era characterised by pluralistic expressions of gender identity and gendered performance, the concept of relational practice offers further insights into gender and emotion in the workplace. Studies of gender in the workplace focus on gendered *ways of talking* as well as how *discourses function to shape* organisational social and cultural processes.

Relational practice is defined as 'the ability to work effectively with others, understanding the emotional contexts in which work gets done' (Fletcher, 1999, p. 2).

Holmes (2006, p. 6) draws a distinction between feminine and masculine interactional styles that are 'strongly associated with middle-class white men and women in the construction of their unmarked gender identity strategies which instantiate and reinforce "the gender order"'. Drawing from research on language and gender, Holmes (2006, p. 6) lists feminine interactional styles as, for example, 'facilitative', 'supportive feedback', 'conciliatory', while listing masculine styles as, for example, 'competitive', 'aggressive interruptions', and 'confrontational'. Holmes (2006) found that both feminine and masculine relational practice styles may be used strategically to achieve workplace goals, while acknowledging that feminine interactional styles tend to go unnoticed. Holmes (2006, p. 103) argued that much relational practice takes place in informal settings '...at the boundaries of meetings, in passing in the corridor, over lunch...' and is typically off-the-record small talk which is perceived as feminine activity. However, within different communities of practice, such small talk may also be perceived as relatively masculine – for example, using humour in a challenging way.

Holmes' interactional style theory provides insight into how a gendered order in the White, middle-class PR industry (Edwards, 2008) is structured in situations where both 'feminine' and 'masculine' styles are deployed with strategic intent, and importantly, *whose* styles are taken seriously when it comes to PRP career advancement. The relational nature of PR work means that successful male and female practitioners pay very close attention to the detail of their interpersonal interactions, including the gendered styles that are likely to pay off through different client interactions as well as the gendered styles that will win the approval of agency bosses (Yeomans, 2013).

Gender analyses also focus on the discourses that shape the social and cultural processes of a profession. Davies (1996, p. 661) argues that 'the key feature of profession is that it professes gender' in the sense that cultural notions of a profession, such as expert knowledge, autonomy, order, detachment, and emotional control, are masculine. Other competences (such as caring) are excluded or seen as support work, thus sustaining gender inequalities. In their study of the legal, management, and teaching professions in the United Kingdom, Bolton and Muzio (2008) found that in these professions, a 'masculine cultural project' dominates. Women managers, in order to progress within a male dominated profession, 'do gender' to the extent that they 'exceed the cultural norms of managing like a man' (p. 291). The authors cite qualitative studies suggesting that in referring to themselves, women adopt male language such as 'I'm still my own man'. On the other hand, in pink-collar work, such as teaching, where men are under-represented, Bolton and Muzio (2008) claim that the masculine cultural project is manifest in both men's occupation at the top of school hierarchies and the devaluation of caring work. Although caring work was traditionally carried out by female primary school teachers, it is now increasingly delegated to (mainly female) learning support assistants. This professionalisation project, according to Bolton and Muzio (2008), therefore serves to redefine the role of educator as a more rational, masculine endeavour. Such observations of the processes of gender segregation in other occupations are not difficult to translate to the PR context. PRPs of either sex who place a value on 'nurturing' relationships in their everyday discourse may well get sidelined at promotion panels.

In her critical discourse analysis of the management consulting profession, Marsh (2009), drawing on the work of Fletcher (1998), identifies two competing discourses: 'the objective professional' which relates to masculine discourse; and the 'trusted adviser' which relates to feminine discourse, where relational practices, processes, social purposes, and emotions are valued. Marsh (2009, p. 281) concludes that the shift from feminine approaches to masculine approaches in what is termed 'modern' or 'scientific management' consulting has:

> led to 'disappearing' of 'feminine' approaches. Women are in a double-bind in enacting a 'feminine' discourse; men doing so may be perceived as doing women's work; both risk being discounted or held in contempt, unless those commissioning also enact a 'feminine' discourse.
>
> (Marsh, 2009, p. 281)

Fitch and Third (2010, p. 6) argue that the PR professionalisation project is 'in part a response generated by a concern about the feminisation of the public relations industry'. Thus, it would appear there is a gendered discourse struggle within the PR profession: a masculine discourse, which appropriates the management discourse of strategy, measurement, and return on investment; and feminine discourse, which adopts the discourse of relationships. Furthermore, while specific personal attributes are ranked as important 'soft skills' for the PR professional role (Tench and Moreno, 2015), paradoxically, some personal attributes, including 'empathy', may be regarded as inherently part of a person's character or instilled as part of their social upbringing. As discussed later in this chapter, the stereotype of woman as 'natural born communicator' (Fröhlich, 2004) is sustained among some female practitioners. While women in PR proudly assert their superior communication skills above those of their male counterparts, in doing so they 'essentialise' communication skills as inherent to female biology, thus potentially positioning themselves as lacking in preparedness for leadership roles. Critiquing Grunig et al.'s (2000) feminist values theory (see also the discussion on page 92), Golombisky (2015, p. 398) argues that while the 'strategic essentialism' of feminist/feminine values theory in PR may not intend to position women as naturally feminine, these values can easily be read as biological destiny.

From this discussion, it is therefore important to consider how processes of gender (Acker, 1992) structure the PR workplace: on the levels of who is included/excluded in terms of gender roles, the gendered discourses of the profession, as well as gendered performance and identity through PRP–client interactions. I now turn to the phenomenon which has preoccupied a number of scholars during the past 30 years: the feminisation of PR; why the gender switch in PR is important to understand from an emotional labour perspective; and why liberal feminism is an inadequate explanation of a neoliberal, postmodern, and gendered occupational culture.

Feminisation of the PR industry and the emergence of feminist theory in PR

In 1949, Mosier argued that women 'with their graciousness and charm, persuasive powers of speech, unaggressive inquisitiveness, and ability to meet with "the soft voice" the "big stick requirements of business" can do well in public relations' (Mosier, 1949, p. 35 cited in Donato, 1990, p. 136). According to Donato (1990), the numerical feminisation of PR that took place in the United States during the 1980s may be attributed to several factors. These factors include: the post-war expansion in PR jobs, including those that required technical and well as managerial skills; increased specialisation in PR work (e.g. such as lobbying); that women were relatively cheap to hire, although PR work was better-paid and more attractive than other semi-professions available to women such as teaching; that female-intensive industries such as banks, hospitals, education, local government – what we would now term 'service industries' – employed the largest share of women; the affirmative action policies of the 1970s which put pressure on employers to hire women; and finally, gender ideology. Donato (1990) does not define gender ideology. However returning to the discussion relating to concepts of gender at the beginning of this chapter, one might infer from Donato's account that gender ideology refers to the 'hierarchical binary' (Dow and Wood, 2006): the prevailing beliefs relating to roles within the workplace and whether these roles are perceived as 'women's work' or 'men's work': in other words, 'gender' is associated with biology, in contrast to a performative understanding of gender as 'fluid, dynamic and constantly negotiated' (Flores, 2006, p. 390).

Donato draws attention to Hochschild's concept of emotional labour, referring to Ghiloni's (1987) study of a Fortune 500 public affairs department in which emotional labour was identified as the most important criterion to assess a public affairs manager's work.[1] Further to this, Donato argued that employers preferred to recruit women to PR because it 'increasingly involves emotional labour' and emotion work was seen as 'women's work':

> The need for emotional labor may be particularly strong after firms admit to engaging in hazardous or socially callous behavior, such as dumping toxic chemicals or selling unsafe intrauterine devices. Public relations specialists must defend such an employer, convincing others that the organization is dependable, responsive to community needs, and operating in the public's best interest.
>
> (Donato, 1990, p. 139)

Thus, the prevailing gender ideology among employers during the 1980s, according to Donato, was that PR required an increasing amount of emotion work. In turn, emotion work was understood as 'women's work'. Since Donato's examination of the factors leading to the feminisation of PR, little attention, if any, was paid to her observation concerning the concept of emotional labour. Toth (2001, p. 240) cites Donato as 'providing a framework by which to assess factors discriminating against women in public relations' but Toth did not recognise, let alone explore, Donato's emotional labour argument. The closest US feminist PR scholars came to discussing emotional labour is in arguing for a superior model of 'feminist values' which links these values – for example, sensitivity, nurturance, and caring – to female gender (Grunig et al., 2000). This raises further questions about the 'essentialising' of female qualities. (I return to Grunig, Toth, and Hon's argument later in this chapter.) The factors that had led to feminisation in PR became causes for concern among feminist scholars. The following discussion traces the subsequent line of enquiry.

One of the early US feminist PR scholars, Creedon (1989) noted optimistically that the 'gender switch' in both PR and journalism had the potential to lead to 're-visioning of gender values' in mass communication (1989, p. 15). She saw that those employed in occupations within mass communication had the power to influence the dominant [gender] values that 'have dictated news values' (1989, p. 15). Cline, also writing in 1989, was less optimistic. Cline, who led the IABC Research Foundation-sponsored *Velvet Ghetto* study, reported that as more women entered PR, salaries were driven down, and men moved on to better-paid jobs in marketing and management (Cline, 1989).

'Feminisation' is a term commonly used to describe a demographic shift in the proportion of women entering a profession, marked by a point in time where there is a dominance of women within that profession. ('Feminisation' is defined differently later in this chapter but at this point, the demographic definition is explored.) As Reskin and Roos explain:

> By definition, occupations' feminization results from their disproportionate recruitment or retention of women workers. Disparate recruitment and retention are the product of changes in the structural features of queues (how employers order workers and workers rank jobs, the intensity of either group's preferences, and the shapes of the labor and job queues); that is, the relative distributions of workers or jobs....all these factors changed during the 1970s, contributing to occupational feminization.
>
> (Reskin and Roos, 1990, p. 29)

While the feminisation of a profession can, on the one hand, be interpreted as a progressive trend, signifying greater opportunity for women and the possibility of influencing gender values within that profession, a structural feature of feminisation, as indicated by Reskin and Roos (1990), is that workers' preferences are part of the phenomenon: women choose a profession because they perceive it as 'women's work' (i.e. perhaps as an opportunity to use the so-called 'soft skills' of relationship-building). In the meantime, men increasingly turn away from the profession for the same reasons, even though it may have been perceived by men as an acceptable occupation when male professionals were numerically dominant.

Observing the tilt towards a feminised profession in the United States during the 1980s, several research projects, funded by the IABC Research Foundation and Public Relations Society of America (PRSA), investigated the situation for women in PR management. The first IABC study, entitled *The Velvet Ghetto: The impact of the increasing percentage of women in public relations and business communication* (Cline et al., 1986), also known as the 'Velvet Ghetto' study, found that men and women's attitudes towards women managers in PR fell into three places on a continuum: at one end of the continuum, women were not seen as a problem, 'we only have people' (IABC, 1986, p. 1); in the middle were those who expressed concern that the feminisation of PR would subject it to stereotyping; and at the other end of the continuum were those who thought that women did not belong to PR management. This study also identified that women perceived themselves as communication 'technicians' rather than 'managers' which the Velvet Ghetto researchers attributed to a 'subtle socialization process' (IABC, 1986, p. 5).

According to Toth (2001), the first IABC study and a subsequent study, *Beyond the Velvet Ghetto* (Toth and Cline, 1989), helped to set the benchmarks for feminist research. These studies identified four gender-related issues: 'threats to the status of the field, a clear pay gap, the "glass ceiling" and the "velvet ghetto" phenomenon' (Toth, 2001, p. 237). Drawing on these and subsequent feminist studies, including two conducted among PRSA members, Grunig et al. (2001) confirmed in a landmark publication, *Women in Public Relations: How gender influences practice,* that gender inequalities existed in terms of salaries, hiring expectations, and promotion prospects to managerial levels: themes which continue to resonate in industry-sponsored surveys within the United Kingdom and elsewhere (e.g. PRCA, 2016; CIPR, 2017b; Shah, 2017).

Feminist and postfeminist perspectives in PR

Feminist studies adopt different ideological positions and assumptions. Rakow and Nastasia (2009) identified six feminist theoretical positions: liberal feminism; radical feminism; socialist feminism; postmodernist feminism; multicultural feminism; and postcolonial feminism. From this classification of feminist positions the authors observed that most feminist analyses in PR have drawn on a liberal feminist perspective, which is the 'dominant paradigm of feminist theory in the Western world'. Notably, liberal feminism supports 'the liberal doctrine of individualism', an approach that advocates the notion that all men and women are rational individuals who are capable

of competing for jobs on an equal footing, assuming that the correct adjust-
ments are made to social structures and gender roles. The main purpose of
PR research undertaken from a liberal feminist perspective is to examine
inequalities and discrimination in work practices, salary, and promotions as
a consequence of feminisation (e.g. Grunig et al., 2001). Ideas for addressing
inequalities involve women practitioners taking individual action in adapting
to social structures, rather than taking collective action to challenge these
structures, as advocated by radical, socialist, or critical theoretical positions.

Within the liberal feminist paradigm is a much-cited article by Grunig
et al. (2000), who, like Creedon (1989) and Rakow (1989), saw the incor-
poration of what they termed 'feminist values' as an opportunity for more
ethical practice in PR. Grunig et al. (2000) proposed a superior model of
women's PR practice, claiming that the 'feminist values' of 'altruism, commitment, equality, equity, ethics, fairness, forgiveness, integrity, justice, loyalty, morality, nurturance, perfection, quality of life, standards, tolerance,
and cherishing children' would help organisations to build better relationships with their 'strategic constituencies' (Grunig et al., 2000, p. 58). Multiple
lists of 'feminist values' are presented in the article; yet the authors appear to
confuse the definitions of the terms 'gender' and 'sex' and conflate "feminine' with 'feminist': even suggesting that 'women's intuition or instincts'
(p. 58) could play a part in better relationship-building, a position critiqued
by Golombisky (2015). In Grunig et al.'s paper, there is little scope for communication as a skill that is learned or an obligation for men practising PR
too. No clear distinction is made between the 'values' or characteristics associated with female gender socialisation, and those values developed through
a feminist perspective. The article attempts to articulate how women might
be a force for change by practising PR more ethically, which, in turn, could
lead to a more reputable profession; but the authors' evident discomfort with
and handling of the topic limits its impact.

In 1995, Linda Childers Hon's study of 34 female practitioners sought their
explanations for discrimination in PR. The issues identified in the study
resulted in a range of 'prescriptions for changes in society, organizations
and public relations' including individual strategies for PR women as well
as strategies for educationalists to raise the consciousness of their (largely
female) students (Hon, 1995, p. 62). Hon's recommendations consciously
augmented liberal feminist strategies with radical feminist ideas to change
societal structures.

Building on Hon's study, Wrigley (2002) argued for a radical feminist lens
through which to interpret women practitioners' acceptance of their lack
of progress in gaining promotion to the highest levels. Despite an increasingly feminised profession, Wrigley identified, through her own study of
female practitioners, the concept of 'negotiated resignation' (Wrigley, 2002)
towards the 'glass ceiling' effect whereby invisible barriers are encountered by
women who aspire to top jobs, even though a clear pathway appears to exist.
Rather than challenge the structures that prevent them from being treated

fairly in the workplace, Wrigley found that women instead question themselves and look to overcome their disadvantaged positions through a variety of strategies including: 'getting along and fitting in, attempting to please by working harder and building consensus, or being a peacemaker in resolving conflicts between co-workers' (2002, p. 49). Wrigley (2002) identified that some women denied that a glass ceiling existed in PR. She interpreted this both as denial of structure and as a survival strategy. Given that the majority of women participating in her study appeared to share a liberal feminist perspective, this adaptive strategy allowed some women to continue in their jobs while non-consciously supporting the status quo or 'hierarchical binary' (Dow and Wood, 2006).

In 2005, Linda Aldoory argued that the feminist PR literature erroneously continued to draw on what she termed an 'androcentric' paradigm. Such a paradigm conceptualised 'a) gender as female b) power as organizational property, and c) diversity/inclusiveness as numerical balance' (2005, p. 672). This paradigm seems to reflect industry assumptions. For example, on the issue of numerical balance, the Public Relations Institute of Australia reported that only 18% of men aged under 25 worked in PR, thus the need to set a target which states: 'the proportion of men aged under 25 rises to 40% by 2025' (PRIA, 2016). There is no justification for the 40% target, nor how realistic it is, given that it relies on recruiting more males to communication degrees and other educational pathways. Nevertheless, the PR industry has a tendency to reach for 'fixes' rather than trying to understand the deeper social and cultural processes that underpin phenomena.

A new feminist or 'emancipatory' paradigm (Aldoory's preferred term, to avoid the pigeonholing effect of 'feminist') for PR theory-building would instead, she argued, seek to understand gender, power, and diversity through the examination of discursive practices and meaning-making between individuals in playing out their professional roles. Thus, gender should be understood as a product of social interaction and as a learned social system; power understood as being legitimised through discursive practice; and diversity understood as situated meanings.

Subsequently, and along similar lines to Aldoory, Rakow and Nastasia's (2009) analysis of the work of Dorothy E. Smith, a Canadian sociologist, argues for a feminist theory *of* PR, rather than a feminist theory *for* PR. The authors assert that feminist PR theory-building, rather than taking for granted the man/woman dichotomy, with a particular focus on the 'lives of women' in PT, would be best served by Smith's concepts relating to the problematisations of: gender; woman/women; power; injustice; and change. Thus, gender research, they argue, should focus on *people*, since 'women as well as men …willingly or unwillingly contribute to the reification of patriarchy, capitalism, Western racism, and colonialism, and there are women as well as men who do not support or accept these' (2009, p. 267). Similarly, some men, as well as women, are the object of institutional discourses that 'have created a patriarchal way of speaking…' becoming '…'common sense' and ubiquitous…' (Rakow and Nastasia, 2009, p. 268). To claim legitimacy for PR practice, the (masculine) language of management (the 'circle of men') from an 'insider' perspective has been sustained by practitioners and educators alike. Thus, the main body of feminist PR research is normative and limited by unexplored assumptions of the profession and its consequences, primarily because a management science paradigm has dominated the field to support efficacy of practice (Aldoory, 2005).

A 'postfeminist sensibility' in PR gender analysis

Later, Fitch and Third (2010) and Fitch (2015) argued that the concept of postfeminism is applicable to contemporary PR. This is based on McRobbie's influential understanding of postfeminism which is: 'a process by which feminist gains of the 1970s and 1980s are actively and relentlessly undermined' while simultaneously appearing to be engaging in a well-informed an even well-intended response to feminism (McRobbie, 2009, p. 12). Fitch and Third (2010, p. 8) supported McRobbie's argument that the postfeminist era has led to assumptions that gender equality has been achieved and that explicit consideration of gender 'is no longer necessary', concluding that the female majority in many professions, including PR, effectively put a stop to gender analysis and theory.

Nonetheless, Rodgers et al. (2016) and Edwards (2018) argue that PR has a postfeminist identity which is reinforced through popular representations of PR work in two television series *Absolutely Fabulous* and *Sex and the City;* therefore to overlook postfeminism is to underestimate how cultural narratives have shaped and continue to shape contemporary feminine subjectivities. In their study of television portrayals of professional femininities, Rodgers et al. (2016, p. 184) found that *Sex and the City* in particular contributed to postfeminist identity construction among young, female PR professionals. Young female participants spoke in admiration of the character of *Sex and the City's* Samantha Jones as being 'strong' and 'authoritative'. One participant related, in performative terms, about actively playing up 'to the PR girl stereotype', when talking to friends:

> You never talk about the day [job] doing coverage reports, or doing content calendars or any of this kind of stuff. Or writing press releases. You talk about the amazing campaign you are about to launch; the event I went to last month.

Gender theorists Gill et al. (2017) subsequently developed the concept of postfeminism as an object of critique within the workplace. These authors argue, following McRobbie (2009), that simply equating postfeminism with anti-feminism overlooks the current 'gender regime' which entangles 'feminist and anti-feminist ideas' (Gill et al., 2017, p. 229). Thus, there is a need to adopt a broad 'postfeminist sensibility', particularly when examining contemporary, lived experiences in organisations (Gill, 2007; Gill et al., 2017). They assert:

> There are a number of broadly agreed upon features of postfeminism as a distinctive sensibility: a focus upon empowerment, choice and individualism; the repudiation of sexism and thus of the need for feminism alongside a sense of 'fatigue' about gender; notions of make-over and self-reinvention/transformation; an emphasis upon embodiment and femininity as a bodily property; an emphasis on surveillance and discipline; a resurgence of ideas of sexual difference.
>
> (Gill et al., 2017, p. 228)

Furthermore, gender scholars argue that postfeminism is strongly associated with the neoconservative and neoliberal ideologies that have shaped Western and non-Western societies and cultures (Rottenberg, 2014; Gill et al., 2017). Such ideologies have, in turn, shaped the discourse of women's lived experience (Adamson, 2017; Gill et al., 2017; Sørensen, 2017). For example, Adamson (2017) analysed four women celebrity CEO autobiographies, concluding that these texts constructed successfully balanced organisational femininity within neoliberal and postfeminist contexts. 'Doing balance successfully' suggests Adamson (2017, p. 323), 'requires women to reclaim and embrace aspects of their femininity, including feminine characteristics and behaviour, attitudes and roles, but to be careful to not "overdo" each of these'. Questions of 'how much' femininity and masculinity is performed within the PR role and why this occurs are highly relevant to interpreting PRPs' lived experiences of negotiating different relationships and managing their identities, which I explore in Chapters 5 and 6.

Postfeminist analyses that interrogate the 'gender regime' in PR, and in particular, the processes underpinning structural issues, such as gender segregation in PR and the PR gender pay gap, offer the potential of more nuanced insights (Yeomans and Mariutti, 2016). Meanwhile, Edwards (2018, p. 193) argues that gender understood as performativity in PR (e.g. Tindall and Waters, 2012; Yeomans, 2013), alongside postfeminism, is a powerful framework for interrogating practitioner experiences within the industry, as they 'illustrate how approaches to gender and feminist theory that depart from the liberal and radical models can open up the theoretical landscape', thus prompting questions concerning 'the alignment of neoliberalism and postfeminist discourses in public relations industry narratives'.

Gendered identity construction and performativity in PR

Female identity

As already discussed, Linda Aldoory called for social constructionist understandings of gender in PR theory-building to 'deconstruct the gendered nature of the work' and to understand how 'professional roles are played out in organizations' (Aldoory, 2005, p. 675). Several researchers have taken up this challenge, either in response to Aldoory's call or concurrently.

Two studies are particularly relevant to understanding gendered emotional labour outside Anglo-American contexts. In Germany, where 69% of PR agency employees were reported as female, the issue of gender stereotypes was examined among 13 women agency practitioners (Fröhlich and Peters, 2007). While participants strongly attributed women's superior communication skills as the reason behind the female majority in PR, participants stereotyped female agency practitioners as 'PR slut', 'PR bunny', or 'PR girly', while distancing their own identities from such a stereotype. Fröhlich and Peters reject the possibility of a model of female superiority associated with 'feminist values' such as 'cooperation, respect, caring, nurturance, interconnection, justice, equity, honesty, sensitivity, perceptiveness, intuition, altruism, fairness, morality and commitment' (Grunig et al., 2000, p. 49). They argue that the degree to which women demonstrate 'exceptional' communication skills and cooperative behaviour should be understood as a consequence of childhood socialisation and 'the result of [women's] limited social power...' (Fröhlich, 2004, p. 72). Indeed, the notion of the 'friendliness trap' (Fröhlich, 2004) that assigns women to using their 'natural born communicator' qualities recodes these qualities as deficiencies in their ability to perform managerial tasks.

Tsetsura's qualitative inquiries among Russian female PR agency practitioners have spawned a body of work (e.g. 2009, 2011, 2014) examining women's perceptions and identity construction from different theoretical positions. In constructing PR as a service profession, practitioners' negotiating strategies included 'educating', 'saving face', and 'compromise' with clients (Tsetsura, 2009, p. 79). The educating strategy, for example, involved practitioners 'constantly educating clients, journalists, and other publics about public relations as a field and about public relations practices'. The requirement for 'educating' was relevant to PR being a relatively young, commercial practice within the Russian context. However, participants attributed their ability to perform particular negotiating strategies to women's historic role within Russian patriarchal society. Tsetsura (2011, 2014) further examined women's perceptions from the perspectives of a 'real job' (2011) and as a 'profession' (2014). While PR was constructed as a 'real job' within the Russian context, it was also constructed mostly as a 'woman's job' (Tsetsura, 2011) and a 'women's profession' (Tsetsura, 2014). Tsetsura argues that her findings are specific to the social, economic, and historic conditions in Russia. However, such analyses highlight the intensive, interactive (as well as gendered) nature of PR as service work, particularly in agencies that are hired as 'arms and legs' (Verčič et al., 2018).

While there are sharp contrasts between the cultural contexts of Russia and Germany and the role of women in these societies, there are problems for female practitioners found in both contexts. Viewed from a critical perspective, the gendered negotiating strategies used by Russian female agency practitioners reinforce the 'hierarchical binary' (Dow and Wood, 2006, p. xvii), forcing women into performing a historic role of doing emotion work (Hochschild, 1983). Furthermore, this work is constructed as a natural extension to female identity. Equally, however, playing with the 'PR bunny' stereotype as recognition of women's exceptional communication skills in agency work means that German female practitioners risk becoming the victims of self-stereotyping and are assigned, or assign themselves, to gender roles that reinforce the status quo.

A non-Western understanding of PR as a service, embodiment and emotional labour, opens up the possibility of further analyses outside Western contexts. However, while a number of descriptive studies of PR in non-Western contexts exist, social constructionist gender studies are yet to emerge. In Japan, for example, where there is a male majority in PR, 'raw sexism characterizes the field [...], rather than the discrimination-despite-feminization status as in the United States' (Cooper-Chen and Tanaka, 2008, p. 103). Cooper-Chen and Tanaka (2008) reported that women who held responsible job titles worked for foreign PR firms, or for non-Japanese based companies in house. They cite a survey of Asian female PRPs in which women denied experiencing gender inequalities, yet were simultaneously 'trying to cope with these issues' (Cooper-Chen and Tanaka, 2008, p. 107). Cultures where face-saving is valued highly pose challenges for the framing of survey questions on gender inequalities; therefore, social constructionist approaches are needed to understand the gender dynamics in non-Western as well as Western PR cultural contexts.

In a comprehensive review of feminist theory-building in PR, Golombisky (2015) identified new directions where gender is defined as socially constructed, is part of an intersectional identity, and is focused on power (e.g. Pompper, 2013; Vardeman-Winter et al., 2013). Nonetheless, such studies are relatively few and Golombisky (2015, p. 408) called for an expansion of intersectional studies reflecting 'ethnicity, class, age, ability, sexuality, gender identity, nationality, and religion', a 'third space' or transnational feminism in PR that questions Western, neoliberal ideology (and corporate PR).

Germane to the studies presented in this book, Golombisky (2015, p. 408) also called for research that examines gender as performativity, thus moving away from gender as sex (interpreted as 'biological determinism or cultural essentialism'). Drawing on the early work of communication theorist Rakow (1986, 1989), Golombisky (2015, p. 403) argues that performativity 'explains the ways people are hailed to enact their multiple identifications, as visible and invisible. Furthermore, each person is always performing multiple intersecting and context-specific identifications'. The professional context of the PR agency is the focus of gendered performance and identity work in this volume, which I argue is intrinsic to PRP-client emotional labour. Yeomans' (2013) findings are re-appraised in Chapter 5.

While relatively few studies have examined women's performativity and identity construction in PR agencies, studies of masculinity/male identity have been almost wholly neglected. Elmer's (2010) autoethnographic account of embodied labour, sexualised labour, and emotional labour in UK government exposed a personal lack of fit with an interview panel's expectations of the 'PR man', and where 'tough guy' performances (i.e. dressed in black motorcycle leathers) could be particularly advantageous when attending meetings.

Tindall and Waters (2012) interviewed 45 openly gay men in the United States about their own career challenges. Using queer theory (Sedgwick, 2003) to discuss themes of identity and performance, Tindall and Waters (2012, p. 465) found that participants 'overwhelmingly revealed internal struggles of being an openly gay man in an overtly heterosexist culture'. Furthermore, they were subject to unwanted stereotyping as 'cultural interpreters' of the LGBT community and similar to women's experience of the glass ceiling were challenged by a 'lavender ceiling' whereby heteronormative expectations of performance limited their advancement unless they hid their sexual identities. Both Elmer (2010) and Tindall and Waters (2012) highlight the problem of organisational contexts where ideas of competence are strongly linked to fixed notions of embodied and performed identity, hence a source of conflict and tension within the practitioner role.

These two PR studies of male identity only partially address the issue of gender as performativity. Since performativity is highly contextual and linked to identity, it is valuable to turn to the broader literature on occupations to further explore male experience and male identity, especially in female-intensive occupations (e.g. Leidner, 1991; Alvesson, 1998; Leidner, 1993; Williams, 1995; Lupton, 2000; Chalmers, 2001; Simpson, 2004). Some of these studies are now discussed.

Male identity in occupational studies

Leidner explored the construction of male identity within occupations that required intensive levels of client or customer interactions (e.g. Leidner, 1991, 1993). In her study of insurance sales agents, Leidner observed that women seemed especially well-suited to the interactive demands of sales work such as establishing and maintaining rapport. However, through sales training, the work was constructed as masculine by emphasising the qualities of 'determination, aggressiveness, toughness in the face of repeated rejection, persistence and stoicism' (Leidner, 1993, pp. 201–202).

Lupton (2000) studied masculine identity among men who had entered, or were about to enter, traditionally female occupations. Lupton's small-scale study comprising nine participants found that 'doing women's work' presented several challenges to masculine identity. The first challenge was that the job could be perceived as low status among friends or future partners; because of this, the male worker could feel compromised in the role.

The absence of other men in the work environment meant that the participants' masculine identity could not be reinforced through everyday conversation. A second challenge to masculine identity was described as a 'fear of feminization' (p. S40) by 'becoming 'invisible as a man', being 'adopted' as a woman, and becoming feminine through working with women.

Lupton found that the strategies that male workers adopted for having their masculine identity challenged included 'reconstructing the occupation' and 'renegotiating masculinity'. In reconstructing the occupation male workers gave their job a different title (e.g. 'temp' instead of 'secretary') and emphasised the hard-edged qualities of the job (e.g. making people redundant as a key aspect of the work of human resource manager). 'Re-negotiating masculinity' meant for some, playing down masculine behaviour, and for others, playing up 'female' behaviour by adopting a camp persona when joining in women's conversations. Participants also identified themselves as being more adaptive to working with women and saw other men, including their friends, as less adaptive, holding traditional views of men and women's roles at work.

In her large-scale study of masculine identity in four occupations: nursing, primary school teaching, library, and cabin crew, Simpson (2004) found that men adopted three strategies to help them combat discomfort with the female image of the job. These strategies included: re-labelling the job (for example, the label 'librarian' with its associated 'dowdy female' image was re-labelled 'information scientist' or 'researcher'); re-casting the job as male to emphasise masculine qualities (for example, emphasising the health and safety role over the service role among cabin crew; focusing on the importance of sport in teaching); and distancing themselves from 'feminine' aspects of the job. 'Distancing' was practised in a number of ways, for example librarians cast female colleagues as non-career orientated (so-called 'second income' earners); nurses emphasised choice of specialism (the 'adrenaline-charged' A&E department; mental health) as well as *choice* of specialism over (largely female) general nursing which was regarded as lower status.

The literature on masculine identity in occupations where there is a numerical female majority spans a range of occupations, from teaching and nursing through to library and clerical work. While there is a body of mainly North American feminist literature on gender in PR, this body of work has paid little attention to women's identity in PR work, while men's identity is perhaps taken for granted. As Lupton (2000, p. S33) observes, 'feminist analyses have tended to "assume" male experience while simultaneously placing men at the centre of their arguments'.

Chalmers (2001) studied the work of male marketing managers in three different organisations. Chalmers found a common pattern in that there was a gendered division between strategic/business and service/support types of marketing. As an aspiring management discipline (similar to PR), marketing could be seen as making a claim to corporate power and status through 'a masculine willingness to push ideas forward forcefully, an aggressive entrepreneurship, and a paternalistic authority'. In contrast to this, 'tasks involving promotions, information gathering, and customer service have been equated with feminine images of passivity, deference, sociability, and housekeeping' (Chalmers, 2001, p. 160). While marketing's position in relation to other functions is subject to power struggles (again, in a similar way to PR), the struggle, according to Chalmers, is also around masculinity. Gendered discursive strategies were invoked by male marketing managers to construct different areas of marketing work differentially as masculine and feminine.

It is reasonable to assume that such discursive strategies may take place in PR practice to legitimise the work of male PRPs, as well as to legitimise the profession itself (as suggested by Fitch and Third, 2010) and Chalmers' work is useful in this respect. Although extensive US research (e.g. Broom, 1982; Broom and Dozier, 1986) into 'roles' in PR established the gendered nature of the so-called 'communication manager' and 'communication technician' roles (mainly enacted by men and women, respectively), the socially accomplished *meanings that construct PR work*, and which are partially revealed by discursive strategies, are underexplored in these early studies.

Thus, 'feminisation' cannot merely be seen as a phenomenon that describes a larger proportion of women than men entering a profession. Men who enter an occupational culture where the feminine, or relational, characteristics of the job, such as rapport-building, educating, empathy, and face-saving are emphasised (e.g. to provide a client service), may find that this type of work presents a lack of reinforcement to masculine identity. Indeed, this type of work may present threats if men have concerns about the external image of the profession and the way they are perceived among friends and potential partners. Male workers therefore manage, or 'work on', their gender identity to reconstruct the occupation as masculine, while re-negotiating their own male identities within the workplace to reduce the misalignment between gender identity and occupational identity.

While the bulk of feminist literature in PR provides considerable knowledge about structural inequalities within the profession and offers strategies to practitioners and educators on how to overcome them, the focus of much research is liberal feminist with a clear agenda for improving efficacy. Constructionist studies of women and men in PR serve to deepen understanding of the profession by examining gender stereotypes, identity, and performativity in PR agency work; however, these studies are still relatively few. Furthermore, they do not examine the concept of emotional labour in professional relationships, nor how such analyses might lead to fresh, critical insights into these dynamic relationships.

Digital labour, gender, and emotion work

The transformation of PR agencies from those specialising in media relations to an increasing emphasis on digital communication within 'emotionally charged media networks' (Beckett and Deuze, 2016), discussed in Chapter 3, inevitably shifts attention away from PRP relationships with trusted journalists to PRP relationships forged online with a myriad of actors including social media influencers. Cultural studies and feminist media studies scholars pose new questions arising from the concept of digital labour. While Fuchs and Sevignani (2013), for example, provide an uncompromisingly Marxist critique of digital labour, in which all users – professionals or not – are viewed as complicit in exploiting their own, unpaid labour on social media sites for commercial gain, others have focused on the gendered and emotional dimensions of digital labour (e.g. Gill, 2002; Duffy, 2015; Arcy, 2016). Such work focuses on women's 'assumed expertise in emotion management—and how that expectation is intensified in the digital realm' (Arcy, 2016, p. 365). This may be through the relational effort of 'gift exchange' (Hochschild, 1983) that goes into 'liking' and 'commenting' on social media platforms, as well as the requirement to build online personal brands to encourage a large following (Duffy, 2015). Duffy (2015) draws attention to the motivations of aspirant female fashion and lifestyle bloggers, including students and graduates of PR and marketing, whose instrumental use of affective relationship-building online holds the potential rewards of social and economic capital, which are unevenly gained.

Turning to PRPs, a study by Bridgen (2011) revealed the contradictory, nuanced features of digital emotional labour. While, on the one hand, practitioners did not regard themselves as exploited, rather recognising the value of self-exploitation for future career prospects, the voluntary nature of work undertaken out of hours meant an increased use of the self as commodity in pursuit of the work for clients: much PRP work was tied up with exploiting 'personal backgrounds and interests in a myriad of relationships' (Bridgen, 2011, p. 73). As digital emotional labour in the form of social media interactions becomes progressively part of mainstream PR practice – if not *the* main contemporary focus of PRP effort – the 'gift exchange' of online relationships out of hours is further intensified, rendering emotion work undertaken in the office and at home as seamless.

For women practitioners, in particular, the phenomenon of 'always on' culture, facilitated by technology (Turkle, 2008), together with the relational burden to maintain bonds with family and friends, is potentially greater and subject to periods of 'interrupted leisure' due to childcare, housework, as well as work-related and nonwork-related distractions from mobile devices (Wajcman, 2015, p. 80). These points are explored in later chapters where I examine the experiences and perspectives of agency directors.

Conclusion

Within this chapter I have pursued an understanding of emotional labour performed through gendered interactions in the workplace. This understanding has been explored through the literature concerning gender (e.g. Rakow, 1986; Butler, 1990; Acker, 1992; Scott, 1999; Dow and Wood, 2006), emotional labour (Hochschild, 1983), discourse approaches to gender (e.g. Marsh,

2009; Fletcher, 1999; Holmes, 2006; Bolton and Muzio, 2008), masculine identity in occupations (e.g. Leidner, 1991; Alvesson, 1998; Simpson, 2004).

More specific to this study, I have reviewed literature on the feminisation of PR (e.g. Grunig et al., 2001; Toth, 2001; Rakow and Nastasia, 2009) and the construction of identities in PR work, including female identity (e.g. Fröhlich and Peters, 2007; Tsetsura, 2014), male identity (e.g. Elmer, 2010; Tindall and Waters, 2012), as well as intersectional approaches to identity (e.g. Pompper, 2013; Vardeman-Winter et al., 2013). Finally, I have briefly examined questions arising from the gendered and emotional aspects of digital labour (e.g. Duffy, 2015; Arcy, 2016) and PRPs' use of social media as emotional labour (Bridgen, 2011).

In this chapter I argued that the feminisation of PR is a more complex phenomenon than it at first might seem. In terms of 'body count', there are more women than men working in PR but the larger concentration of women at the lower and middle levels of PR agencies illuminates a gendered hierarchy, as both the industry and scholars have noted. Less acknowledged in the PR literature are the processes that construct and gendered institutions and organisations (Acker, 1992). These processes include decisions and procedures on who is included/excluded in terms of gender roles, the gendered discourses of the profession, as well as gendered performance and identity construction through PRP-client interactions. The gendered discourse of the PR professional project (Fitch and Third, 2010) suggests parallel struggles: a struggle, on the one hand, towards professional legitimacy (a 'respected' profession and a management function) which is enacted by professional membership associations, educators, and PRPs alike, in relation to *other professions*; and a more subtle gender struggle *within* the 'pink ghetto' through PRPs' day-to-day relations with clients, journalists, colleagues, and online influencers. Postfeminist analyses, and an understanding of gender as performativity, enable an interrogation of the 'gender regime' in PR. Finally, digital emotional labour – identified as another area of gendered work – should be understood as the focus of PRP effort as 'seamless' online relationships increasingly define PR practice.

Note

1 Moloney (2006) defines public affairs as a specialism within the broader field of public relations. The focus of PA practice is on building relationships with government ministers, officials, as well as other opinion formers on matters of public policy.

References

Acker, J. (1988) Class, gender, and the relations of distribution. *Signs*, 13, pp. 473–497.
Acker, J. (1990) Hierarchies, jobs, bodies: A theory of gendered organizations. *Gender and Society*, 4 (2), pp. 139–158.
Acker, J. (1992) From sex roles to gendered institutions. *Contemporary Sociology*, 21, (5), pp. 565–569.

Adamson, M. (2017) Postfeminism, neoliberalism and a 'successfully' balanced femininity in celebrity CEO autobiographies. *Gender, Work and Organization*, 24 (3), pp. 314–327.

Adkins, L. (2000) Objects of innovation: Post-occupational reflexivity and re-traditionalisation of gender. In S. Ahmed, J. Kilby, C. Lury, M. McNeil, and B. Skeggs, eds. *Transformations: Thinking through feminism*. London, Routledge, pp. 259–272.

Aldoory, L. (2005) A re-conceived feminist paradigm for public relations: A case for substantial improvement. *Journal of Communication*, 55 (4), pp. 668–684.

Aldoory, L. and Toth, E. (2002) Gender discrepancies in a gendered profession: A developing theory for public relations. *Journal of Public Relations Research*, 14 (2), pp. 103–126.

Alvesson, M. (1998) Gender and identity. Masculinities and femininities at work in an advertising agency. *Human Relations*, 51 (8), pp. 969–1005.

Arcy, J. (2016) Emotion work: Considering gender in digital labor. *Feminist Media Studies*, 16 (2), pp. 365–368.

Beck, U. (1992) *Risk Society: Towards a new modernity*. London, Sage.

Beck, U. and Beck-Gernsheim, E. (2002) *Individualization*. London, Sage.

Beckett, C. and Deuze, M. (2016, July–September) On the role of emotion in the future of journalism. *Social Media + Society*, 2 (3), pp. 1–6.

Bolton, S. C. and Muzio, D. (2008) The paradoxical processes of feminization in the professions: The case of established aspiring and semi-professions. *Work, Employment and Society*, 22 (2), pp. 281–299.

Brady, A. and Schirato, T. (2011) *Understanding Judith Butler*. London, Sage.

Bridgen, L. (2011), Emotional labour and the pursuit of the personal brand: Public relations practitioners' use of social media. *Journal of Media Practice*, 12 (1), pp. 61–76.

Broom, G. M. (1982) A comparison of sex roles in public relations. *Public Relations Review*, 8 (3), pp. 17–22.

Broom, G. M. and Dozier, D. M. (1986) Advancement for public relations role models. *Public Relations Review*, 12 (1), pp. 37–56.

Butler, J. (1986) Sex and gender in de Beauvoir's second sex. *Yale French studies*, 72, pp. 35–49. Available from: https://www.jstor.org/stable/2930225?seq=1#page_scan_tab_contents Accessed 28 October 2018.

Butler, J. (1990) *Gender Trouble: Feminism and the subversion of identity*. New York and London, Routledge.

Chalmers, L. (2001) *Marketing Masculinities: Gender and management politics in marketing work*. Westport, CT, Greenwood Press.

Chartered Institute of Public Relations (2017a) *PR and pay equality: A qualitative study into challenges and perspectives on gender pay*. London, CIPR. Available from: https://www.cipr.co.uk/sites/default/files/10932_PR&PAY_Equality_Report.pdf Accessed 29 December 2017.

Chartered Institute of Public Relations (2017b) *State of the profession*. London, Chartered Institute of Public Relations. Available from: https://www.cipr.co.uk/sites/default/files/10911_State%20of%20PR%202017_f1.pdf Accessed 29 December 2017.

Cline, C. G. (1989) The $1 million penalty for being a woman. In P. J. Creedon, ed. *Women in Mass Communication: Challenging gender values*. Newbury Park, CA, London, and New Delhi, Sage, pp. 263–275.

Cline, C. G., Masel-Walters, L., Toth, E. L., Turk, J. V., Smith, H. T., and Johnson, N. (1986) The velvet ghetto: The impact of the increasing percentage of women in public relations and organizational communication. San Francisco, IABC Foundation.

Collinson, D. L. and Hearn, J. (1996) *Men as Managers, Managers as Men: Critical perspectives on men, masculinities and managements.* London, Thousand Oaks, CA, and New Delhi, Sage.

Cooper-Chen, A. and Tanaka, M. (2008) Public relations in Japan: The cultural roots of kouhou. *Journal of Public Relations Research*, 20, pp. 94–114.

Cornwall, A. and Lindisfarne, N. (1994) Dislocating masculinity: Gender, power and anthropology. In A. Cornwall and N. Lindisfarne, eds. *Dislocating Masculinity: Comparative ethnographies.* London, Routledge, pp. 11–48.

Creedon, P. J. (1989) The challenge of re-visioning gender values. In P. J. Creedon, ed. *Women in Mass Communication: Challenging gender values.* Newbury Park, CA, London, and New Delhi, Sage, pp. 13–33.

Cronin, A. M. (2000) *Advertising and Consumer Citizenship: Gender, images and rights.* London, Routledge.

Davies, C. (1996) The sociology of professions and the profession of gender. *Sociology*, 30 (4), pp. 661–678.

Donato, K. M. (1990) Keepers of the corporate image: Women in public relations. In B. F. Reskin and P. A. Roos, eds. *Job Queues, Gender Queues: Explaining women's inroads into male occupations.* Philadelphia, PA, Temple University Press, pp. 129–144.

Dow, B. J. and Wood, J. T. (2006) The evolution of gender and communication research: Intersections of theory, politics, and scholarship. In B. J. Dow, and J. T. Wood, eds. *The Sage Handbook of Gender and Communication.* Thousand Oaks, CA, London, and New Delhi, Sage, pp. ix–xx.

Duffy, E. (2015) The romance of work: Gender and aspirational labour in the digital culture industries. *International Journal of Cultural Studies*, 19 (4), pp. 441–457.

Edwards, L. (2008) PR practitioners' cultural capital: An initial study and implications for research and practice. *Public Relations Review*, 34 (4), pp. 367–372.

Edwards, L. (2018) *Understanding Public Relations: Theory, culture and society.* London, Sage.

Elmer, P. (2010) Re-encountering the PR man. *Prism*, 7 (4). Available from: http://www.prismjournal.org/fileadmin/Praxis/Files/Gender/Elmer.pdf. Accessed 28 October 2018.

Evans, M. (2003) *Gender and Social Theory.* Buckingham, Open University Press.

Fallaize, E. (1998) *Simone de Beauvoir: A critical reader.* London and New York, Routledge.

Fitch, K. (2015) Feminism and public relations. In J. L'Etang, D. McKie, N. Snow, and J. Xifra, eds. *The Routledge Handbook of Critical Public Relations.* Abingdon, Oxon, Routledge, pp. 182–199.

Fitch, K. and Third, A. (2010) Working girls: Revisiting the gendering of public relations. *PRism*, 7 (4). Available from: http://www.prismjournal.org/index.php?id=gender. Accessed 5 October 2018.

Fletcher, J. (1999) *Disappearing Acts: Gender, power, and relational practice at work.* Cambridge, MA, MIT Press.

Flores, L. (2006) Gender with/out borders: Discursive dynamics of gender, race and culture. In B. J. Dow, and J. T. Wood, eds. *The Sage Handbook of Gender and Communication*. Thousand Oaks, CA, London, and New Delhi, Sage, pp. 379–396.

Fröhlich, R. (2004) Feminine and feminist values in communication professions: Exceptional skills and expertise or 'friendliness trap'? In M. de Bruin and K. Ross, eds. *Gender and newsroom cultures: Identities at work*. Cresskill, NJ, Hampton Press, pp. 65–77.

Fröhlich, R. and Peters, S. B. (2007) PR bunnies caught in the agency ghetto? Gender stereotypes, organizational factors, and women's careers in PR agencies. *Journal of Public Relations Research*, 19 (3), pp. 229–254.

Fuchs, C. and Sevignani, S. (2013) What is digital labour? What is digital work? What's their difference? And why do these questions matter for understanding social media? *Triple-C*. 11 (2), pp. 237–293.

Ghiloni, B. W. (1987) Women, power and the corporation: Evidence from the Velvet Ghetto. In G. W. Domhoff and T. Dye, eds. *Power Elites and Organizations*. Newbury Park, CA, Sage, pp. 21–36.

Gill, R. (2002) Cool, creative and egalitarian? Exploring gender in project-based new media work in Europe. *Information, Communication & Society*, 5 (1), pp. 70–89.

Gill, R. (2007) Postfeminist media culture: Elements of a sensibility. *European Journal of Cultural Studies*, 10 (2), pp. 147–166.

Gill, R., Kelan, E., and Scharff, C. (2017) A postfeminist sensibility at work. *Gender, Work and Organization*, 24 (3), pp. 226–244.

Golombisky, K. (2015) Renewing the commitments of feminist public relations theory from Velvet Ghetto to social justice. *Journal of Public Relations Research*, 27 (5), pp. 389–415.

Grunig, L. A., Toth, E. L., and Hon, L. C. (2000) Feminist values in public relations. *Journal of Public Relations Research*, 12 (1), pp. 49–68.

Grunig, L. A., Toth, E. L., and Hon, L. C. (2001) *Women in Public Relations: How gender influences practice*. New York, The Guilford Press.

Hochschild, A. R. (1983) *The Managed Heart: Commercialization of human feeling*. Berkeley, CA, University of California Press.

Hochschild, A. R. (2008) Emotion work, feeling rules, and social structure. In M. Greco and P. Stenner, eds. *Emotions: A social science reader*. Abingdon and New York, Routledge, pp. 121–126.

Holmes, J. (2006) *Gendered Talk at Work: Constructing gender identity through workplace discourse*. Malden, MA, Oxford, Victoria: Blackwell.

Hon, L. C. (1995) Toward a feminist theory of public relations. *Journal of Public Relations Research*, 7 (1), pp. 27–88.

Howard, J. A., Risman, B., Romero, M., and Sprague, J. (1999) Series editors' introduction. In M. M. Ferree, J. Lorber, and B. B. Hess, eds. *Revisioning Gender*. Thousand Oaks, CA, London, and New Delhi, Sage, pp. xi–xiv.

IABC Velvet Ghetto summary report. (1986) Available from: http://www.iabc.com/researchfoundation/pdf/VelvetGhetto.pdf. Accessed 26 May 2010.

Leidner, R. (1991) Serving hamburgers and selling insurance: Gender, work and identity in interactive service jobs. *Gender and Society*, 5 (2), pp. 154–177.

Leidner, R. (1993) *Fast Food, Fast Talk: Service work and the routinization of everyday life*. Berkeley, University of California Press.

Lupton, B. (2000) Maintaining masculinity: Men who do 'women's work'. *British Journal of Management*, 11, special issue, pp. S33–S48.

Marsh, S. (2009) *The Feminine in Management Consulting: Power, emotion and values in consulting interactions.* Basingstoke, Palgrave Macmillan.

McRobbie, A. (2009) *The Aftermath of Feminism: Gender, culture and social change.* London, Sage.

Moloney, K. (2006) Public affairs. In R. Tench and L. Yeomans, eds. *Exploring Public Relations.* Harlow, Pearson Education, pp. 446–463.

Mosier, J. (1949) Opportunities for women in public relations. *Public Relations Journal,* 5 (6), pp. 33–40.

Pompper, D. (2013). Interrogating inequalities perpetuated in a feminized field: Using critical race theory and the intersectionality lens to render visible that which should not be disaggregated. In C. Daymon and K. Demetrious, eds. *Gender and Public Relations: Critical perspectives on voice, image, and identity.* London, Routledge, pp. 67–86.

Public Relations and Communications Association (2016) *PRCA census 2016.* London, PRCA. Available from: http://prmeasured.com/wp-content/uploads/2016/06/PRCA-PR-Census-2016.pdf. Accessed 28 October 2018.

Public Relations Institute of Australia (2016) Diversity and inclusion policy. Available from: https://www.pria.com.au/public/38/files/Education/Diversity%20and%20Inclusion/Diviersty%20and%20Inclusion%20policy.pdf. Accessed 10 January, 2018.

Rakow, L. F. (1986) Rethinking gender research in communication. *Journal of Communication,* 36, 11–26.

Rakow, L. (1989). From the feminization of public relations to the promise of feminism. In E. L. Toth and C. G. Cline, eds. *Beyond the Velvet Ghetto.* San Francisco, CA, IABC Research Foundation, pp. 287–298.

Rakow, L. F. and Nastasia, D. I. (2009) On feminist theory of public relations: An example from Dorothy E. Smith. In Ø. Ihlen, B. van Ruler, and M. Fredriksson, eds. *Public Relations and Social Theory: Key figures and concepts.* New York and Abingdon, Oxon, Routledge, pp. 252–277.

Reskin B. (2000) The proximate causes of employment discrimination. *Contemporary Sociology,* 29 (2), pp. 319–328.

Reskin, B. and Padavic, I. (1994) *Women and Men at Work.* Thousand Oaks, CA, Pine Forge Press.

Reskin, B. F. and Roos, P. A. (1990) Queuing and changing occupational composition. In B. F. Reskin and P. A. Roos, eds. *Job Queues, Gender Queues: Explaining women's inroads into male occupations.* Philadelphia, PA, Temple University Press, pp. 29–68.

Rhode, D. L. (2017) Gender stereotyping and unconscious bias. In S. R. Madsen, ed. *Handbook of Research on Gender and Leadership.* Cheltenham, Northampton, MA, Edward Elgar, pp. 316–327.

Rodgers H., Yeomans, L., and Halliday, S. (2016) The 'gogglebox' and gender: An interdiscursive analysis of television representations and professional femininities. In C. Elliott, V. Stead, S. Mavin, and J. Williams, eds. *Gender, Media and Organization: Challenging mis(s)representations of women leaders and managers.* Charlotte, NC, Information Age Publishing, pp. 169–196.

Roper, M. (1996) Seduction and succession: Circuits of homosocial desire in management. In D. L. Collinson and J. Hearn, eds. *Men as Managers, Managers as Men: Critical perspectives on men, masculinities and managements.* London, Thousand Oaks, CA, and New Delhi, Sage, pp. 210–226.

Rottenberg, C. (2014) The rise of neoliberal feminism. *Cultural Studies*, 28 (3), pp. 418–437.

Scott, J. W. (1999) Some reflections on gender and politics. In M. M. Ferree, J. Lorber, and B. B. Hess, eds. *Revisioning Gender*. Thousand Oaks, CA, London, and New Delhi, Sage, pp. 70–96.

Sedgwick, E. K. (2003) *Touching Feeling: Affect, pedagogy, performativity*. Durham, NC, Duke University Press.

Shah, A. (2017) Why do PR firms pay women, people of color less? The Holmes Report, 12 September. Available from: https://www.holmesreport.com/long-reads/article/why-do-pr-firms-pay-women-people-of-color-less. Accessed 20 April 2018.

Simpson, R. (2004) Masculinities at work: The experiences of men in female dominated occupations. *Work, Employment and Society*, 18 (2), pp. 349–368.

Skeggs, B. (2004) *Class, Self, Culture*. London, Routledge.

Sørensen, S. O. (2017) The performativity of choice: Postfeminist perspectives on work-life balance. *Gender, Work and Organization*, 24 (3), pp. 297–312.

Tench, R. and Moreno, A. (2015) Mapping communication management competencies for European practitioners. *Journal of Communication Management*, 19 (1), pp. 39–61.

Tindall, N. T. J. and Waters, R. D. (2012) Coming out to tell our stories: Using queer theory to understand the career experiences of gay men in public relations. *Journal of Public Relations Research*, 24, pp. 451–475.

Toth, E. L. (2001) How feminist theory advanced the practice of public relations. In R. L. Heath, ed. *Handbook of Public Relations*. Thousand Oaks, CA, London, and New Delhi, Sage, pp. 237–246.

Toth, E. L. and Cline, C. G. Eds (1989) *Beyond the Velvet Ghetto*. San Francisco, CA, IABC Research Foundation.

Tsetsura, K. (2009) How female practitioners in Moscow view their profession: A pilot study. *Public Relations Review*, 36 (1), pp. 78–80.

Tsetsura, K. (2011) Is public relations a real job? How female practitioners construct the profession. *Journal of Public Relations Research*, 23 (1), pp. 1–23.

Tsetsura, K. (2014) Constructing public relations as a women's profession in Russia. *Revista Internacional de Relaciones Públicas*, 8, (4), pp. 85–110.

Turkle, S. (2008) Always on/always on you: The tethered self. In J. E. Katz, ed. *Handbook of Mobile Communication Studies*. Boston, MA, MIT University Press, pp. 121–138.

Wajcman, J. (2015) *Pressed for Time: The acceleration of life in digital capitalism*. Chicago, IL, and London, The University of Chicago Press.

Walters, S. D. (1999) Sex, text, and context: (in) between feminism and cultural studies. In M. M. Ferree, J. Lorber, and B. B. Hess, eds. *Revisioning Gender*. Thousand Oaks, CA, London, and New Delhi Sage, pp. 222–257.

West, C. and Zimmerman, D. H. (1987) 'Doing gender'. *Gender and Society* 1, pp. 125–51.

Williams, C. (1995) *Still a Man's World*. Berkeley, University of California Press.

Wood, J. T. (2006) Gender and communication in interpersonal contexts. Thousand Oaks, CA, London, and New Delhi: Sage, pp. 1–8.

Wrigley, B. J. (2002) Glass ceiling? What glass ceiling? A qualitative study of how women view the glass ceiling in public relations and communications management. *Journal of Public Relations Research*, 14 (1), pp. 27–55.

Vardeman-Winter, J., Tindall, N., and Jiang, H. (2013) Intersectionality and publics: How exploring publics' multiple identities questions basic public relations concepts. *Public Relations Inquiry*, 2, pp. 279–304.

Verčič, D., Tench, R., and A. T. Verčič (2018) Collaboration and conflict between agencies and clients. *Public Relations Review*, 44 (1), pp. 156–164.

Yeomans, L. (2013) Gendered performance and identity work in PR consulting relationships: A UK perspective. In C. Daymon and K. Demetrious, eds. *Gender and Public Relations: Critical perspectives on voice, image and identity*. London, Routledge, pp. 87–107.

Yeomans, L. and Mariutti, F. G. (2016) Different lenses: Women's feminist and post-feminist perspectives in public relations. *Revista Internacional Relaciones Publicas*, 6 (12). Available from: http://revistarelacionespublicas.uma.es/index.php/revrrpp/article/view/430. Accessed 28 October 2018.

5 'Skilled emotion workers'

PRPs' emotion management in everyday professional relationships

Introduction

The chapter begins with an analysis of the agency office environment in which professional norms, or feeling rules, and relationships between public relations practitioners (PRPs) and their directors and colleagues are discussed. Bolton's typology of workplace emotion is used to examine PRPs' motivations associated with these norms. 'What it means to be an agency practitioner' begins with a discussion of participants' biographies in the processes of becoming a practitioner, before moving on to discuss the notions of being professional, in which gender, identity, and performance are brought into the analysis. 'Being yourself' in public relations (PR) agency relationships is closely examined in relation to theoretical notions of the self in emotional labour theory. The chapter then moves on to discuss the emotion management strategies of PRPs. The specific situations that require 'emotional control' in PR, as well as 'educating' and 'empathising', are examined. The chapter draws to a conclusion in reference to Hochschild's 'alienation of the self' theory to question whether PRPs' emotional labour constitutes such alienation.

Although aspects of this study have been published elsewhere (i.e. Yeomans, 2010, 2013, 2016), the findings presented in this chapter provide the basis for ongoing developments of emotional labour/emotion management theory in public relations, which continues in Chapter 6 with the study of agency directors. In presenting multiple realities of PR within these two chapters, the reader should be able to understand the relationships between the two studies.

Negotiating understandings of PR within the PR agency office environment

'Feeling rules' in PR agencies

As discussed in Chapter 3, 'feeling rules' are the expected attitudes and modes of employee behaviour of an organisation's management, communicated through company orientation programmes, ongoing training, and supervisors' surveillance of workers performing the service role (Hochschild, 1983, pp. 57–59). Bolton (2005) distinguishes between *professional* and *organisational* feeling rules, arguing that the feeling rules arising from the 'dual demands' (p. 126) of a person's profession and employing organisation may well be in conflict with each other. However, in my study, there was little, if any, suggestion of the dual demands of profession and organisation suggested in the literature. Working in an agency environment (as opposed to an in-house PR department within a large corporation), practitioners were surrounded by colleagues who were also engaged in PR work. Indeed, working in a PR agency sustained participants' confidence and sense of a professional community. It was perceived as a safe haven from external pressures as evidenced by the 'relaxed' culture depicted by some participants and the informal, sometimes close and mutually supportive relationships, which two participants described as a 'family atmosphere' (Alison; Pamela).

Yet the agency environment had a contradictory dimension that may have partly arisen from the need to maintain a 'friendly' mood (Alison; Pamela). Internal pressures arose from frustrations with colleagues for not 'pulling their weight' (Graham) and an antipathy towards 'spoon-feeding' junior executives to meet external demands (John; Alison). In addition, there was the stress of gendered, professional rivalry: 'there are *so* many women' (Gill) and discomfort with managing junior colleagues (Graham, Gill, Pamela, Emma). Within the agency environment, senior agency directors played a highly influential role as informal mentors and guides in developing the professional practice of the participants in this study; therefore the feeling rules and emotional climate could be said to spring from their attitudes and example.

Agency directors and feeling rules

The personalities and expectations of agency directors carried a special significance for participants. The influence and importance of some regional agency bosses emerged in terms of their business and media networks; their PR expertise and experience; and their impact, perceived both negatively and positively, on the career development of their young staff. For example, Emma expressed respect for her managing director's entrepreneurship 'she started in her back bedroom'; Graham admired his two directors' extensive professional networks based on their years of experience; and John cited his managing director's coaching role in the careers of young account managers who were now leading other agencies:

> I like to think of him as my mentor; I told him so. You may or may not be aware that he's the unspoken 'godfather of PR' in [City A] simply because every... single... one and I'm pretty sure in saying that, of the heads of all the big agencies have been coached by [him] at some point or other in their career. All of them; they've all come through [his] door at some point.
>
> (John)

Here, there is a strong resonance with Kaiser et al.'s (2008, p. 34) study of management consulting firms where senior colleagues ('superiors') acted as 'powerful role models' and therefore as internal emotional socialisation agents. Therefore, agency directors' expectations could be interpreted as synonymous with both organisational *and* professional feeling rules that were particular to the agency and its professional relationships. However, the subtlety of feeling rules within the agency context requires further examination.

As already discussed in Chapter 3, there are no barriers to entry to PR in the United Kingdom, in terms of qualifications, despite the efforts of professional membership organisations. Therefore, the different feeling rules, or behavioural norms, promoted by agency directors: 'make the client happy' (John); 'be yourself but be professional' (Gill); 'use the charm' (Emma); 'challenge the client' (Graham; John) were determined by different professional cultures. This point was especially noted by John, the most senior practitioner interviewed, after reading my collated 'description of practice' (Personal communication, 18.01.2012). Such feeling rules were developed in relation to the specific client contact, the specific client relationship, and the specific situation.

Kaiser et al. (2008, p. 314) assert that the '"client first" orientation' of consulting firms suggests that the clients act as *external* socialisation agents for young consultants. They argue that clients are ' "emotionally contagious" in that they 'provoke or elicit emotions'. Therefore, the notion of a 'feeling rule' within a small PR agency context could be overstating the agency's claim on practitioners' emotional displays. Perhaps one can talk about agency directors' 'signals' or cues (Hochschild, 1983, pp. 221–222) that act as more implicit 'guides for action'. Such cues, in turn, provide practitioners with a certain latitude for interpretation in different client situations (Bolton, 2005, p. 110). This latitude for interpretation is shown in expressions of trust. Both John and Emma emphasised their MDs' trusting management approach in which they felt 'empowered' to manage client relationships without interference:

> It's very relaxed, my boss...she started in her back bedroom kind of 16 years ago and it just growed [sic] to 12 people without her setting any business plans or anything. She puts a lot of trust in her staff. It's very much we do the work and get the results, how we go about it is very much up to us. We don't have timesheets.
>
> (Emma)

> [...] it's almost on a trust basis. The MD, he is very relaxed and believes in empowering people. Which is I think is the thing that's helped me to progress my career.
>
> (John)

The 'timesheets' referred to by Emma are indicative of one aspect of agency culture. For example, Gill and Alison had to fill in daily timesheets at the end of each day to account for the amount of time they had spent on client work. This information was used by the agency to inform the client billing procedure as standard practice within the PR industry (PR Moment, 2017). Therefore, the looser approach adopted at Emma's and John's agencies implied a higher level of trust between the MD and account handlers.

Although some agency directors were perceived as *lacking* in openness and trust in their account handlers, their concerns were paramount. Therefore, 'upward management' strategies were equally as important as elsewhere: 'And I always go into their office…just to double check things and advice and things like that' (Pamela). Within the relatively small regional agency environment, agency directors were understood to possess the power and authority to limit or support a practitioner's aspirations for promotion within the agency (Gill; Alison) or to another agency (Pamela), by virtue of their own social capital as agency heads located within regional networks (Ihlen, 2009). The multiple levels of checking and sign-off required for client work suggested that final approval from an agency director signified recognition of the account manager's effort. Importantly, agency directors' influential role was recognised as providing career development opportunities for those who were candidates for 'fast-tracking'.

The flirtatious client handling encouraged by Emma's female managing director ('Use the charm and you can get away with things if you're a woman') suggested that her otherwise sober law and engineering clients enjoyed the 'bubbly' 'creative' and 'happy' aspects of PR when it suited them and their own corporate image. Yet, at the same time, these clients expected a business-like, professional service that involved achieving the media coverage to promote their business, and in some cases, lead to direct sales: 'it does help the bottom line' (Emma). Here, there are echoes of the gendered service expectations of Alvesson's (1998) 'bureaucratic-rational' advertising executives' clients. Interestingly, however, the 'use the charm' advice was adopted only up to a point by Emma. While she recognised the need to adapt herself to different clients' expectations and to use every day small talk, she could not 'play on the woman' (with its negative connotations of seductress) as this conflicted with her own self-identity as a 'serious' person. Therefore the 'use the charm' feeling rule within this agency context may be regarded more as a 'guide for action' given its negotiated status (Bolton, 2005, p. 110). By contrast, the agency feeling rules of 'challenging the client' and 'not being a Yes man', illustrated in John and Graham's discourse, suggested that their agency directors' ideas of 'making the client happy' involved emphasising expertise and value to their business in taking a more challenging stance, particularly with male clients. This, in turn, drew on and reinforced a masculine notion of professionalism during client interactions and in client relationships (Simpson, 2004).

Colleague relationships

The so-called 'relaxed' and 'friendly' environment in the agency office allowed participants to air their frustrations among colleagues, and there was shared humour and 'banter', but only up to a point: there was a line beyond which they, as ambitious practitioners, risked being perceived as unprofessional by their bosses, their peers, and their juniors. This implied PRPs' dependency on emotional cues to guide their behaviour. For example, in Gill's narrative, a perceived atmosphere of surveillance prevailed at her 'competitive' agency office. Gill felt she was being judged by those around her: if she 'moaned' about clients or journalists too much, did not show initiative or come up with creative ideas and 'profile' herself sufficiently with agency bosses (made explicit in her agency's structured training and her line manager's feedback), then it would be noted in her appraisal and this might limit her chances of promotion.

In work settings where *professional norms* are dominant, collective emotional labour is more likely to take place outside of work (Lewis, 2005). 'Collective emotional labour' refers to situations where service workers seek out spaces for mutual support within the workplace to help them cope with difficult emotional situations (Korczynski, 2003). Within this study, however, only Pamela's account of regularly socialising with colleagues suggested any notion of mutual support outside the office environment. For Pamela, such socialising might have been a welcome release from the 'dysfunctional' directors at her agency who kept account handlers in the dark on business matters and yet expected them to devote themselves towards vaguely specified goals. Other study participants made efforts to maintain a clear dividing line between personal and work life. While not averse to socialising with and confiding in colleagues (i.e. peers) occasionally, it appeared that most study participants preferred to draw boundaries between their personal and work lives as a means to both preserve their professional status and unwind from the daily pressures of office life. The separation of home and work life may have been a characteristic of regionally based PR during the period of the study.

Graham, Gill, Pamela, and Emma all expressed the problems of being too friendly with junior members of their teams in a small office. This suggested that preserving status as well as escaping the pressures of work was the motive for keeping personal and work life separate. However, most of this study took place between 2008 and 2012, when social media platforms and the use of smartphones were only just beginning to be incorporated into PR practice. The notion of 'always on' work culture, discussed in Chapter 3, had yet to make an impact on the lived experience of PRPs. Nonetheless, since colleague relationships were experienced as stressful in this study, due to individualised careers and a competitive agency environment, the notion of mutual support or collective emotional labour, it would seem, was limited to situations where a 'them' (directors) and 'us' (PRPs) workplace culture had developed, as related by Pamela.

Motivations associated with feeling rules within PR agencies

A central feature of Bolton's typology of workplace emotion is motivation: 'it recognises the motivations of organisational actors to enact the feeling rules in distinct ways'. Professionals adhere to feeling rules for a variety of reasons and motives: for example, material gain, status, and sometimes for altruistic reasons. Importantly, motivations are also linked to 'broader frameworks of action' (Bolton, 2005, p. 93). Here, Bolton is referring to institutionalised practices, power hierarchies, and social positioning. However, 'broader frameworks of action' could also refer to the wider professional sphere in which practitioners seek to gain recognition that will, in turn, raise their status within their particular PR agency.

Two of the six participants, Alison and Pamela, self-identified as 'high flyers' and in the case of Graham, his rapid advancement from junior account executive to account manager in less than a year (less than two years after graduating), implied a 'high flyer' status. In addition, John, Pamela, and Alison had won PR industry awards. Pamela and Alison had achieved Young Communicator of the Year for their region. During the timescale of my fieldwork (2008–2012), all participants, four of whom were under the age of 30, had been promoted at least once within the agency structure or, in the case of John, had moved to an in-house role. Therefore, the study participants could be characterised as young, ambitious practitioners, for whom there was a strong motivation to adhere to the agency's expectations, to gain recognition, promotion, and raised status within their agency, as well as recognition and enhanced career mobility within the wider PR professional sphere.

Motivations for recognition and raised status varied among participants. John, for example, strongly identified himself as an entrepreneur, and in the first interview emphasised his role as deputy to his managing director in running a small business; almost 'MD-in-waiting'. Gill emphasised her preparedness for more 'strategic' work, expressing frustration with the non-strategic work that some clients expected her to undertake:

> I'm the second most senior person on the account and should be doing more strategic things…and she asks me to make sure that all the cells are equal [on a spreadsheet] and just really petty things and you think 'is that all you're bothered about?' and 'surely you've got more important things that you should be worrying about?'.

Alison, meanwhile, saw herself as a strong advocate for PR as a management function and emphasised her 'comfortable' relationships with her agency's senior management, thus positioning herself for a leadership role.

As suggested, the importance of professional status to practitioners (perhaps more so than any other motives) may explain why practitioners, in different ways, made considerable efforts to prevent negative emotions from impacting on their own work as well as the reputation of the agency. In claiming that they did 'not take things personally', both Gill and Alison were able to adopt a professional 'mask' (Goffman, 1959, p. 30) that helped them to buffer 'egotistical' journalists as well as difficult clients. Learning not to say 'yes' automatically to journalists was not merely about responding realistically to their demands; it was an effort to prevent the likely consequence of looking foolish in the eyes of the journalists as well as peers when a demand could clearly not be met. Alison's 'empathising' strategy (see page 129) served not only to build a good relationship with her client but simultaneously to prevent blame which would be passed on by the client to her bosses if she did not make the effort to empathise. Pamela, too, prevented blame and potential embarrassment by copying in her bosses on all emails where there was an 'issue' with a client. John avoided blame and potential humiliation from his boss or the client by ensuring that the client had 'no surprises' and that he was 'upfront' when the media coverage gained had not shown a good return on investment for the client.

As discussed in Chapter 2, the social emotion of 'shame' includes variations of this emotion (e.g. humiliation, embarrassment, and feelings of rejection or failure) that arise from situations where there is a social disconnection from others: a 'threat to the social bond' (Scheff, 2000, p. 97). The fear of experiencing shame will, in turn, drive social actors to take avoiding action in order to prevent difficult social situations from arising. Such motivation will apply especially within the organisational or professional context but also in relation to the 'interior monologue in which we see ourselves from the point of view of others' (Scheff, 2000, p. 95).

I argue that this interactional perspective on the presentation of self may be heightened among PRPs whose core function is to present their client in the best possible light to external publics. Thus, the 'looking-glass self' (Cooley, 1922) that makes a judgement of the self: a self that reflexively monitors and regulates personal behaviour from the perspective of others could be seen to operate among PRPs. Indications that such self-monitoring took place could be found in the accounts of four participants, who in their drive to be the best in their everyday practice were particularly self-critical: 'I need to start being more sort of strict with my time-planning' (Gill); 'I beat myself up more than anyone else would' (Pamela); 'I'll be honest I'm a bit of a perfectionist' (John); 'Maybe put myself under quite a bit of pressure' (Graham). Given the career focus among participants, and the need to look to the next career move or promotion, there was a clear motive behind 'careful management of the self' (Illouz, 2007, p. 66).

In summary, a discussion of the professional context is important to identify the organisational and professional feeling rules that PRPs attend to (or not) in their emotion management. From this study a complex picture emerged. Regional PR in this study had an entrepreneurial identity in which agency directors often played an influential and highly personal socialisation role as guides and mentors in setting expectations for their account handlers. In small, owner-managed regional agencies these expectations, feeling rules, or emotional cues were implicit 'guides for action' which were informal and negotiated in relation to the client relationship and situation. For some practitioners, working in agencies that were part of larger networks, feeling rules were explicitly communicated through a structured training and appraisal system, as discussed below. This suggests that 'emotion management is performed in particular ways by different members of the same profession' (Bolton, 2005, p. 124). Some practitioners in this study were motivated by recognition and professional status; therefore, as implicit and explicit feeling rules become internalised, emotion management is more likely to be self-regulated by the more experienced practitioner to anticipate and prevent difficult situations from arising.

What it means to be an agency PR professional

Becoming a PRP: education and training

Becoming a PRP was a deliberate decision for all participants in the study: they had not 'fallen' into PR, which Graham had observed, to his surprise, was the case for some of his older, more experienced colleagues. My participants were typical, in that at the time of the study, 86% of new recruits to PR were graduates (Lepper, 2012). Less typical was that most had some form of educational qualification in PR. Four had gained a bachelors or masters degree in PR, and a fifth had studied for a professional PR certificate. Gill, the only participant who had not undertaken a course of study in PR, felt that her absence of formal PR training or education had resulted in a lack of confidence at the early stages of her career.

Different participant conversations revealed different attitudes to education and training. While Alison identified her master's education as providing an understanding of PR as a management function ('I got this from doing my master's more so than people who haven't actually studied [PR] as a discipline'), John questioned the relevance of his PR masters education to his PR work, although acknowledged that 'it taught me how to write and structure a proposal, that's one thing it *absolutely* taught me to do'. Pamela saw the relevance of some of the learning experiences she had gained on her three-year PR degree course, yet went on to assert that learning on the job 'was second to none' because this taught her 'what works well and what doesn't work'. Hence, the suggestion was that 'expertise' in the PR agency was 'seen as constituted and transmitted through practice' (Pieczka, 2002, p. 321), even when some participants had gained a PR education.

Gill and Alison both engaged in regular, structured training and development designed by their agency to inculcate a corporate culture across an international network:

> There's a huge talent scheme so each person has their own, like, talent calendar for the year. And there's workshops that are kind of toured around the country and all the different offices. So we are all getting the same training on all different subjects. [...] So each level goes away for, like, two and a half days on this awayday to a nice hotel where you have training sessions and team building exercises, that sort of thing. We have a social budget and flexi-time – you are encouraged to use flexi-time to your advantage so then you can start late or leave early.

This structured training and development also served to reinforce a professional PR culture, for example, in setting ethical standards across the agency. However, among those interviewed, the 'talent scheme' described by Gill was the exception to common experience within the regional PR agency setting. Experiences of structured training and development in other regional agencies varied considerably: they were non-existent (Emma and John); used as a reward in lieu of a salary rise (Pamela); or based around internal staff presentations on given topics (Graham).

Two participants, Graham and Alison, were members of the Chartered Institute of Public Relations (CIPR), which has a professional code of conduct; however, this code of conduct continues to be limited to the CIPR's 9,000 or so members and is not applicable to the majority of practitioners who are neither members of the CIPR nor the Public Relations and Communications Association (PRCA). Therefore, a relatively weak association with the 'knowledge model' of a profession (van Ruler, 2005, p. 161) was suggested by participants' variability of experience and opportunities in professional training and development and the relatively limited impact of professional associations in their lives at the time of the study. The model of profession suggested by agency PR is an 'entrepreneurial' model, as argued by Muzio et al. (2008). Therefore, Bolton's argument concerning the 'dual consciousness' arising from professional codes of conduct and organisational feeling rules was not evident.

Some agency bosses, as small business entrepreneurs, appeared to hold little regard for supporting the career development of their staff through structured business or PR training, yet were often understood to be supportive managers and mentors in 'learning on the job', particularly in learning how to manage relationships: '…it's all from the people above me really and watching how they do it, and yeah doing the same thing. It's all on the job' (Emma). Graham listened to and observed the behaviours of his bosses during their interactions with others. This meant that as a young practitioner in his first year of full-time paid work, he had a template to work to, that could be reinterpreted to suit his own personality and style of communication: 'listen in to them and then almost try to make a mental script and then use it again for when I'm trying to do it' (Graham).

Theories of social learning and self-efficacy suggest that by observing the behaviour of others, including role models, social actors work out how to handle the kinds of situations that are most likely to bring them success or rewards (Bandura, 1977, 1997). If learning on the job for PRPs involved learning the observed behaviours and feeling rules that are appropriate for specific situations then, referring back to Bolton's typology in Table 2.1, it was the 'presentational' emotion management that was frequently used to become a successful agency PRP. Presentational emotion management responds to social feeling rules defined as 'the implicit traffic rules of social interaction' (Bolton, 2005, p. 133). PRPs have to skilfully interpret those traffic rules within a diverse range of situations: where there is a lack of cooperation from the client; when the client has an idea that the practitioner believes will not work; when the client needs to be convinced that a media strategy will work; and when a journalist is rude or elusive.

Presentational emotion management involves more than a set of personal qualities and skills: it is the embodiment of these resources that contribute to 'cultural capital' (Bourdieu, 1997). Cultural capital, as a resource, generates 'symbolic capital' which affords access to dominant social groups through shared language, norms, values, dress, and behaviours (Edwards, 2008). Edwards (2008, p. 371) contends that PRPs in the United Kingdom have 'high levels of cultural capital' based on indicators including parental occupations and practitioners' educational qualifications ('institutional capital'). Although my study did not examine other resources such as the cultural activities and tastes of practitioners, their social class, indicated by educational attainments as well as parental occupations, suggested that these practitioners were well-placed to 'mix with a variety of people, securing extensive social networks that could lead to better results or new clients' (Edwards, 2008, p. 371).

In bringing the issues of social class and educational attainment into the analysis, the meaning of 'presentational emotion management' becomes more clearly defined in that, as Bolton (2005, p. 157) argues, some social actors are already prepared, through early socialisation, to 'play according to the company's rules of social interaction' than others. So, for example, as a middle-class, well-educated woman, Emma did not need to be instructed how to dress in the office when meeting a journalist or attending a client pitch; furthermore, she observed that the trend of wearing jeans in the office was *too* casual for her because 'you never know who might come in': *she* did not wish to be caught off guard (another indicator of embarrassment) in the presence of a client and was able to re-interpret the dress code to suit her own idea of being professional.

Illouz (2007, p. 64) argues that 'emotional capital' is the 'most "embodied" part of the embodied forms of cultural capital'. Emotional capital, in turn, converts into a commodified form of emotion, that of 'emotional intelligence' which is a 'type of social intelligence that involves the ability to monitor one's own and others' emotions, to discriminate among them, and to use the information to guide one's thinking and actions' (Mayer and Salovey, 1993, p. 433, cited in Illouz, 2007, p. 64). Furthermore, Hughes (2010) argues that emotional intelligence (EI) shifts the focus away from the 'feeling rules and scripts' of emotional labour to individuals developing competences that rely on self-regulation. This 'individualisation of emotion' requires people be true to their authentic selves and emotionally reflexive, expressing themselves in ways that are 'appropriate', even though this brings the added pressure of negotiating complex situations (Hughes, 2010, p. 41).

In summary, becoming a successful agency PR professional, based on participants' biographies and understandings in this chapter, may have owed more to the personal skills and qualities acquired through earlier socialisation, than to the knowledge derived from PR education. Further, learning on the job within the agency context, watching how others handled relationships, and responding to relational cues helped to shape practitioners' existing relational skills so that they became relevant to the task in hand. This process, in turn, helped to generate an embodied form of PR 'expertise' (Pieczka, 2002, p. 32) suggestive of an 'emotional–intelligence' model of professionalism (van Ruler, 2005).

While an 'emotional–intelligence' proposition could be challenged by scholars and practitioners due to the growing technical knowledge and skills base required to practise PR in a digital age, I argue that PR will continue to use legitimisation strategies through client interactions. As discussed in Chapter 3, interpersonal legitimisation strategies are used to both justify PRP expertise in handling client accounts as well as client organisations' contributions to society (Waeraas, 2009; Merkelsen, 2011). Arguably only skilled emotion workers can perform this kind of work. Not only are skilled emotion workers required to interact with clients and others remotely, using digital networks, they are also required to understand the norms of online emotional expression (Waterloo et al., 2018) in order to communicate effectively with target publics. Therefore, the PRP's capacity to leverage personal symbolic capitals, holding the 'right' credentials for PR work within neoliberal capitalism, will continue to hold sway in the PR field (Edwards, 2014).

Being professional: gender, identity, and performance

The image of the PR profession in the United Kingdom has, to a large extent, been influenced by media representations. The gender stereotypes of the male political 'spin doctor' and the female 'PR girl' are depicted in popular television culture, ranging from political satires to sitcoms and romantic comedy-dramas (Rodgers et al., 2016). Indeed, the identities of the participants in this study were intersubjectively constructed *in relation to* the gender stereotype of the 'PR girl' as I discuss later.

Participants' professional identities were influenced in other ways. Agency directors as informal mentors and role models may have been the 'folk symbols' that participants aspired to emulate (Becker, 1970 cited in Bolton, 2005, p. 124). It is also conceivable, drawing on the 'folk symbol' idea that practitioners borrowed the identities and norms of other, related professions to 'define the way they think about themselves' (Bolton, 2005, p. 124). PR agencies continue to recruit ex-journalists whose own occupational culture and identities are constructed as more autonomous (Kovach and Rosenstiel, 2001 in Pieczka, 2006; Richards and Rees, 2011; Hopper and Huxford, 2015) and 'masculine' (Steiner, 1998 in de Bruin, 2000; Jenkins and Finneman, 2018). Such identities contrast with PRPs' identities as 'shapeshifters' which is more fluid and adaptable: 'at the heart of the shapeshifter identity is relationships with others and how they conceive of you as an expert' (Reed, 2013, p. 245).

'Being professional' had multiple meanings. While participants in the study were advised by their directors to 'be themselves' (a 'social' feeling rule) yet 'be professional' ('professional/organisational' feeling rule) during client interactions, the elasticity of the term 'professional' meant performing emotion and other work in response to whatever the situation demanded (de

Bruin and Ross, 2004; Hughes, 2010). While Bolton (2005) suggests that the likely framework for professional behaviour is a code of conduct, such a code was not explicitly referred to. Gill and Alison referred to the importance of client confidentiality, and this may have stemmed from their agency's statement of values which claimed to have 'helped shape industry standards' over the years through its commitment to being open and ethical. However, it was generally understood among participants that professionalism meant 'behaving well' in specific contexts. This echoes Fournier's (1999) notion of personal conduct as a professional competence. Pamela articulated professionalism in the following way:

> a line of professionalism that shouldn't be crossed in terms of going from a client's PR relationship to like more "matey". You always have to be very careful with that. Erm…doing your job *well*, giving the results that they want, or trying to give the results that they are wanting to achieve. Whether it's speaking to a journalist, going to dinner with a client, going to an event. I think professionalism is 100% caught up in everything.

However, as noted from Pamela's narrative, '100% professionalism' could be re-interpreted according to context: for Pamela, it could mean 'not getting drunk' with clients but, on the other hand, allowing her guard to drop with journalists because some journalists were counted as friends. This contingent view of professionalism reinforces Bolton's notion of 'discretion and autonomy in the interpretation of professional feeling rules' (2005, p. 126). Further, Hughes (2010, p. 51) argues that the implementation of EI ideas in contemporary workplaces has effectively changed the emotional rules for work, demanding a 'reflexive emotional self that increasingly has to take account of a far more complex array of considerations'. Professionalism in PR agency work therefore suggests a form of EI that PRPs use to adapt to different situations and relationships.

Sociologists (e.g. Davies, 1996; Bolton and Muzio, 2008) argue that the concept of 'professional' is gendered, which nuances the meaning of the word from an emotion management perspective. They argue that the concept of 'professional' is informed by a masculine cultural project and its discourse, which denotes objectiveness and rationalism. Viewed from this perspective, the women participants in this study emphasised their 'professional' 'serious' or gender-neutral attributes and aligned their performances to a 'masculine' notion of a profession (Bolton and Muzio, 2008; Marsh, 2009; Fitch and Third, 2010). In making this assertion, I should mention how some 'gender-neutral' narratives in this study were co-created. My question 'When does being a woman/man influence the way in which you interact with (journalist, client etc)?' consistently invited defensive reactions from female participants, echoing Wrigley's (2002) 'denial' of gender findings. However, 'seriousness' was emphasised in relation to other questions too, including how participants dealt with difficult clients or journalists. Gill and Alison claimed that they 'did not take it personally' when clients and journalists were difficult or rude. Emma ensured that her 'serious' side was emphasised when dealing with engineering and legal clients. According to Alison, it was imperative to come across to senior colleagues and clients in a pitch situation as '100% professional' by which she meant formal, well-prepared, and business-like. Gill stated it was important to self-monitor and 'profile' herself in the presence of agency directors to enhance her promotion prospects. These aspects of identity were carefully worked on, it would appear, in order to counter the perceived stereotypical image of the 'PR girl' (Fröhlich, 2004; Fröhlich and Peters, 2007). Such performances were also motivated by claims to professional status and rewards such as 'proving yourself' (Gill) in competition with (other female) colleagues, discussed earlier in this chapter (Bolton, 2005).

As I argued in Chapter 3, masculine identities in PR have received limited attention in the literature. In this study, the discourse and performance of male participants were intertwined with the preservation of masculine identity within the context of a female-intensive profession (Alvesson, 1998). Similarly to advertising, an occupational identity perceived as 'feminine' in agency PR presents challenges to men working in the industry. John, rather unusually, worked with an all-male team and asserted his masculine identity extensively through his discourse of 'confrontational' encounters with clients, claiming that this earned him the (male) client's respect (Leidner, 1993). Some of John's male clients were small business owners ('I can totally and utterly empathise with the fact that he has a family business') who, perhaps, encapsulated 'entrepreneurial ideologies and discourses' of capital accumulation and traditional ideas of male and female roles (Mulholland, 1996, p. 149). This consideration of clients' demands could be regarded as a pressure on the male PRP to perform the 'proper enactment of gender, since masculinity is often associated with toughness and detachment' (Leidner, 1993, p. 200). Therefore, John invoked a 'take it or leave it' brinkmanship strategy[1] to force the client into accepting or rejecting his PR advice.

Similarly, Graham's interactions with male marketing managers also called upon him and his senior male colleagues to 'challenge' the client using a brinkmanship strategy; therefore, consciously or not, both John and Graham and his male bosses played on 'being a man' to preserve their professional status and their masculinity as well as to achieve the desired outcome with the client. Although he too ascribed to 'not being a Yes man' in a similar way to John, Graham further defined his PR role as masculine (Simpson, 2004) by emphasising his online PR specialism. Digitally focused PR agencies were relatively new phenomena when this study was undertaken (2008–2011). By adopting the language and techniques of the digital agency, Graham effectively distanced his practice from what he repeatedly called the 'traditional', and perhaps, feminised agencies. Furthermore, in the case of Graham's agency, PR's claims to online expertise was contested by online marketing strategists within the client organisation, thereby raising the question of jurisdictional claims (Abbott, 1988) to corporate power (Chalmers, 2001). Upon receiving the 'description of practice' which was sent to participants to validate my account of PR practice, it is worth noting here that one female participant commented that female, not just male practitioners, were expected to 'challenge' clients. My response to this is that the word 'challenge' did not feature once in the narratives of female participants; therefore 'challenge' might be attributed to a specific gendered interactional style (Holmes, 2006), as well as a process of masculine identity construction with me as a female researcher.

As I discuss later in this chapter, both John and Graham in different ways wished to claim a more equal balance of power with journalists. In identifying their practices with male journalists, it may be argued that John and Graham's respective discourses of masculine newsroom culture (Steiner, 1998 cited in de Bruin, 2000; Jenkins and Finneman, 2018) and knowledge management (Wenger, 2000) served to construct, and perhaps to reinstate, a masculine professional identity and status, taken within the context of earlier PR history as a male-dominated occupation (L'Etang, 2015).

As Williams (1993) argues, there is a tendency for both men and women to be rewarded for distancing themselves from femininity. From the foregoing discussion, female participants practised distancing by disassociating themselves from the 'PR girl' stereotype and aligning their identities with the masculine discourse of the objective professional (Marsh, 2009). Interestingly, both male participants had in rather different ways constructed a masculine version of PR that both distanced their work from the predominantly feminised agencies and acted as a defence to any possible perceptions of doing 'women's work' (Lupton, 2000; Simpson, 2004). Paradoxically, much relational work in agency PR (as discussed later in this chapter), performed by both men and women, employed the strategies of 'empathising', 'educating', and 'managing expectations' which, in turn, closely align with the feminine discourse of the trusted adviser (Marsh, 2009, cited in Yeomans, 2010). However, as previously discussed, relational work as a skill on its own is undervalued unless it accompanies a technical skill; therefore, PR work has to be constructed as doing more than emotional labour.

Being yourself: the role of personality and 'the self' in agency relationships

As discussed in Chapter 2, Hochschild (1983, pp. 185–198) made a distinction between 'true' and 'false' selves. She argued that emotional labour in service work alienated workers from their 'authentic' selves or true feelings because they were engaged in 'deep acting' performances that suppressed the 'true self'. The binary of the 'true' and 'false' self has been critiqued by recent theorists who argue that people enact multiple identities at work; find spaces where they can be themselves; find humour through shared emotional labour and in doing so subvert cultural norms within the workplace (e.g. Shuler and Davenport Sypher, 2000; Bolton and Boyd, 2003; Guerrier and Adib, 2003; Korczynski, 2003).

Some theorists argue further that specific occupations are a means of self-identity expression or the means to improve actors' social standing and economic success (e.g. Korczynski, 2003; Schweingruber and Berns, 2005), while others claim that emotional labour is a necessary part of being a professional (e.g. Mann, 2004; Ogbonna and Harris, 2004; Anleu and Mack, 2005; Mastracci et al., 2006) arising from the 'dual demands' of organisational and professional feeling rules (Bolton, 2005) as well as ascribed gender roles (Bellas, 1999; Bolton and Muzio, 2008).

Within this study the notion of 'being yourself' was associated with 'being professional' by some participants. These two ideas could well be seen as incompatible since 'being yourself' denotes freedom of emotional expression during social interactions while 'being professional' suggests emotional control; but, as argued earlier, agency PRPs bring the 'basic socialised self' to their relational work, drawn from 'a lifetime's social guidance' (Bolton, 2005, p. 133). Fournier (1999, p. 287) also links socialisation to being a professional: 'conducting or constituting oneself in an appropriate manner', a characteristic of professional competence. In agency PR, the socialised self, which involves the ability to manage the emotions of self and others, is a resource in its own right and includes emotional resources that help PR firms to manage client and journalist relationships.

'Being yourself' could mean exhibiting 'personality' (John, Gill and Graham) and 'friendliness' (Pamela, Gill) but it could also mean 'adapting your style' to different social situations (Alison and Emma), which was an 'essential' part of the job (Graham). Participants consistently strove to build informal and easy-going relationships with clients, while recognising that not all clients wanted that kind of relationship. Gill, in particular, viewed her own personality as being part of the service that clients 'buy into' during the business pitch:

> people have approached me [to do] PR work who have never actually worked with me but just know me and so they come to me. Which is quite odd really because they don't know if I can do it or not but just because they buy into you, you have to be yourself.
>
> (Gill)

Personality, or 'personal chemistry', is part of what clients buy when they buy PR services (Gabbott and Hogg, 1996; Pieczka, 2006; Sissons, 2015). Mart and Jackson (2005) found that clients of *smaller* agencies expected higher levels of service and more frequent communication as well as more informal, enjoyable relationships. Poor communication would be a possible reason for switching agencies. Clients expected high levels of interaction, which my participants labelled as 'over-servicing', a financial as well as an emotional construct. Not only did participants express feelings of injustice in that clients were not prepared to pay a proper rate for PR services, but also that their PR skills were being exploited. However, over-servicing was mostly accepted as part of the job: 'we all over-service our clients' (Alison). John felt that the London agencies were 'heck of a lot stricter' in their billing arrangements in comparison to his regional agency but that over-servicing was a 'very difficult thing to manage' once the client's expectation had been established.

Thus, it could be argued from this study that 'personality' helped to differentiate the service offer during and after the client pitch. As interactions were likely to be more informal, due to small agency size, and less a standardised 'professional business transaction' (Mart and Jackson, 2005, p. 11) then clients could expect a more flexible, tailored relationship. This, in turn, had implications for emotion management within the client-agency relationship. Not only did practitioners have to 'go the extra mile' to 'make it easy' for the client, they also had to overcome their feelings of frustration concerning over-servicing the client, and, beyond that, sometimes a lack of recognition (from the client) for the results they had gained. Embedded within these interactions is the notion that participants in this study had to actively work on their feelings and identities to successfully carry out their professional tasks and rationalise their decisions to work in PR.

Enjoyment in agency life: 'learning something every day'

For most participants, much of the enjoyment and rewards of agency life sprang from dealing with a variety of client sectors and different personalities. Practitioners frequently talked of 'learning so, so much' every day in terms of building up knowledge about different businesses through reading newspapers and carrying out background research into their clients' sectors. Emma was most animated when talking about her legal clients 'with law firms you're learning about something every day 'cause the law changes all the time. There are all these new things happening, new cases', adding 'that's why I've stuck at it for so long' (Emma), perhaps hinting that she might have moved to an in-house role otherwise. Alison more overtly talked of the downsides and compensations of agency life:

> I work long hours and maybe don't get paid as much as some of my friends doing a thing like accountancy…and you kind of rationalise that by saying: 'Well I *learn* so much every day that will help me in my future career. I am doing something I really want to be doing and I enjoy doing and get a lot out of, and feel passionately about' […]
>
> (Alison)

Typically, a strong sense of enjoyment arose from seeing the tangible 'results' of practitioners' efforts: 'making the client happy […] I feel particularly proud when the client says 'Yeah, good job, well done'; 'keeping clients happy, getting results and seeing the results' (John); 'when you get a new business pitch, that's a good feeling!' (Gill). The 'results' translated into media coverage, through the print, broadcast, or online media.

Five years into her career and several promotions on, Pamela continued to enjoy seeing media coverage: 'Still love getting cuttings for my clients and sending it over' (Pamela). Emma elaborated further: 'it's a real challenge getting across complicated issues that they are talking about in a really simple press release; in a straightforward article. Well, I like that challenge' (Emma).

Enjoyment: being a trusted adviser

Rewards for practitioners also came through building closer relationships with clients as a result of successful advice or coverage, so that 'they come to you' [for advice] (Gill, Alison). As account director and second-in-command at his agency, John articulated his idea of a good PRP-client relationship thus: 'You get to a point where you are an extension of the client's team [...] I really thrive on doing that and providing best advice and the client listens to it and accepts it'. John gave an example of how this ideal relationship worked:

> I'll have almost daily conversations for an hour on the telephone. Throwing ideas around, chatting about stuff, bouncing stuff around. I will then take all of that, and he says this: 'tripe', streamline it, manage it, and pull it together into some level of meaning. And that can be developed into a press release, features, opinion pieces etc. And that is fairly typical.
>
> (John)

'Getting your teeth into' (Gill) a client's project, however, was often difficult due to other clients' demands. Having a range of client demands heightened the risk of 'being spread a bit too thinly' (Pamela) or 'scratching the surface' (Emma). The actual experience of working in-house in Gill's case and the perceptions (Emma; Pamela; John) that working in-house would bring a 'deep understanding' of the business sometimes led to thoughts of moving in-house as the next career move. A year on from their first interview, neither Pamela nor Emma had moved to an in-house role but they had both been promoted to account director; John, meanwhile, had moved in-house to work for a long-standing client. It seemed that as long as agencies provided a promotion incentive, PRPs remained in agency PR and were prepared to put up with the feeling of sometimes being the 'middle-man' between clients and journalists (Alison; Emma) and not always 'in control' of events (Emma). Despite the pressures, PR agency work was a deliberate, preferred, career choice, and perceived as a means of identity expression (Korczynski, 2003). While stressful, PR was not experienced as 'alienation'. As such, PR as emotional labour could be said to represent 'a complicated version of freedom' (Hesmondhalgh and Baker, 2011).

The emotion management strategies of PRPs

Faking it: surface acting in PR

Practitioners' rapport-building performances, or 'surface acting' (Hochschild, 1983), involved numerous, everyday informalities to 'warm up' the client or the journalist to encourage a 'receptive' attitude. Graham gave an account of his agency sending flowers to a client at the client's work premises (even though the flowers were intended for his wife). This gesture evocatively demonstrates what Bolton (2005, p. 82) regards as a 'cynical' performance where the actor knows that they are faking sincerity but realise its instrumental importance in managing the feelings of others to achieve a desired outcome. The gesture of sending flowers to a client, favoured by Emma's managing director, could also be construed as an example of a 'gender display' (Reskin and Padavic, 1994). A PRCA guide that was in print at the time when my interviews were conducted reinforced this approach: 'Your relationship may be purely about business, but that doesn't mean you can't treat your client like a friend. Little things do count, like sending a card or flowers on their birthday' (PRCA, 2009). Conversely, John responded with a tone of angry disdain when I questioned him about using personal gestures with clients:

> I mean, yeah it is important to remember a client's birthday. But in the grand scheme of things, is it *really*? I think really it's about delivering on what your objectives are, doing damned good business and making the client happy with the business that you're pushing forward.

Surface acting was also demanded in situations where participants had to fake an interest in their clients' ideas, while finding a way of getting them to change their ideas:

> But I'm just sitting there thinking [*quiet, small voice*] "It's awful…we can't take a national journalist to this" [*then laughs out loud*] but it just means putting those feelings to one side and steering them round to another course of action!
>
> (Pamela)

Participants' cynical discourse also centred around male journalists whose egos had to be 'pandered to' (Alison), not only in terms of providing them with worthwhile stories or ideas for features through the process of 'selling-in' (Yeomans, 2013), but also in terms of maintaining an attitude of friendliness and openness, to ensure future cooperation. Cooperation was needed, for example, when the journalist had discovered information that was potentially damaging to a client's reputation (Pamela).

Feelings of frustration

During the research interviews, expressions of 'frustration' often served as a proxy term for emotions ranging from anger to irritation. 'Frustration' was typically used to describe situations that could not be controlled or where there was a lack of understanding of the PRP's position (e.g. from clients). However, the PRP's emotion management role was to 'get rid' of feelings of anger

(Hochschild, 1983, p. 90) by empathising with the journalist or client. To act on the anger would 'threaten the social bond' (Scheff, 2000, p. 97) and cause the practitioner to lose face and perhaps, their client's account. It could be argued that a degree of 'masking' took place with me as researcher because participants' accounts of their emotions were 'politically sensitive performances of their selves' (Coupland et al., 2008, p. 343) as serious-minded professionals.

Some accounts of interactions demanded more from PRPs than 'going into robot' to create a friendly tone (Hochschild, 1983, p. 129). In navigating around journalists' professional identities as autonomous news-gatherers, however inaccurate this identity may be (de Bruin, 2000; Davies, 2008; Beckett and Deuze, 2016), practitioners had to learn to absorb rude rebuffs and worse, an absence of any response from the journalist:

> […] sent her loads of information, she wanted specific statistics, I'd spent ages researching that. And then, got her fine on the phone. And she kind of went into a black hole after that. There are only so many times you can push.
>
> (Emma)

The busy journalist could not use Emma's story, but did not get back to her to let her know. Emma's feelings of frustration and disappointment continued as the relational focus shifted back to the client. Somehow the absence of a piece of coverage had to be justified to the client. A complete absence of explanation from the journalist appeared as a snub: the breaking of a 'social bond' in a situation where there was a perceived social contract (Scheff, 2000). A visceral illustration of PR as emotional labour is John's account of asking a journalist for their guidance on improving the story, so that the client had an explanation for the absence of their story in print:

> You've got to do the thing that I really hate about PR, that is grimacing through a nice big smile. And going 'Oh hi it's la la la.' When really you want to say: 'Right you're gonna listen to me'. You've just got to keep…I always say persistence pays off. And if it's a good story, persistence will pay off.
>
> (John)

The struggle to maintain a veneer of politeness and friendliness in eliciting feedback from a journalist about a story that she had rejected illustrates a moment where the authentic self is confronted by and bows to the demands of the job, in a similar way to Hochschild's flight attendants who are trained to focus not on their feelings of anger, but on the passenger's situation (Hochschild, 1983, p. 196).

Both Alison and Gill effortfully practised detachment from their emotions ('not taking things personally'), and this appeared to be part of their training. It was their way of dealing with rejection from a journalist, and yet like

Emma and John, they still had to 'persist' to elicit feedback from the journalist that would be useful to their client while avoiding 'pestering' the journalist in the process. Emma's phrase 'there are only so many times you can push' suggested how emotionally demanding it could be for the practitioner to avoid 'pissing off' the journalist, an action that risked a loss of respect from the journalist, a loss of trust from the client (in the practitioner's ability to tap into media channels), and, ultimately, a threat to professional status for the practitioner in not getting the job done.

Hochschild (1983, p. 113) observes that to rid oneself of anger towards someone, 'the recommended strategy is to focus on what the other person might be thinking and feeling: imagine a reason that excuses his or her behaviour'. This empathetic emotion management strategy was evident in practitioners' accounts of relationships with journalists as well as clients. Therefore, in dismissing some journalists' brusque manner as 'egotistical' while trying to understand journalists' own pressures in meeting news copy deadlines (Gill, John, and Alison), practitioners were practising 'deep acting' (Hochschild, 1983, p. 38).

Empathising

For empathy to work successfully during journalist or client interactions, the practitioner had to strongly identify with their problems and put themselves 'in their shoes' (Alison). It is therefore, perhaps, no coincidence that John described his working environment as 'run almost like a newsroom, people shouting upstairs and downstairs' (John). In emulating a fast-paced, masculine news environment, John and his team were more able to mirror the urgency of the task, and construct their male journalist contacts as counterparts in the news-creation process, even though the power balance in the relationship may in fact lie with the journalist. In recognising the 'imposed relevance' of PR's frequent asymmetrical relationship with journalists, John made efforts to take control by making journalists' interests of 'intrinsic relevance' to him and his team (Schütz, 1970).

Graham, who worked for an agency specialising in digital communication, frequently used the term 'collaborate' when discussing relationships with journalists. 'Collaborate' is a term borrowed from the knowledge management field to denote systems through which organisational knowledge sharing and social learning may take place (Wenger, 2000). Within a media relations context, the use of the term 'collaborate' may serve to construct a more equal balance of power between the PRP and the journalist to create a story, albeit in a somewhat romanticised fashion. (It is unlikely that journalists themselves would see PRPs as fellow 'collaborators', given the political connotations as well as the implication of less than autonomous news-gathering.) Nevertheless, Graham's distinctively differentiated discourse among my participants highlights the importance of empathising with the needs of online journalists as a 'community of practice' where knowledge sharing is valued 'in informal processes, such as conversations, brainstorming and pursuing ideas' (Wenger, 2000, p. 244). Again, such empathising may be seen as a means to take control of an otherwise asymmetrical relationship between PR and journalism.

A further example of empathetic performance was Alison's account of her 'difficult' client (Yeomans, 2013, 2016). In researching her client's job and learning not to 'blame' her client for being unhelpful in providing information that Alison requested in order to do her job, Alison succeeded in changing her own negative attitude towards her client. Alison was subsequently congratulated by her bosses for the 'brilliant' relationship, and for succeeding where others had failed: 'I've invested quite a lot of time in making sure that for example, I don't blame her if we don't get information through' (Alison). Alison's justification for approaching her client in this way suggested highly complex and reflexive emotion management that was intensively focused on achieving a positive outcome, both for the client and the agency.

Deep acting

Hochschild (1983) regards empathic interactions, as outlined previously, as 'deep acting' and a profound threat to the actor's sense of self because of the potential 'emotive dissonance' (p. 90) between producing the 'right' feeling and getting rid of an actor's more 'authentic' feeling, which may be one of frustration or anger towards the client. However, some theorists argue, in contradiction to Hochschild, on this point that such a 'transformation of the self' builds 'emotional capital' (Cahill, 1999) which may be regarded by actors as an important skill in 'becoming a better self' (Schweingruber and Bern, 2005, p. 680).

Alison believed: 'you have to adapt yourself to different situations anyway and it kind of makes you a better person to be able to do that'. Alison's assertion not only suggests that she saw herself becoming 'a better self' through adapting herself; here, there are also resonances of du Gay's assessment of the commercial organisation reconstructed around the sovereign consumer, where 'work is construed as an activity through which people produce and discover a sense of personal identity' (du Gay, 1996, p. 78). Although it is not accurate to portray all the participants in this study as discovering a sense of personal identity through deep acting, acting deeply suggests that some practitioners may not experience the 'alienation' to which Hochschild refers. To be praised, as in Alison's case, for cultivating a 'brilliant relationship' with a difficult client, could be interpreted as affirmation of a valuable, transferable, emotion management skill that helps to build personal self-esteem.

Educating

'Educating' the client was another typical emotion management strategy. This process is well illustrated in Pamela's narrative (Yeomans, 2013, p. 96) where the value of PR work, 'rather than being couched in business terms as financial benefits (for example, using business terms such as 'return on investment'; 'advertising value equivalents'), is instead a careful exercise in the status enhancement of the 'reluctant' client' while teaching him about the value of PR to his law firm. Pamela's 'nurturing' narrative also illustrates a feminine interactional style (Holmes, 2006) in 'challenging the client' when the issue of the value of PR advice arose:

> Nurturing them, nurturing *him*...gave him time, gave him examples of what other departments in the law firm had done and showing him the results so that he started to come round. Talking to him about what he wanted to achieve, not in a PR sense, but just generally, and then talking him through how PR could help with that, help him achieve what he wanted to achieve and... then end up getting to the stage where he was more comfortable with us and I thought: 'why don't we set up a meeting with [*name omitted*] magazine?'...so got out of him some newsworthy angles, ok, set up a meeting, and managed to get him...got his comments on the front cover of [*name omitted*] magazine, which of course was straightaway 'Right, ok, I can see the benefits' [...] and from then on he was willing to work with us on everything.
>
> (Pamela)

'Educating' was part of an approach which involved 'talking through' a process or a problem and was part of 'managing expectations' to ensure that client expectations were grounded in a realistic understanding of the contingent nature of public relations. In this study, participants regularly used an 'educating' approach in order to make the case for PR, or to justify a different PR campaign strategy. Graham asserted that education was essential to 'showing [clients] the benefits [of social media] and demonstrating the benefits with previous case studies that we'd done with previous clients in the same sector'.

'Educating' was a key negotiating strategy for participants in Tsetsura's study of Russian female practitioners. 'Educating' was constantly required with 'clients, journalists and other publics' because PR was a young field (Tsetsura, 2009, p. 79). Ashra (2008, p. 145) argues that educating and advising is not only a form of persuasion in convincing others about the value of professional communication but also an identity device, 'a deliberate manoeuvre on the part of the practitioner to be perceived as an expert and therefore someone who is potentially a key contributor to organisational events, thereby making them central or integral to organisational events'. In turn, the process of 'educating' suggests that the practitioner is engaged in a continuous process of legitimisation (Waeraas, 2009; Merkelsen, 2011), selling themselves, their personal expertise in reaching target publics, as well as that of their PR agency.

As I have already shown, the emotional demands of PR work meant that there was a continuous pressure on PRPs to draw on their social identities as friendly, approachable people in order to manage their own feelings and the feelings of others in response to the requirements of the situation. The emotion management strategy of 'managing expectations', including the expectations of agency directors and colleagues, was *central* to practitioners' emotion management strategies due to the highly contingent nature of PR work: results could not be guaranteed and only parts of the entire PR account managing process could actually be controlled by the PRP (e.g. writing press releases that were relevant to the target media) since much relied on the successful handling of relationships.

It is worth noting that the gendered performances of 'empathising' (Alison) and 'educating' (Pamela) well illustrate what Marsh (2009) refers to as the feminine discourse of the 'trusted adviser' in management consulting. Crucially, as Marsh (2009, p. 269) asserts, the 'trusted adviser' discourse is more than 'embracing the emotional dimension of apparently objective work': it is a feminine discourse that privileges the processes of 'relational practice' in their own right (Fletcher, 1998). Relational practice contributes to 'results' in public relations; this is especially true given that there are also journalist relationships to foster in the 'backstage' work for the clients of PR firms, and, increasingly, social media influencers. However, a significant amount of the work of male and female PR consultants constitutes 'relational practice' which, as argued throughout this chapter, draws on practitioners' identities in different contexts.

Conclusions

The emotional cues of senior colleagues and peers were the implicit 'feeling rules' (Hochschild, 1983; Bolton, 2005) of agency work that were, in turn, internalised by practitioners and guided their professional practice, especially in the small PR firms, towards a 'client first' orientation (Kaiser et al., 2008). Learning on the job and observing others helped to shape not only practitioners' technical skills but also their relational skills so that they became relevant to the specific problem or situation. The process of developing and honing the relevant relational skills to deal with clients, journalists, and others, in turn, helped to generate 'emotional capital' (Cahill, 1999; Illouz, 2007) as an embodied form of PR 'expertise' (Pieczka, 2002, p. 32) which supports the notion of an 'emotional intelligence' model of professionalism (van Ruler, 2005).

'Being a PR professional' meant drawing on multiple identities to negotiate relationships. Different identities were enacted in order to meet the different expectations of how PR professionals should conduct themselves (Fournier, 1999), as well as to achieve recognition and status rewards for the practitioner (Bolton, 2005). Practitioners drew on 'professional' identities (e.g. 'behaving well'), social identities (e.g. as friendly people, even 'personalities'), as well as gender identities. Practitioners working in small, regional agency offices had a particular need to draw on different identities with different clients, because frequent, informal communication is part of the service offer (Mart and Jackson, 2005) and personal 'chemistry' plays an important role in service differentiation (Mart and Jackson, 2005; Pieczka, 2006; Sissons, 2015). Practitioners' identities were also shaped by structural notions of the individual as 'entrepreneur of the self' (Gordon, 1987, p. 300), as competitors in the labour market for PR jobs; as cultural intermediaries in promotional culture (Hodges and Edwards, 2013); and as consumers in their own right within the culture.

The professional performance of 'managing expectations' was *central* to practitioners' emotion management strategies due to the highly contingent nature of PR work where 'results' for the client, such as positive media coverage, could not always be guaranteed. The performance of 'educating' in PR agency work serves to highlight the importance of legitimisation of expertise (Waeraas, 2009; Merkelsen, 2011) as well as gendered 'relational practice' (Fletcher, 1998). Much of the work of male and female PR consultants constitutes 'relational practice'. This raises questions about whether the certain emotion management skills required of practitioners in their everyday work is regarded as women's work and therefore not a 'real job' (Tsetsura, 2011). A perception that PR is feminine work, sustained by 'PR girl' stereotypes, may explain why the male practitioners, in particular, framed their relational work in masculine terms, a practice found in other occupations where there is a female majority (Alvesson, 1998; Lupton, 2000; Simpson, 2004).

In this study, deep and surface acting were commodified aspects of the self in regional PR work (Hochschild, 1983). In addition, female practitioners learned to both deny their gender and their feelings to be perceived as 'serious' and 'professional'. However, in contrast to Hochschild's concerns surrounding the alienation of the self through repeated 'deep acting' performances, it would appear that commodified performances in PR agency work formed part of professional identity development: practitioners learned to exert control over their social interactions rather than be victim to them. Such processes support an EI model of PR professionalism whereby the practitioner becomes known for their client handling skills. Through repeated performances of surface and deep acting in everyday social interactions, PRPs therefore become 'skilled emotion managers who are able to juggle and synthesize different types of emotion work dependent on situational demands' (Bolton, 2005, p. 289).

Note

1 Perhaps along the lines of the Boston Consulting Group's *Brinkmanship in Business*.

References

Abbott, A. (1988) *The System of Professions*. London, University of Chicago Press.
Alvesson, M. (1998) Gender and identity. Masculinities and femininities at work in an advertising agency. *Human Relations*, 51 (8), pp. 969–1005.
Alvesson, M. and Willmott, H. (2002) Producing the appropriate individual. Identity regulation as organizational control. *Journal of Management Studies*, 39 (5), pp. 619–44.

Anleu, S.R. and Mack, K. (2005) Magistrates' everyday work and emotional labour. *Journal of Law and Society*, 32 (4), pp. 590–614.

Ashra, N. (2008) *Inside stories: Making sense of the daily lives of communication practitioners.* [Ph.D. thesis]. University of Leeds.

Bandura, A. (1977) *Social Learning Theory.* New York, General Learning Press.

Bandura, A. (1997) *Self Efficacy Theory in Changing Societies.* Cambridge, Cambridge University Press.

Becker, H. S. (1970) *Sociological Work: Method and substance.* Chicago, IL, Aldine.

Beckett, C. and Deuze, M. (2016, July–September) On the role of emotion in the future of journalism. *Social Media + Society*, 2 (3), pp. 1–6.

Bellas, M. (1999) Emotional labor in academia: The case of professors. *The ANNALS of the American Academy of Political and Social Science*, 1, pp. 561–596.

Bolton, S. C. (2005) *Emotion Management in the Workplace.* Houndsmill, Hampshire, Palgrave Macmillan.

Bolton, S. C. and Boyd, C. (2003) Trolley dolly or skilled emotion manager? Moving on from Hochschild's Managed Heart. *Work, Employment and Society*, 17 (2), pp. 289–308.

Bolton, S. C. and Muzio, D. (2008) The paradoxical processes of feminization in the professions: The case of established aspiring and semi-professions. *Work, Employment and Society*, 22 (2), 281–299.

Bourdieu, P. (1997) The forms of capital. In A. H. Halsey, H. Lauder, P. Brown, and A. Stuart Wells, eds. *Education, Culture, Economy, Society.* Oxford, Oxford University Press, pp. 46–59.

Bruin, de, M. (2000) Gender, organizational and professional identities in journalism. *Journalism*, 1 (2), pp. 217–238.

Bruin, de, M. and Ross, K. (2004) Introduction: Beyond the body count. In M. de Bruin and K. Ross eds. *Gender and Newsroom Cultures: Identities at work.* Cresskill, NJ, Hampton Press, pp. vii–xiv.

Cahill, S. E. (1999) Emotional capital and professional socialization: The case of mortuary science students (and me). *Social Psychology Quarterly*, 62, pp. 101–116.

Chalmers, L. (2001) *Marketing Masculinities: Gender and management politics in marketing work.* Westport, CT, Greenwood Press

Cooley, C. H. (1922) *Human Nature and the Social Order.* New York, Scribner's.

Coupland, C., Brown, A. D., Daniels, K., and Humphreys, M. (2008) Saying it with feeling: Analysing speakable emotions. *Human Relations*, 61 (3), pp. 327–353.

Davies, C. (1996) The sociology of professions and the profession of gender. *Sociology*, 30 (4), pp. 661–678.

Davies, N. (2008) *Flat Earth News: An award-winning reporter exposes falsehood, distortion and propaganda in the global media.* London, Vintage Books.

Edwards, L. (2008) PR practitioners' cultural capital: An initial study and implications for research and practice. *Public Relations Review*, 34 (4), pp. 367–372.

Edwards, L. (2014) Discourse, credentialism and occupational closure in the communications industries: The case of public relations in the UK. *European Journal of Communication*, 29 (3), pp. 319–334.

Fitch, K. and Third, A. (2010) Working girls: Revisiting the gendering of public relations. *PRism*, 7 (4). Available from: http://www.prismjournal.org/index.php?id=gender. Accessed 5 October 2018.

Fletcher, J. (1998) Relational practice: A feminist re-construction of work. *Journal of Management Inquiry*, 7 (2), pp. 168–186.

Fournier, V. (1999) The appeal to professionalism as a disciplinary mechanism. *Sociological Review*, 47 (2), pp. 280–307.

Fröhlich, R. (2004) Feminine and feminist values in communication professions: Exceptional skills and expertise or 'friendliness trap'? In M. de Bruin and K. Ross, eds. *Gender and Newsroom Cultures: Identities at work*. Cresskill, NJ, Hampton Press, pp. 65–77.

Fröhlich, R. and Peters, S. B. (2007) PR bunnies caught in the agency ghetto? Gender stereotypes, organizational factors, and women's careers in PR agencies. *Journal of Public Relations Research*, 19 (3), pp. 229–254.

Gabbott, M. and Hogg, G. (1996) Purchasing public relations: The case of the public relations industry in Scotland. *Journal of Marketing Management*, 12, pp. 437–453.

du Gay, P. (1996) *Consumption and Identity at Work*. London, Thousand Oaks, CA, and New Delhi, Sage.

Goffman, E. (1959) *The Presentation of Self in Everyday Life*. London, Penguin Books.

Gordon, C. (1987) The soul of the citizen: Max Weber and Michel Foucault on rationality and government. In S. Whimster and S. Lash, eds. *Max Weber: Rationality and modernity*. London, Allen and Unwin, pp. 293–316.

Guerrier, Y. and Adib, A. (2003) Work at leisure and leisure at work: A study of the emotional labour of tour reps. *Human Relations*, 56 (11), pp. 1399–1417.

Hesmondhalgh, D. and Baker. S. (2011) 'A very complicated version of freedom': Conditions and experiences of creative labour in three cultural industries. *Poetics: Journal of Empirical Research on Culture, the Media and the Arts*, 38 (1), pp. 4–20.

Hochschild, A. R. (1983) *The Managed Heart: Commercialization of human feeling*. Berkeley, University of California Press.

Hodges, C. M. and Edwards, L. (2013) Public relations practitioners. In J. Smith Maguire and J. Matthews, eds. *The Cultural Intermediaries Reader*. London, Sage, pp. 89–99.

Holmes, J. (2006) *Gendered Talk at Work: Constructing gender identity through workplace discourse*. Malden, MA, Oxford, and Victoria, Blackwell.

Hopper, M. K. and Huxford, J. E. (2015) Gathering emotion: Examining newspaper journalists' engagement in emotional labour. *Journal of Media Practice*, 16 (1): 25–41.

Hughes, J. (2010) Emotional intelligence: Elias, Foucault, and the reflexive emotional self. *Foucault Studies*, 8, pp. 28–52.

Ihlen, Ø. (2009) On Bourdieu: Public relations in field struggles. In Ø. Ihlen, B. van Ruler, and M. Fredriksson, eds. *Public Relations and Social Theory: Key figures and concepts*. New York and Abingdon, Oxon, Routledge, pp. 62–81.

Illouz, E. (2007) *Cold Intimacies: The making of emotional capitalism*. Cambridge and Malden, Polity Press.

Jenkins, J. and Finneman, T. (2018) Gender trouble in the workplace: Applying Judith Butler's theory of performativity to news organizations. *Feminist Media Studies*, 18(2), 157–172.

Kaiser, S., Müller-Seitz, G. and Cruesen, U. (2008) Passion wanted! Socialisation of positive emotions in consulting firms. *International Journal of Work Organisation and Emotion*, 2, (3), pp. 305–320.

Korczynski, M. (2003) Communities of coping: Collective emotional labour in service work. *Organization*, 10 (1), pp. 55–79.

Kovach, B. and Rosenstiel, T. (2001) *The Elements of Journalism*. London, Guardian Atlantic.

Leidner, R. (1993) *Fast Food, Fast Talk: Service work and the routinization of everyday life.* Berkeley, University of California Press.

Lepper, J. (2012) Do you need a degree to work in PR? PR Week, 1 March. Available from: https://www.prweek.com/article/1119695/need-degree-work-pr. Accessed 8 February 2019.

L'Etang J. (2015) 'It's always been a sexless trade'; 'It's clean work'; 'There's very little velvet curtain': Gender and public relations in post-Second World War Britain. *Journal of Communication Management,* 19 (4), pp. 354–370.

Lewis, P. (2005) Suppression or expression: An exploration of emotion management in a special care baby unit. *Work, Employment and Society,* 19 (3), pp. 565–581.

Lupton, B. (2000) Maintaining masculinity: Men who do 'women's work'. *British Journal of Management,* 11, special issue, pp. S33–S48.

Mann, S. (2004) People work: Emotion management stress and coping. *British Journal of Guidance and Counselling,* 32 (2), pp. 205–222.

Marsh, S. (2009) *The Feminine in Management Consulting: Power, emotion and values in consulting interactions.* Basingstoke, Palgrave Macmillan.

Mart, L. and Jackson, N. (2005) Public relations agencies in the UK travel industry: Does size matter? *Prism,* 3 (1). Available from: http://www.prismjournal.org/vol_3_iss_1.html Accessed 2 May 2018.

Mastracci, S. H., Newman, M. A., and Guy, M. E. (2006) Appraising emotion work: Determining whether emotional labor is valued in government jobs. *American Review of Public Administration,* 36 (2), 123–138.

Merkelsen, H. (2011) The double-edged sword of legitimacy in public relations. *Journal of Communication Management,* 15(2), pp. 125–143.

Mulholland, K. (1996) Entrepreneurialism, masculinities and the self-made man. D. L. Collinson and J. Hearn, eds. (1996) *Men as Managers, Managers as Men: Critical perspectives on men, masculinities and managements.* London, Thousand Oaks, CA, and New Delhi, Sage, pp. 123–149.

Muzio, D., Ackroyd, S., and Chanlat, J.-F. (2008) Introduction: Lawyers, doctors and business consultants. In D. Muzio, S. Ackroyd, and J.-F. Chanlat, eds. *Redirections in the Study of Expert Labour.* Basingstoke, Palgrave Macmillan, pp. 1–30.

Ogbonna, E. and Harris, L. C. (2004) Work intensification and emotional labour among UK university lecturers: An exploratory study. *Organization Studies,* 25 (7), pp. 1185–1203.

Pieczka, M. (2002) Public relations expertise deconstructed. *Media Culture & Society,* 24 (3), pp. 301–323.

Pieczka, M. (2006) 'Chemistry' and the public relations industry: An exploration of the concept of jurisdiction and issues arising. In J. L'Etang and M. Pieczka, eds. *Public Relations: Critical debates and contemporary practice.* Mahwah, NJ, and London, Lawrence Erlbaum Associates, pp. 303–327.

PR Moment (2017) How timesheets waste time. *PR Moment,* 4 May. Available from: https://www.prmoment.com/category/pr-insight/how-timesheets-waste-time. Accessed 28 October 2018.

Public Relations Consultants Association (2009) *The frontline guide to a career in PR.* London, PRCA.

Reed, C. (2013) *Becoming a profession: Crafting professional identities in public relations.* [Ph.D. thesis]. Cardiff University.

Reskin, B. and Padavic, I. (1994) *Women and Men at Work.* Thousand Oaks, CA, Pine Forge Press.

Richards, B. and Rees, G. (2011) The management of emotion in British journalism. *Media, Culture & Society*, 33 (6), pp. 851–867.

Rodgers, H., Yeomans L., and Halliday S. (2016) The 'gogglebox' and gender: An interdiscursive analysis of television representations and professional femininities. In C. Elliott, V. Stead, S. Mavin, and J. Williams, eds. *Gender, Media and Organization: Challenging Mis(s)representations of Women Leaders and Managers*. Charlotte, NC, Information Age Publishing, pp. 169–196.

Scheff, T. J. (2000) Shame and the social bond. *Sociological Theory*, 18 (1), pp. 84–99.

Schütz, A. (1970) *On Phenomenology and Social Relations*. Chicago, IL and London, University of Chicago Press.

Schweingruber, D. and Berns, N. (2005) Shaping the selves of young salespeople through emotion management. *Journal of Contemporary Ethnography*, 34 (6), pp. 679–706.

Shuler, S. and Davenport Sypher, B. (2000) Seeking emotional labor: When managing the heart enhances the work experience. *Management Communication Quarterly*, 14 (1), 50–89.

Simpson, R. (2004) Masculinities at work: The experiences of men in female dominated occupations. *Work, Employment and Society*, 18 (2), pp. 349–368.

Sissons, H. (2015) Lifting the veil on the PRP-client relationship. *Public Relations Inquiry*, 4 (3), pp. 263–286.

Steiner, L. (1998) Newsroom accounts of power at work. In C. Carter, G. Branston, and S. Allan, eds. *News, Gender and Power*. London and New York, Routledge. pp. 145–159.

Tsetsura, K. (2009) How female practitioners in Moscow view their profession: A pilot study. *Public Relations Review*, 36 (1), pp. 78–80.

Tsetsura, K. (2011) Is public relations a real job? How female practitioners construct the profession. *Journal of Public Relations Research*, 23 (1), pp. 1–23.

van Ruler, B. (2005) Commentary: Professionals are from Venus, scholars are from Mars. *Public Relations Review*, 31 (2), pp. 159–173.

Waeraas, A. (2009) On Weber: Legitimacy and legitimation in public relations. In Ø. Ihlen, B. van Ruler, and M. Fredriksson, eds. *Public Relations and Social Theory*. New York and London, Routledge, pp. 301–322.

Waterloo, S. F., Baumgartner, S. E., Peter, J., and Valkenburg, P. M. (2018) Norms of online expression of emotion: Comparing Facebook, Twitter, Instagram and WhatsApp. *New Media and Society*. 20 (5), pp. 1813–1831.

Wenger, E. (2000) Communities of practice and social learning systems, *Organization*, 7 (2), pp. 225–246.

Williams, C. ed. (1993) *Doing 'Women's Work': Men in nontraditional occupations*. London, Sage.

Wrigley, B. J. (2002) Glass ceiling? What glass ceiling? A qualitative study of how women view the glass ceiling in public relations and communications management. *Journal of Public Relations Research*, 14 (1), pp. 27–55.

Yeomans, L. (2010) Soft sell? Gendered experience of emotional labour in UK public relations firms, *PRism*, 7 (4). Available from: http://www.prismjournal.org Accessed 28 October 2018.

Yeomans, L. (2013) Gendered performance and identity work in PR consulting relationships: A UK perspective. In C. Daymon and K. Demetrious, eds. *Gender and Public Relations: Critical perspectives on voice, image and identity*. London, Routledge, pp. 87–107.

Yeomans, L. (2016) Imagining the lives of others: Empathy in public relations. *Public Relations Inquiry*, 5 (1), pp. 71–92.

6 Professional relationships in public relations

Agency directors' perspectives of emotion management

Introduction

In Chapter 5 I theorised that emotion management strategies of public relations (PR) executives are performed in response to the emotional cues (Hochschild, 1983) of agency directors, as well as the perceived relational demands of clients and journalists. I also argued in Chapter 3 that social media influencers (SMIs), as recent entrants to the PR-media ecology, place further emotional demands on public relations practitioners (PRPs). In this chapter I extend the scope of my inquiry by examining the emotion management of the self and others explored from the perspectives of the directors and partners of PR firms. I view agency directors as the 'emotional experts' (Kleres, 2015) who set the tone of their enterprises, drawing on their own experiences of occupational socialisation within the PR industry, their professional identities, as well as personal aspirations for the firm, particularly when it is theirs to shape.

The empirical content in this chapter draws on semi-structured interviews with directors and partners of PR agencies. Participants were White British, comprising six women and two men, with a median age of 40. Interviews were supplemented by observational notes drawn from visits to four London agencies, where I attended meetings and took part in informal discussions with a further 12 employees (for further details of methodology see the Appendix, page 205). The research questions driving this study were: how do participants view their professional identities? How do participants understand and manage professional relationships within their own firms? What are the 'feeling rules' that apply to different situations and contexts? And what are participants' expectations of their employees in these different contexts?

The research took place in 2016, thus enabling analysis of emotions in the workplace set within an era of technology-enabled devices, 'always on' work culture, and PR management processes that increasingly integrate technology and people (Wajcman, 2015). While emotional labour theory provides both an entry point and ongoing interpretive framework for this exploration, I extend the relational focus by linking it to other relevant literature, including that of aesthetic labour (Witz et al., 2003). Further, the 'social shaping of technology' approach (Wajcman, 2015) enables a critical examination of the material world of PR, including physical spaces (Hirst and Schwabenland, 2018) and ICT that are intended to support the efficiency of the PR management process. While material objects are not the central focus of this chapter, their role as 'agents' in mediating professional relationships is and will be of increasing importance. Furthermore, gender perspectives, as discussed in Chapter 4, bring in a highly relevant lens to interpret professional relationships in the PR agency to offer further insights into the structuring of PR as a profession. It is the existing and emerging socio-emotional norms of interaction in PR agency practice that I examine in this chapter.

The chapter begins with a discussion of the entrepreneurial identities of agency directors. Understanding the process of becoming an entrepreneur in PR, and with it the process of becoming embedded within the neoliberal PR agency context, is essential to gain insight into self-perceptions and the shaping of directors' own practice. I then move on to examine the agency environment which I theorise as the site of identity performance (Rakow, 1986; Butler, 1990). The performativity of agency directors and PRPs is shaped by physical space, technology, as well as expectations of attitude and dispositions within the client relationship. Participants' understandings and strategies for a successful client relationship are examined before discussing how they are adapting to the perceived and actual demands of millennials as employees. A shifting 'PR logic' (Fredriksson et al., 2013) based on journalist relationships is then explored in relation to the intensified focus of relationships with SMIs. The chapter closes with a discussion of the pressing need for agencies to strive for business growth, and the ways in which they do this.

Entrepreneurialism, identity, and gender: 'doing the best work for your clients'?

I questioned participants about their family, education, and early influences in forming their professional identities as agency practitioners. Participants' constructions of identity drew on entrepreneurial discourse, which Gherardi (2015, p. 650) defines as a 'multi-discursive construction' that intersects with other identities including gender, race, religion, class, and geography. An entrepreneurial identity, argues Gherardi (2015):

> is not something that one possesses; rather, it is a process of becoming, undertaken in the course of a life project, situated in time and space, and designed by the choices made in historical and cultural circumstances.

While the findings presented in this chapter were not analysed from a discourse perspective, I have adopted a gender-sensitive approach to participants' discourse because this sheds light on why agency directors and men and women construct their identities in particular ways. For example, Lewis argues that the discourse of female entrepreneurs tends to reflect 'a strong belief in merit and the neutrality of business' (Lewis, 2006, p. 458), while Gherardi (2015) argues that female entrepreneurs author their entrepreneurship as 'life projects' in ways that combine work with family.

In discussing their early influences, two participants, Jane and Pauline, attributed their own business ethos to their fathers' success in business: 'He commits, so he's a 12-hour-a-day man to get the job done right, and I probably am' (Jane). 'I was his marketing assistant. I was helping him deal with some of the customers, deal with the sales team, but I was also understanding about competitor analysis and things like that. I learnt quite a lot' (Pauline). These biographical narratives resonate with Gherardi's 'second generation' identity narratives in which female entrepreneurs (in her own project) expressed a continuation of a family tradition (Gherardi, 2015). More typically, however, my participants had no familial influence of working in business or PR, but had worked in PR agencies from an early stage of their career, or since graduating from university. Starting out in junior roles in PR agencies, participants cited senior managers or directors as exerting a 'huge influence' (James) in learning about agency work: 'You're in awe of what they know and how they handle things' (Tim). Jane, a partner, who had spent most of her career with the same agency, learning from its 'brilliant' founders, proudly asserted the company's values as:

> very much clients first, excellence first, it's a meritocracy, doesn't matter who you are, where you've come from, it matters about what you do and how well you do it, no matter who you are. And that was borne out. I worked hard and that came: 'the harder I work, the luckier I get' philosophy.
>
> (Jane)

Jane's inference to 'no matter who you are' invoked a portrayal of less valued cultural capital (Edwards, 2008): she had not attended an elite university, and had moved to London from another part of England. Therefore, despite her White, middle-class credentials, which might be assumed to provide particular advantages (Edwards, 2014, 2015), Jane attributed her success to hard work and merit. A neoliberal, meritocratic attachment to women defining 'their own identities independent of their relations to others', is, according to Budgeon (2013, p. 284), characteristic of 'late modern culture' in which the 'idealized subject' is 'flexible, individualised, resilient, self driven and self made'.

In becoming entrepreneurs themselves, similarly to Emma's boss (in Chapter 5), both James and Helen, as founders of their own businesses, recalled feelings of isolation, working initially in their 'back bedroom' before they were ready to venture further in growing their business. As founders of PR firms, some participants were driven to run their own businesses because it offered them choices about which clients to work with; quite often these were clients they had successfully worked with at previous agencies. It also offered them choices about their lifestyle, and as discussed later in this chapter, the opportunity to balance work and home life, offering the promise of 'flexibility' as well as freedom. However, as Mandy related:

> We had no idea when we started this how difficult it was. We were very naïve. It was perhaps fortunate because had we known how difficult it is to run an agency we might never have done it but we just thought 'yeah it'll be fun, it'll be easy'. And it's not.
>
> (Mandy)

A common aspiration among all participants was the desire for 'fun' and 'enjoyment' while providing a good service to the client: 'I just want to work for really good people and do great stuff and enjoy myself' (Tim). Participants consistently expressed creative enterprise activity as the source of personal enjoyment and motivation. This was accomplished through *competing for new business*: 'I love pitching a new business' (Jane), 'I still like winning business. I still get competitive' (Pauline), 'Pitching gives me a big buzz' (Mandy); *generating creative ideas for campaigns*: 'Coming up with ideas and making them happen' (Charlotte); and *working with others, particularly young people*: 'I get a real kick out of sharing that knowledge and experience' (Sarah); 'What gives me the most buzz is working with these bright people' (Mandy). James referred to his employee: 'I actually enjoy getting up and coming to work because I'm working with someone who gets it'.

Leadership identity and gendered experience

I questioned participants about their leadership role and what this meant to them. James had a clear view of what his leadership role meant: 'it's your professionalism, your reputation and your track record'. James asserted that he offered his clients 'authority' based on years of experience in PR, which enabled his business to stand out among competitor businesses. Sarah and Charlotte, occupying board level roles in large agencies, expressed their leadership in terms of a strong desire to develop younger generations of PR professionals, as well as play a wider public role through their involvement with professional membership organisations. However, while Charlotte claimed to be 'passionate' about the value of PR, she felt more motivated to participate in a women's networking association than the 'male dominated' professional membership organisations. In professional membership organisations, from her perspective, women lacked a voice and were overlooked as guest speakers, particularly if their interests did not sit with a 'corporate affairs bias'. Charlotte perceived such discriminatory mechanisms, whereby only certain senior people were invited to participate in the profession, as 'backward' and lacking in openness to 'innovative' trends.

Sarah enjoyed playing a leading role as mentor in a women's networking organisation. As senior partner in her agency, she made conscious efforts to support junior colleagues, particularly women, who she perceived as 'lacking a voice'.

> I know that women often feel that it's quite difficult in a room in an industry of quite senior people, predominantly male and often find it quite hard to put their point of view across, or we all do... Women generally do have this sense of what we want to say is not good enough. I think there is still a tendency to give way to our male colleague who, maybe, will speak a bit louder.

From Charlotte and Sarah's accounts of their experience, not only was a subtle process of gender discrimination at play in PR (Acker, 1992), protecting the 'masculine professional project' (Davies, 1996; Bolton and Muzio, 2008; Fitch and Third, 2010), but also a jurisdictional strategy to protect PR's claim to a certain type of expertise (Pieczka, 2002; Edwards, 2018). In this case, expertise in 'corporate affairs' was perceived to assume more weight in the eyes of the PR profession (in contrast to consumer-focused or other types of PR). Therefore, historical distinctions between the public (coded as masculine) and domestic (coded as feminine) realms of PR appeared to be sustained (Fitch and Third, 2013; L'Etang, 2015).

Other participants expressed resistance to perceptions of themselves as leaders in the industry. Tim related: 'for me it's always been just actually about my own business or whatever business I'm working in and my clients', while Pauline asserted: 'I think it is about doing the best work you can for your clients'. Mandy's leadership focus was purely on the day-to-day: 'Just keeping the agency afloat to be honest is quite an achievement'. Similarly, Helen stated: 'It is just keeping things moving really'. Therefore, despite three participants, Mandy, Helen, and Pauline, being regular recipients of industry awards (with its association of 'best practice' within their sector), an understanding of leadership in agency PR, particularly as a small business entrepreneur, was one that fulfilled participants' desires for business success based on client approval. This suggests an alignment with definitions of PR (PRCA, 2018) as an 'industry' in its central role of servicing the market, as opposed to a 'profession' or occupation with a broader public service remit (Muzio et al., 2008). As argued in Chapters 4 and 5, a market-driven, client-focus is the professional norm which PRPs learn in agencies, promoted by the self-interest and visions of agency directors whose priority is the success of the business.

Physical space, attitude, and embodiment in the PR firm

Open offices, emotion management, and gender

In Chapter 5, the PR agency open plan office was characterised as a spatial norm, believed to enable open communication and transparency and opportunities for shared humour. These office spaces were simultaneously experienced by some PRPs as somewhat oppressive, competitive, surveillance environments in which one's every move could be observed and interpreted by junior and senior colleagues, as well as peers. In this second study, the spatial norm of the shared, open plan PR office prevailed. Workstations were typically organised in rows, with desks pushed together, where one row of workstations (comprising four or more positions) faced another row, organised with the intention of facilitating interaction with the person seated opposite. Small team discussions took place in separate rooms, some entirely closed and private, others with transparent glass walls, so that it was visible who was involved in the discussion.

Formal, private meetings were held in separate rooms or in quiet spaces elsewhere on the premises. Although some participants as owners, partners, or MDs had access to their own private office, three participants in this study were deliberately seated among their teams:

> [...] there's nobody sitting in gilded cages, we're all very much on the floor [...] we sit within all of our teams, which I think is really important and that sort of sets a certain level of just making everyone feel like we're all the same, which is good.
>
> (Charlotte)

> I think it makes conversations easier [and although] everyone probably emails everyone, I probably stand up and shout at everyone (laughs). Yeah, what's happened to that? [...] I think, open plan's a much healthier environment... [although] ideally we'd need more private offices so people can go and focus and do quiet work when they want to.
>
> (Pauline)

> I still sit downstairs. [Senior colleague] has now moved upstairs and got an office but I still sit downstairs with everyone else because [...] I just like to be part of the group. And I just like to hear what's going on. I'm nosy basically and I think I would miss out on too much if I sat in a different room. For [senior colleague] it's a concentration thing so he gets a lot more done in his office. I've got an office. I just never use it. Because I'd rather know what's going on downstairs and not miss out.
>
> (Mandy)

Helen, who occupied a private office at her agency, expressed a desire to be more visible and seated among her team for an impending office move: 'one of my key priorities is making sure we've got an open plan space that I am actually *in* the open plan space'.

The open plan office as 'conceived space' for PR agency practice is one of democratic design to facilitate relationship-building (Hirst and Schwabenland, 2018, p. 162). The preferred 'spatial practices', or routines, of Charlotte and Helen were to sit and work among their teams. Pauline liked that she could 'shout at everyone' from her seat among the team, particularly as she operated 'hands-on' on one client account. Mandy, in particular, identified as being part of the group in the open plan space 'downstairs' rather than associating with her senior colleague by occupying her private office 'upstairs'. While Mandy shared her feelings of ambivalence towards her status as 'boss': 'We don't feel like bosses [...] we're just one of [them]', there was also a hint that she felt more in control by not 'missing out' on everyday group interactions that took place 'downstairs'. Having a visible presence seated among the team not only reminded her employees who was running the business but that Mandy was also 'one of them': accessible, should a problem arise, and available to manage the emotional atmosphere more sensitively. In celebrating the open plan office's democratic and communicative potential, participants' 'lived space' was imagined as social interaction, 'deep relationship building', and reduced hierarchies according to 'new office' design principles (Hirst and Schwabenland, 2018, p. 159).

Some theorists argue that gendered emotion work is established through spatial practices, so that dominant forms of emotion work are performed as masculine in some spaces, rendering other spaces as feminine (Lewis, 2008). While the open plan office may be designed as gender neutral to fit the 'ideal worker', Hirst and Schwabenland (2018, p. 174) argue that physical spaces shape action 'in myriad ways, both implicit and explicit' so that gender is 'constantly in contestation'. In the case of Mandy, her desire to be seated among her team 'downstairs' may signal a more *or* less powerful position than her male partner whose private office was upstairs. A collaborative and accessible bodily presence, coded as 'feminine' interactional style (Holmes, 2006), might be construed as the more powerful action but this would likely depend upon context.

In characterising her business-to-business (B2B) agency, Helen contrasted its quiet, 'academic' work environment: 'you can hear a pin drop sometimes' to that of a 'buzzy' consumer agency. Helen attributed her quiet work environment to its highly specialist focus which involved 'translating' technical documents and trawling through research reports. My office observations at two specialist agencies handling B2B and healthcare accounts revealed relatively long periods of silence or low-volume discussion among colleagues, peppered with louder, light-hearted Monday morning banter, or an audible, lengthy phone conversation. My presence as researcher may well have influenced conduct at Agency A, where one PRP's outburst of swearing, when reading information about a forthcoming conference: 'what the f...' was quickly hushed by the office manager seated nearby. Although I was present as observer, I felt the need to join in some of the small talk in order to make people feel at ease around me, while trying not to disturb the flow of conversation.

Pauline's assertion that 'everyone probably emails everyone' within the same office was plausible: there was much keyboard activity at workstations.

Her comment about shouting across the office: 'Yeah, what happened to that?' implied that vocal social interaction was no longer the norm and that emailing, even with people in the same office, was a preferred mode of communication. Within 'open office' redesigns, Bernstein and Turban (2018, p. 6) found that electronic interactions increased by 50%, while face-to-face interactions decreased by 70%. Overall interactions diminished, leading to a lowering of productivity (Bernstein and Turban, 2018, p. 6). These findings suggest that face-to-face communication at an emotional level could be diminished too. Frequent emailing, which emerged across my study as the most common form of PRP communication with both clients and journalists, suggested a far more *intra*personal, individualised and emotionally demanding endeavour (Tait, 2018) than the imagined 'much healthier', face-to-face interactional office. Increased online activity, including managing clients' social media accounts on Twitter, Facebook, and Instagram, includes the requirement to learn the online norms of emotion expression on different platforms (Arcy, 2016; Waterloo et al., 2018), and using this knowledge to 'attune' to different publics in different contexts. Therefore, the volume of electronic interactions that I observed suggests that some practitioners were engaged in an *intensified* and *individualised* emotional labour. On the other hand, the experienced PRP who becomes trusted for being able to talk through issues over the phone with clients who are lacking in PR expertise is valued, as attested by the MD at Agency A when she called upon her 'excellent' colleague to 'hand hold' a client.

Agency B, a consumer-focused agency, fulfilled Helen's description of 'buzzy'. During my visit, the vast, open plan floor was animated with people coming and going and, occasionally, dominated by loud male voices. Much PRP activity was at workstations with laptops and PCs, while multiple small team discussions took place in comfortable, pub–snug style seating areas where laptops could be used for note-taking. In this large space, meals and snacks from the nearby shop could be brought in with groups of tables and chairs to facilitate dining. Board level, confidential meetings took place in private rooms on the same floor; however the décor in the directors' meeting room was purely functional and minimalist. White walls and furnishings were informally arranged: comprising a wall-mounted TV, a low level coffee table, and comfortable, dark sofas. There appeared to be little concern for formalities at this agency: while meetings were scheduled in the diary, there was a feeling of perpetual movement and spontaneity as the MD's focus shifted from resourcing issues to specific client campaigns, bringing different members of the team into the meeting room for updates when necessary.

Learning the 'right' attitude

In Chapter 5 PRPs learned the feeling rules for managing professional relationships largely 'on the job' through observing and listening to senior colleagues, as well as through direct interactions with clients, through which they learned how to 'adapt their style'. In the small PR firm environment, informal mentoring from agency directors was highly influential to the occupational socialisation of some PRPs. They learned how to emotionally 'attune' themselves (Scheff, 1990; Burkitt, 2014) to different clients, different personalities, and different situations. Attuning drew on the 'presentational self' (Bolton, 2005), which requires social, cultural, and emotional resources that equip PRPs to learn how to relate to the clients: this could be described as presenting the 'right attitude'.

In my second study, participants, as agency directors, had themselves learned to become attuned to relationships from observing senior colleagues in their own careers: 'you just learn from your own personal experience of where you know you cross the line and where you don't' (Timothy). Timothy explained how 'the line' between appropriate and inappropriate professional conduct (Fournier, 1999) could shift from client to client.

> you're dealing with such a variety of different characters and personalities, that the lines are constantly different for everyone. I mean, we had a client once which they'd take us out for a meal, which then would turn into an enormous drinking party and a client that was acting really atrociously. I mean, they were just being complete idiots and half dressing and sloshing drinks everywhere and being very rude and crass and you could, if you wanted to, quite easily go to that level and join in and they wouldn't think anything of it. I wouldn't because again it comes back to the values and for me, that way of acting was wrong, so I'm not going to do that anyway.
>
> (Timothy)

Timothy's narrative suggested that not only was professional conduct learned from those he admired, but also he brought the 'presentational self' to the situation, drawing on earlier socialisation experiences, through which personal values were instilled (Bolton, 2005).

Participants, as agency directors, required that team members, and particularly junior recruits, demonstrated the desired personal attributes for the job. The personal attributes looked for in an account handler were broad, as might be expected from the diversity of agencies represented, ranging from 'inquisitiveness', 'entrepreneurial flair' through to 'commitment', 'enthusiasm', and articulacy. Positive emotions were associated with the 'right attitude', described as: 'the make it happen approach' (Timothy); 'switched on and engaged' (Helen); 'they want to work hard but they also want to have fun' (Mandy); and 'someone who can think on their feet, has some kind of entrepreneurial flair' (Sarah).

Participants looked for attitude above skill, particularly in junior recruits because: 'you can teach skill but you can't teach attitude' (Mandy). The wrong attitude, or people who 'don't care that other people think they are shirkers', on the other hand, could be 'toxic', contagious, and detrimental to other team members, as well as embarrassing in client situations (Helen). Thus, some participants' strategies for dealing with 'problem' attitudes among employees included providing one-to-one coaching, asking PRPs questions about the situation that has caused them to have a client problem, as illustrated in Pauline's account:

> I would say, come on, sit down, think about it, why is the client behaving like that? What have we done? Have we not thought about this properly? As I said, you've just delivered a piece of coverage in *The Sun*, her readers don't read *The Sun*, [they read *The Times*] that's why the client's being difficult. So, there's a little bit of that.
>
> (Pauline)

Jane's account further illustrates how 'the wrong attitude' had implications for gender relations. A young, male junior employee had openly expressed frustration with a (female) client's 'stupidity' and, while he was 'so bright and so clever', he was particularly disrespectful and difficult to manage, particularly for senior women in the PR firm, raising questions about who should be responsible for mentoring and coaching him.

> I'm sensible enough to know if that [a telling off] comes from me, he might leave, but if it comes from [senior male colleague], it'll all be fine. I don't know what to think about that. It's not right but it's my reality: if I want to keep him, I'm going to have to have him work with more men.
>
> (Jane)

While Jane expressed frustration: 'it's not right but it's my reality' with her need for the 'redistribution of authority' to a male colleague (Hochschild, 1983, p. 178), she did not feel an urge to challenge the status quo. This was possibly due to a collective desire to retain 'bright and clever' people. Retaining 'bright' people was important to all participants who had employees. Recruitment was an expensive process, tying up many director-level hours. Further, having selected who they thought was the right person, agencies wanted to believe they had made the correct choice. For Mandy, however, a person with a bad attitude had to be 'got rid of' to avoid unsettling the whole team. James, running a two-person micro agency, was attracted to the idea of recruiting a junior employee, but he did not want to take the risk. James related, 'they speak in a different language – a lot more informal': there was little time for him to coach a younger person to meet his and the client's expectations of appropriate tone, manner, and dress.

Appearance, dress, and demeanour

A smart-casual, generally relaxed dress code among account handling staff could be observed across all agencies. The least conventional office-like attire included a full set of highly coordinated, fluorescent striped sportswear, including a hoodie (drawn up) and trainers. This outfit was worn by a board level member at Agency B. His affiliation with a client's sports brand was highly visible as he walked the floor, indicative of a self-authored 'streetwise' aesthetic, denoting informality, even 'fun'. And yet, for a board director to embody the client's brand in the manner described suggests a powerful, imposed, presentational norm (Warren and Fineman, 2007).

By contrast, participants servicing corporate, financial, and B2B clients wore relatively formal clothing when I visited their offices: for women, this was a tailored dress or jacket and skirt. Yet these contexts were also subject to processes of informalisation (Wouters, 2009). Pauline claimed 'I rarely put on a suit nowadays'. According to Mandy, even her corporate clients' dress codes were changing: 'Nobody ever wears ties. It's just open collar. You don't see many suits in this business anymore'. James remarked that his agency was making the transition from corporate and B2B clients ('very suit and tie') to taking on more 'fluffy' work, by which he meant consumer PR work. 'Fluffy' is also newsroom slang for the type of work that involves 'soft news' (consumer or human interest) stories that are largely allocated to women journalists in the gendered newsroom (North, 2016). After many years of wearing a suit and tie to the office, both as a journalist and later as a PR man working in a large agency, James was in a position where he felt he could wear trainers and jeans, at least on days with no clients.

While Witz et al.'s (2003) analysis focused on the importance of aesthetic labour and embodied dispositions in consumer relationships (typically, the retail sales floor), I argue that a variety of embodied dispositions are *especially* important to PRP-client alignment and the wider relational habitus of the PR field. This includes both corporate and consumer client contexts that shape the occupational identities of PR actors. James' occupational identity was partly formed by the media newsroom and its 'masculine heterenormativity' (Jenkins and Finneman, 2018, p. 170), as well as corporate PR.

Therefore, a switch from corporate to 'fluffy' PR not only suggested a gradual gender switch, or 'feminisation' of his own practice, but also the need to maintain control of his masculine identity as a former journalist (Jenkins and Finneman, 2018).

The appropriate embodied disposition that is relevant to PRP-client alignment also includes performances such as 'fast talk', as illustrated by the vignettes in Boxes 6.1 and 6.2. These vignettes illustrate the importance of 'sounding right' in some PR roles, especially those roles which call upon the White, middle-class (and gendered) aesthetic of the retail sector (Williams and Connell, 2010). Furthermore, in exhibiting a shared 'self-surveillance' that involved working on the self to adapt to the client and media context: 'everyone talks like this', it could be argued that the two account executives were constructing subjectivities that were consistent with both a postfeminist sensibility *and* neoliberalism (Gill et al., 2017, pp. 230–231).

Box 6.1 Fast talk in a PR agency

Two young, White female account executives introduce themselves to me. They talk very quickly in a mannered style. They are aware of this and one asks me if they are talking too quickly. To them, perhaps, I'm not only an academic and remote from their world, but someone who is much older and only an occasional visitor to the London 'bubble'. One of them discloses 'everyone talks like this' (meaning the professional context of PR and possibly the London fashion world). They tell me with some amusement that when they go back to their family homes in the regions, their friends and relatives find their fast talk difficult to understand. They seem to like the idea that their embodied disposition – an acquired, rapid speech pattern – is a marker of their professional demeanour and identity as upwardly mobile London PR girls.

(Author's notes, May 2016)

PRP-client emotion management: 'chemistry', managing expectations, and reducing emotional risk

A successful client relationship was generally seen as long-term (e.g. 5–15 years) and respectful of professionalism on both sides. Participants emphasised their long-term relationships, quite often having gained business through word-of-mouth referrals. They described much of their time spent on new business, with the most regular 're-/pitching' taking place in consumer or fast-moving consumer goods (FMCG) environments. Getting to know a potential client sometimes involved long periods of relationship-building. Mandy considered this process very important: 'we've got examples of lunching and dining with people for six or seven years before anything comes of it'. The ability to build a personal relationship beforehand could be hampered by lack of time, or procurement protocol, which I go on to discuss below. While Helen's and Pauline's agencies handled a large number of international clients remotely through email, internet video, or by phone, these relationships were considered not possible without initial face-to-face meetings and annual face-to-face meetings to renew both professional and social relationships. Some of Helen's international clients had become friends over many years; she described these relationships as stronger than local client relationships.

'They are treating us like commodities': threats to agency-client 'chemistry'

Agency B adopted a more formal approach to relationship-building, known as 'chemistry' whereby the client and the agency were able to get to know the brief and each other before a pitch. I was surprised to see that a room, with a door labelled 'chemistry' was dedicated to this type of meeting. In placing a sign on the room, the tacit understanding of good relationships through 'chemistry' had been formalised. Through this session, the MD explained 'you'll pretty much know whether it's the right fit, and if it's something you want to go for...on a good pitch process you can meet them three or four times...which is really good'.

'Chemistry' is a key ingredient of the PRP-client relationship (Pieczka, 2002; Sissons, 2015); therefore testing the relationship by formalising the process in this way acknowledged its importance to a potential PRP-client contract. However, considerable frustration arose from a trend, in sectors such as FMCG and healthcare, towards 'procurement'. Here, the potential client's procurement department handles the tendering and shortlisting for new business, including the 'pitch', the process through which creative ideas for strategic communication are presented to the potential client. Dealing with procurement departments at these early stages often meant that the PR agency was forbidden direct access to the client contact such as the head of communications.

The buyer-supplier arrangement, according to Mandy, did little to facilitate a good client relationship and test the chemistry: 'they are treating us like commodities', a point echoed in several opinion pieces in the UK trade magazine, *PR Week* (e.g. Thomas, 2016; Burne James, 2018). The trend of PR's integration with other marketing services meant that agencies sometimes faced over-servicing clients at heavily reduced fees, a process known as 'reverse auction', which 'ranks agencies according to how low they bid' (Sudhaman, 2015). In spite of industry growth, the level of competition among agencies, according to the former WPP chairman Martin Sorrell, was severe: 'Competition is fierce and as image in trade magazines, in particular, is crucial to many, account wins at any cost are paramount' (Sudhaman, 2017).

At Agency B, existing, large PR accounts were routinely re-pitched for. Frustrated discussions about the tendering process took place during a board level meeting: the outcome of one major client bid (in terms of brand prestige as well as its monetary value) still had not been decided after a 6-month process and this led to concern among directors about whether they might lose that lucrative account all together.

Managing client expectations and minimising emotional risk

As discussed in Chapter 5, a key tenet of emotional labour theorising of PRP-client relationships is managing expectations, which Verčič et al. (2018) assert is primarily the agency's responsibility. Expectation management takes place at the beginning and throughout the handling of the client's account in order to minimise risk, including the emotional risk to a trusting relationship. Everyday 'small things' as relational practice (Fletcher, 1999) were part of display (Hochschild, 1983) that helped to make the client feel important, as emphasised by Sarah:

> By being responsive, by giving them time, by not keep looking at your BlackBerry when you're in a meeting, by not being on the phone, respond to emails quickly, just little things often, it's often really, really small things and even if you don't, you can't answer what they want immediately, at least you can say 'thanks, I got it, I'm on it'.
>
> (Sarah)

Equally important, however, were strategic, transactional approaches that were an attempt to 'manage' the client relationship smoothly from the beginning, to keep surprises to a minimum and to avoid problems with the client further down the line. At Pauline's agency this strategy was referred to as 'client alignment'; at Helen's agency it was called 'scoping'. There were similarities in these approaches, whereby information was gathered at the outset, including the client's objectives as well as ideas on how the client measured success. The client's expectations could be explicitly written down, together with the services that could be provided by the agency in support of those expectations. This detailed process could be linked to the time estimated on the account and the fees charged. The contract could be reviewed and updated according to changing demands on the account throughout the year. Both Pauline and Helen found this to be a very effective way of managing client expectations: 'It's a really useful exercise for actually understanding the dynamics within the client relationship' (Pauline). 'It makes it very, very easy for us to justify fee increases, scope increases' (Helen). On the other hand, the approach had to be flexible to client demands: Helen never turned down additional work outside of 'scope' as long as her client understood that the fee would have to be re-negotiated later. Furthermore, the 'client alignment' process did not necessarily prevent the problem of 'over-servicing', an issue highlighted by participants in Chapter 5, and Pauline:

> suddenly I look at the overservicing and it's ridiculous, so I'll probably go off on one [...] I look at it and say ooh, maybe I should have paid attention to that and then I'll go, okay guys, this isn't on, why are we doing this?
>
> (Pauline)

The success of the agency-client relationship in winning and keeping business was not restricted to a specific client contact. It was equally important for PRPs to picture and understand the relationship dynamics that lay *beyond* their main client contact. In earlier work, I theorised that the process of 'imagining the other' is part of the practitioners' empathic or perspective-taking skill (Yeomans, 2016). In the process of selling-in a proposal, perspective-taking is required because the practitioner has to step into the shoes of their client contact to imagine possible scenarios that might prevent the agency's proposals from being accepted by decision-makers. Such scenarios were borne out of participants' past experience. In some circumstances, there was a lack of trust in a client contact's ability to 'sell in' the agency's proposals to senior colleagues or board members:

> I'm trying to give [the client] the script, if I think they need it, to talk internally about the sort of work we are doing for them, because I fear for them being my advocate…if I can see they're probably not going to do that job very well.
>
> (Jane)

Mandy related: 'Sometimes they want to sell it themselves internally and it goes wrong…sometimes you can salvage it; sometimes it's gone'. Timothy recalled how a highly successful media campaign, gaining national coverage, led to a client sacking the agency because the client's company chairman disagreed with the news angle: 'I should have started to find ways to talk to the chairman…to get an understanding of what his values were and the sort of thing he was expecting'. Therefore, while directors preferred to be brought into the client organisation to present their proposals in person to those who might need further convincing, this was not always possible or desirable due to availability and time constraints on both sides. Furthermore, there was a suggestion among some participants that PR agencies were deliberately kept at arm's length by some in-house client contacts. In-house contacts were typically heads of corporate communication who were perceived to have a limited influence when it came to approving budgets. Jane found this arm's-length relationship frustrating: 'You need access to the people you need to impress'. The people agency directors needed to impress were those who ultimately held the large budgets: chief marketing officers or chief executive officers (CEOs). The suggestion of 'arm's length' PR consultant/agency influence resonates with the work of Sissons (2015, p. 283) who found in a detailed ethnographic analysis of the PRP–client relationship during a time of financial crisis that the relationship 'is one of struggle for limited influence often among competing interests, where personal agendas can interfere with or prevent the acceptance of solutions suggested by the PRP'.

Charlotte, Timothy, Mandy, James, and Helen asserted that they only worked with 'good' clients, or people they felt could do business with.

> We don't work with a lot of clients on purpose; we would rather work with fewer and do better work […] you get into all sorts of trouble when […] they just don't get it and they think they know best and you can't tell them anything […] and that becomes a fruitless relationship.
>
> (Charlotte)

Sometimes the individual client contact, as discussed in Chapter 5, did not understand PR and therefore did not comprehend the expertise the PR agency had to offer. While PRPs as trusted advisers frequently engaged in a process of 'educating' the client about the value of their PR expertise (Yeomans, 2010, 2013), the directors in my second study expressed impatience with clients who didn't 'get it'. James explained:

> they still think it's advertising, and it doesn't matter whether it's someone who's a one-man band or a CEO of a global company, it doesn't matter; they think it's advertising and we have that time and time again and you have to explain to people in quite simple terms.
>
> (James)

Here were further echoes (as in Chapter 5) of the need for PRPs to legitimise their expertise to clients through continuous interactions (Waeraas, 2009). Other participants saw relationship failures as a misalignment of values: 'you don't have to push yourself with people who share your values' (Timothy). Mandy's agency made its own values of 'mutual respect', a point of differentiation from competitors in order to retain staff:

> You try and find out before you pitch whether that is someone you want to pitch to…we've turned down pitches just because friends have said 'don't touch it, it's poison'. And they might have lost a whole team over it.
>
> (Mandy)

Mandy recognised that rejecting clients at a very early stage limited the growth of the business but it was an important price to pay to retain good staff: 'so when we've found ourselves in that situation with clients making people's life a misery, we've dealt with it and we've resigned the business because of it. We've handed money back before'.

The prospect of losing 'a whole' team was too much to risk. Charlotte also had her team in mind when a client relationship was not working out: 'if the team lose their enthusiasm for it, then we're not the right people to be selling their company'. Helen related how she had resigned a client account due to the client's unreasonable behaviour with her teams: 'numerous team members over the years…had been very upset by the client'. Helen, Pauline, and Mandy saw themselves as first line of defence in protecting their teams: 'I've had some hard conversations on the phone with the client trying to protect the team' (Pauline). James, on the other hand, with just one employee, was able to decide very quickly who he wanted to work for, based on past experience: 'if someone rings me up and they're looking for PR and I don't like the sound of them, for whatever reason, then I don't have to meet them. I can choose who I work for'.

In sum, participants' early stage, informal decisions about which clients were suitable to work with, as well as formal business processes (e.g. 'chemistry'), together with processes for client management ('alignment' and 'scoping'), were attempts to reduce over-servicing, as well as to limit difficult emotional exchanges. Given the evident pressures on agencies to win new business, this is a surprising though nevertheless strong theme to emerge from this study. Participants' unwillingness to venture into 'fruitless' relationships may reflect confidence in the PR role in the larger agencies and a wish to maintain happy teams, as well as a desire among directors of smaller PR firms for a healthier work-life balance, as people who win new business through referral and enjoy long-term relationships with their clients.

Anxiety in the agency: emotion management in the absence of key client account staff

Participants spent a considerable amount of time on client work; for example, Jane estimated that 80% of her work was devoted to clients. Participants were involved in generating new business through networking or pitching, maintaining contact with existing clients, and for some, even in larger agencies, throwing in their weight when required by continuing to direct day-to-day work on a client account. A recurring metaphor was the extent to which participants were 'hands-on' or got 'their hands dirty': 'I may not get my hands quite as dirty as the others but I will' (Pauline). While this work was time-consuming, participants understood that contact with the client, particularly at a senior level, was essential to help the client to feel comfortable: 'yeah, client contact with the Director of Comms or the CEO, they often like the reassurance of a senior person talking to them, so I do definitely keep my hand in' (Sarah). Charlotte explained her own involvement:

> I tend to get involved with clients quite a lot at the beginning of relationships, so where everyone's a bit unsure of stuff and you're trying to get everyone used to each other and make them feel calm and get that first bit of work out that makes everyone feel pleased and excited about the relationship and so I tend to get involved at that point, and then as and when I'm needed. So, whether it's evaluation meetings or selling of campaigns, it tends to be the beginning and the end, not necessarily through the middle of campaigns.
>
> (Charlotte)

Anxiety arising from the absence of senior personnel became the subject of unfolding 'crises' at two agencies during my observation visits. At Agency A, an account handler's concern about a senior colleague's absence due to a highly contagious virus gradually accelerated from his checking with the office manager about the next day's diary, and which senior people were available to cover the meeting, to queries to the MD about 'what to say to the client'. The absence of a key contact could potentially reduce confidence in the agency, which the account handler seemed well aware of, and a meeting between the client and a senior-level substitute needed to be scheduled for the following day. The frequent checking and seeking advice on 'what to say to the client' suggested that the account handler was concerned about possibly raising anxieties about the contagious virus and was therefore seeking ways to emotionally 'attune' with the client (Bloch, 2010; Burkitt, 2014). Avoiding embarrassment in a client relationship, as discussed in Chapter 3, is important to the preservation of a PRP's self-respect and a professional identity (Bloch, 2010). Could it be helpful for the account manager to simply tell the client the facts of the situation? In this case, the MD was pragmatic: 'There is no other way of explaining why people are not there'.

At Agency B, feelings of surprise and concern were intense from the start, prompted by the sudden and unexpected resignation of a board director. A series of meetings ensued to discuss how that director's absence could be covered by another colleague to ensure continuity with her clients. There was a need to 'plug gaps' quickly for an upcoming pitch. At the same time, directors struggled to understand and therefore provide responses to their clients as to why their colleague had suddenly resigned: within the confines of a private meeting room they shared their own opinions and reasons for the surprise departure – perhaps her domestic situation and her husband's job?

These examples, at two different agencies, of missing key personnel support the notion that PRPs need to continually legitimise their expertise through appropriate personal conduct. This might include checking what *is* appropriate conduct for the situation (Fournier, 1999). While a director's resignation carries more significant implications than illness, these two insights demonstrate that the ongoing management of a client's expectations is essential for directors who may already experience an elevated state of anxiety about the business such as awaiting the outcome of a re-tendering process with a major client. Such emotion management strategies are thus highly relevant to engendering client trust, long term (Yeomans, 2010).

Employee relationships: adapting to the surprise of the 'millennial' generation

In being deliberately selective about their clients, some participants attributed this to their own concerns for work-life balance and job satisfaction, as well as concern for the work-life balance and job satisfaction of their employees. Concern for one's own work–life balance could be attributed to personal family responsibilities, which Helen and James discussed as one of the benefits of running their own business. It offered flexibility. Others stressed the need for their companies to be focused on 'people' issues. Sarah, a partner in a large, established London agency emphasised '…there's been a real effort to be more aware that we are a people business and we need to make sure that we look after our people, so there has been quite a big change actually'. Helen, who ran a small, regional agency, emphasised her people-focused approach: 'we have flexible working for a number of working parents. You know, we offer staggered starts and finishes…people have a life outside work and…we have to get the balance right'.

Some participants strove to move away from past, often negative, experiences in PR agencies, characterised by excessive workloads, bullying, stress, and long working hours cultures, as well as negative attitudes towards family responsibilities. Enjoyable work environments were seen as a key priority, where not only were the employees keen to commit their time and energies but also the directors of the agencies themselves. For some, the decision to become entrepreneurs was a deliberate lifestyle choice: 'I am choosing to be at work rather than being a mum…so actually I want a nice environment to work in' (Helen). 'I keep office hours, I'm in at half nine to, depending on childcare, four, five or whatever it is' (James). Timothy related, 'if everyone around me is happy with what's going on and my clients are happy, I'm quite happy and I go back home to my family and enjoy a nice evening' (Timothy).

Some of the working conditions could be managed through more productive, respectful client relationships, as discussed, and also through adopting human resources (HR) policies such as flexible working arrangements to better suit employees' personal commitments. The dearth of so-called 'talent' in PR was common knowledge among UK practitioners (PR Moment, 2017; Holmes, 2018). Some participants acknowledged high turnover of staff in the PR/communication field in sectors such as healthcare: 'it's an employee's market' (Mandy), and so people-friendly policies and benefits were essential to recruit and retain good people. Jane's narrative was the most explicit about the recruitment challenges facing the PR industry:

> [we are] constantly interviewing junior people that could join the agency, because we constantly need them. And that's because in our experience, we'll have around 25 percent turnover of those entry level people in the first year because you get most of it right, but for some people […] comms isn't for them, or PR isn't for them or media work isn't for them or it wasn't what they expected, so we're constantly having to recruit.
>
> (Jane)

In discussing the so-called millennial generation in Chapter 3, I referred to one of the research questions posed by Thomas et al. (2014, p. 1577): 'what currency do different generational categories have within organizations?' The attributes and demands of the 'super confident' (Sarah) millennial generation were a topic of explicit discussion with four participants (Mandy, Charlotte, Sarah, and Helen) as well as some of their colleagues. While confident, entrepreneurial people, deemed as characteristic of millennials, were positively sought by agencies when recruiting new staff, some participants noted, with surprise, that millennials brought different attitudes and expectations such as valuing hard work and fun in the workplace as well as personal well-being: 'they're more about experiences and health and fitness…we have mindfulness sessions and yoga and massages' (Charlotte). Concern with personal well-being among millennials meant that they were not enticed by the perceived 'perks' of agency life such as 'booze and parties' experienced by directors in their own youth. Reinforcing the image of the health-conscious agency, I observed that the bright, open space of the kitchen area in Agency C included piles of fresh fruit set out in bowls. There were large refrigerators stocked with drinks for employees to help themselves to, as well as a coffee machine. Similarly, Agency B had its own small shop where one could buy healthy drinks, snacks, and hot meals. The shop's main food brand, which was akin to the Innocent brand, communicating 'playfulness, friendliness and fun' (The PAD Research Group, 2016, p. 303), was stocked, perhaps, with the millennial employee (as customer) in mind.

It was remarked at Mandy's agency that sometimes giving a pay rise wasn't enough; young people wanted to negotiate and ask why the pay was not higher: they appeared to value their worth and were more assertive than previous generations. The same discussion, involving an HR and finance director, revealed surprise at the demand for shared parental leave from a male employee. In 2015, new rights were granted to UK workers for shared parental leave of up to 37 weeks paid leave which meant that fathers could take more time off to care for a new baby (Peachey, 2015). The surprise emanated from the fact that a male employee was demanding this right so soon after the new legislation had come into effect.

'Flexibility', as a neoliberal concept, tends to 'carry positive overtones' (Eagleton-Pierce, 2016, p. 81). However, this raises questions about flexible working arrangements, for whom they are intended and under what conditions they operate. While flexible working in this study was seen to benefit the lives of some agency directors in their personal drive to manage work-life balance, the 'surprise' millennial employee demand for shared parental leave (raising possible questions around commitment to the job) may not always be welcome. Furthermore, 'flexible working' could still involve working intensively at unsocial hours, even if starting times were adjusted (see Box 7.1). As Chung (2017, p. 9) points out, the 'gift exchange' (Kelliher and Anderson, 2010) of employers' flexible work arrangements and the greater effort expended by employees in return, can lead employees to 'work harder and/or longer hours'. This is particularly true where flexible working is not equally available to all and generates a fear of being stigmatised by those wishing to take it up, e.g. in long hours cultures (Chung, 2017).

As discussed in Chapter 3, Meng et al. (2017, p. 68) found millennial PR professionals to be 'a contradictory generation, desiring independence, flexibility, and challenges balanced with clear expectations, regular evaluation, and safety nets in case of failure'. While all participants in Meng et al.'s study struggled with work-life balance, a workplace culture that was 'friendly, supportive and enjoyable' (p. 80) could make the difference to how they felt about the job. These findings may explain why some agency directors in my study felt compelled to find ways in which their businesses could adapt to younger employees such as operating flexible working and 'wellbeing' policies. Further, a small business working environment that becomes formalised through processes such as project management systems and 'scoping' to set out client expectations in writing could be seen as attempts to squeeze out time-consuming and costly events and potential relational conflict (i.e. the possible scenario of discontented employees *and* clients). As argued previously, such an environment perhaps reduces surprises and emotional risk.

The PRP-journalist relationship: shifting emphasis and employee resistance

Typically for participants as agency directors or partners, personal contact with journalists was minimal or infrequent. Their time was spent with potential clients, existing clients, or dealing with pressing HR matters. However, it was deemed useful to maintain personal contacts with high profile journalists or, in Jane's case: 'when there is an interesting piece of work which means facing off against a city or a corporate journalist on a difficult issue. But mostly I don't'.

Three participants, however, maintained regular contact with journalists, sometimes out of necessity, due to the small size of their agency (James), or because they felt that personal contact with journalists at MD level was essential to maintain important relationships (Mandy and Helen). While Mandy asserted that her personal investment in the PR agency ritual of 'dinners' with key health correspondents continued to prepare the way for selling in good stories, Pauline, by contrast, saw wining and dining journalists as a thing of the past and that if the story was good enough, it could be talked through over the phone by a highly experienced member of the team specialising in media relations:

> When I started, you took a journalist out for lunch and drank a bottle of wine with them, it doesn't happen anymore, and yet we still seem to be delivering. [My colleague] never takes a journalist out, never ever ever. I've worked with him for 25 years, and only once did he take a journalist out for lunch. And yet if there's anyone that's going to get us on to the BBC, *The Times, The FT*, it's him.
>
> (Pauline)

As outlined in Yeomans (2010, 2013), media relations work involving certain journalists – for example business editors of local newspapers, or those working for national newspapers – instilled fear among junior PR agency staff as well as wariness among experienced PR agency staff. This was also reflected in Sarah's narrative as senior partner of a large PR firm: 'I think that I'm really happy not having to sell-in stories and I've really done that, been there: I'm not sorry to say goodbye to that side of it'. However, the emotional labour of learning how to deal with 'difficult' and sometimes 'angry' journalists, and using effective strategies to approach them, was traditionally an expected part of PRPs' on-the-job training: it was a rite of passage of occupational socialisation, somewhat comparable to the 'bollockings' received by journalists themselves as an everyday newsroom experience (Aldridge, 1998). In the case of the PRP-journalist relationship, the journalist, in turn, reprimanded the PRP for a misplaced and untimely phone call.

Re-visiting the field in 2016 revealed a shifting emphasis on the PRP-journalist relationship. This shift included resistance among agency employees to build relationships with journalists using 'traditional' techniques, including phone calls and meeting them face to face. Some agency directors reported that young staff were more comfortable sending emails to both clients and journalists and neither saw the need to make a phone call, nor to network and build personal relationships, not even in situations where they might genuinely pay off such as at trade fairs.

> I find more and more, particularly with young people, they can't…they can't use the phone, they don't know how to. It's just all texts and messaging and emails.
>
> (James)

> I say to them if you want to line up a day out of the office, get yourself out of here, line up a few media briefings. You know you've got budget, you've got expenses to take people out to lunch, go out for a beer, whatever you want to do just make it happen. But very few people actually do it.
>
> (Helen)

Participants' experiences and responses to the management of PRP-journalist relationships could be said to reflect the rapidly changing media environment and the context-specific logics of PR practice. While Helen, who relied on good media relationships for her B2B clients, regretted resistance, especially among younger employees to build what she saw as important personal relationships with journalists through telephone or face-to-face means, others, such as Pauline and Charlotte, did not see relationships with the news media as a priority for some of their clients. For them, a shifting emphasis towards SMIs, particularly for consumer clients, meant re-deploying the time and efforts of their teams towards building highly productive relationships elsewhere, thus drawing on the perceived 'strengths' of the millennials in using digital channels.

The rise of SMIs: getting them excited about the brand

In some client sectors, as I argue in Chapter 3, PRPs' emotional effort has been diverted to the demands of SMIs, as more powerful endorsers of PR messages to consumers and other stakeholders. A subtheme that emerged from my questions to agency directors about news media was the increasingly important role of SMIs, including bloggers and vloggers who are active on digital and social media channels. Within a consumer environment, SMIs are understood as more influential in youth markets than mainstream media channels. A growing body of literature supports this depiction of consumer PR (e.g. Smith, 2010; Lahav and Roth-Cohen, 2016). However, 'thought leaders' within the professional (or B2B) environment, according to Pauline, could also be useful intermediaries:

> most of the time my team are dealing with bloggers as much as they are journalists. Bloggers are so influential, certainly on the consumer side,

and even in the professional space, there are some key thought leaders, I think I would describe them that, rather than bloggers; they just happen to use a blog as a way of communicating their thoughts, which wouldn't have happened six, seven years ago.

(Pauline)

In my study of PR executives (see Chapter 5), Graham was the only PRP whose employer specifically dealt with online journalists and bloggers. This 'digital PR' firm, located within an English city region, was considered innovative when the study was undertaken. According to Graham, who worked for clients in the technology sector, bloggers represented a group that demanded *even more* careful and sensitive handling than journalists when pitching a story:

I mean, the principles are the same; you're telling them something in the first paragraph, the first couple of minutes of them reading your pitch why this is of interest to you and why it's of interest to them. But it's important to be quite informal, and very personal, calling them by name etc. you know, almost personalise it as well, but don't look too desperate, you know 'I really enjoyed the articles. I thought this would be of interest to you, I was passing by etc'. And I think the key with bloggers is they love to be treated…going back to that personality of the blogger… I think they like to be treated as VIPs. So, they like to be given behind the scenes content, or content I think journalists wouldn't be able to get their hands on etc.

(Graham)

Charlotte, who I interviewed in 2016, explained that agency relationships in a consumer environment could mean flying a group of SMIs to a fashion show in New York, where 'exclusive' content involved providing the SMIs with rich experiences:

Influencers could choose the outfits that went down the catwalk. While the brand would normally be so controlling over something like a fashion show, it was like, influencers *absolutely* given the control, plus they're put in the most prestigious place on the front row. Whereas *Team Vogue* and all these [fashion] publications would normally sit there, it's actually putting them [SMIs] on the pedestal, giving them involvement and creating experiences for them […] the media coverage is a nice-to-have addition to it, but as long as we've got the social channels excited and engaged in it, then we've done our job, really.

(Charlotte)

The New York fashion show provides an example of shifting roles in the new media ecology. Not only were SMIs given preferential treatment to the fashion media in being able to 'curate' the fashion shows (Duffy and Hund, 2015), they were also physically occupying the prestigious viewing positions on the front row, once the exclusive domain of the fashion media (i.e. *Team Vogue*). This illustrates the perceived influence of the social media channels and those who are active on them; influencers literally pushed out the glossy publications whose editors (especially in fashion) once held sway among consumers.

'Experience', as Eagleton-Pierce (2016, p. 65) argues, is a further concept of neoliberalism. It is strongly identified with a philosophy which describes 'phenomena in terms of human consciousness' (Husserl, 1973/1939). Returning to SMIs, the stage-management of pleasurable experiences through immersion in a fashion show designed to stimulate their emotional responses illustrates a key tenet of experiential marketing theory (Holbrook and Hirschman, 1982). Blogger/vlogger storytelling, based on their immersive brand experiences, is therefore a way of communicating 'passion' for the brand. A further illustration of the attention routinely lavished on fashion bloggers as a particular type of 'VIP' influencer is well-illustrated in the following vignette drawn from my observations at Agency B.

From the PRP perspective, organising exclusive consumer 'experiences' for SMIs as well as thinking about underwear products to target 'bridal' bloggers (as in Box 6.2) all requires emotional effort, and especially in the light of the hinted-at fickle and volatile demands of these new 'VIPs', as related by Graham. Keeping the 'social channels excited and engaged' suggests even greater demands for emotional labour for PRPs in dealing with fashion

---

Box 6.2 Getting fashion bloggers and fashion media excited about the brand

The account manager joins us. We sit on sofas in a busy open space and the account team discuss plans for a forthcoming campaign for a major bra brand aimed at brides-to-be. The bra samples budget is £1,000 and they discuss which bras to send to bloggers who are getting married. The execs want to 'excite' the bloggers about the brand and they share product images on a laptop. They also discuss media alerts (visual press releases with minimal text) for a major bridal magazine. The agency arranges photography for the media alert. A good bridal PR image, which emulates the images used on the bridal magazine cover, is 'likely to go down well' with the target magazine.

Not only are the account team planning to 'excite' their target bloggers and fashion media about the brand through providing tailored, appealing product samples, in embodying a London fashion PR identity through rapid talk (see Box 6.1), they are also working up their own levels of excitement in an effort to display expertise and strong affiliations with the brand they are representing.

(Author's notes, May 2016)

---

bloggers. Bloggers are a group of entrepreneurs in their own right who are passionate in sharing exclusive content on their blog, while competing for attention and prestige with other bloggers and well-known celebrities in the fashion world (Duffy and Hund, 2015). This necessarily involves PRPs negotiating the 'deal' with their client, the fashion brand, fulfilling the blogger's need to feel recognised (including a possible scaling up of demand for compensation in return for writing a positive blog, based on their own precarious employment situation), and managing expectations with all parties.

Growing the business: the economic imperative

The 2008 global financial crisis had affected some agencies almost overnight. According to some participants, the impact of the crisis, including decisions to make staff redundant, had deeply affected some board level colleagues' mental health. A continued anxiety about sustainable business growth prevailed.

When I undertook fieldwork in 2016, agencies placed at the top of the UK's *PR Week* Top 150 rankings averaged at around 10% growth for that year; however, growth was not consistent among all agencies (Suleman, 2016). In 2018, by contrast, 'aggregate growth was at the lowest rate since the recession in 2009' (Harrington and Rogers, 2018). PR's sensitivity to the fluctuations of the market, and the political–economic conditions influencing the market, was evident from these results.

Three London agencies that I visited in 2016 invited me to meetings in which the financial position of the firm was under discussion, while the MD of the fourth agency provided a personal explanation of what was happening in her business. While some agencies in 2016 were struggling to meet the demands of growth, which, in the case of the first agency, meant a strain on their 'digital' team, there seemed little complacency about financial health, prompting intense discussion at a senior practitioner meeting. A range of ideas were put forward to 'monetise' advisory or database services, linked to existing services, that could be offered to clients as stand-alone products, thus making the best use of the company's extensive knowledge base. This section of the meeting generated considerable debate. Ideas such as facilitating 'introductions' to certain client contacts for a fee were met with scepticism by one senior partner, raising questions about ethics and the reputation of the firm. Senior practitioners were keen to suggest other possible ideas that could attract revenue such as undertaking reputation audits, offering scenario-planning for cyberattacks, as well as offering 'thought leadership' in the form of free online content.

At the second agency, all 30 or so staff were called to a meeting and introduced to a comprehensive campaign that would enable a large sales push by involving every member of staff. A clear financial target was set and with some gentle humour and graphics presented on a TV screen, one of the MDs introduced a range of initiatives, explaining his 'top tips' on winning new clients/more business. Among his 'top tips' was a strong graphic image that included a picture of a gravestone with 'Email RIP' written on it, followed by a picture of a man shouting: 'It's scary picking up the phone, but it is not cold calling, just creating opportunities to meet and hear their problems over coffee'. (This example further alluded to millennials' unwillingness to use the telephone.) The MD used the gendered term 'nurturing' as a term for client development (see also reference to 'nurturing' in Chapter 5, p. x), the argument being that looking after the needs of existing clients was important to grow new business. To ensure that everyone was aware of the explicit income target for the year, the MD announced that he would install a large barometer graphic on the wall of the kitchen to show sales gains. Clear expectations for generating sales leads were set, including writing case studies for the website, and while delivered with some humour: 'I'm not telling you off', the message was serious. Some staff appeared uncomfortable about being singled out for their perceived unresponsiveness to the call for case studies.

At the third agency, a dip in the position of the agency within the *PR Week* rankings at the time was the basis of directors' concern. There was a call for some time to think about 'easy [client] wins' but the same conversation generated concerns about the need to find new 'talent' (i.e. employees) to support existing clients' work, as well as to focus existing staff on meeting the key performance indicators. This particular vignette illustrates the frenetic disposition of the PR firm in an intensely competitive consumer sector.

One of the main concerns of the MD at the fourth agency was to ensure that the company was placed on a sound financial footing for the future. The MD's approach to this was to enable the process of gradual acquisition by a large strategic marketing and communications firm, which already held a stake in the company. In preparation for the planned acquisition, more streamlined, technologically enabled processes were being adopted, and a successor to the MD's role was in place. Therefore, while the agency's staff were not seemingly under pressure to grow the business, as depicted in other agencies, transformation of the business was underway.

In summary, agency PR is part of a highly competitive setting, characterised by structural changes within the PR/marketing services and news media industries, as well as changes in a variety of client sectors. Agency directors were not only working within an unstable set of environmental circumstances, including unpredictable markets and technological innovation, but also managing professional relationships that brought their own dynamics and challenges.

Conclusions

In this chapter I critically examined professional relationships in PR, grounded in the experiences and understandings of directors and partners in PR agencies in the United Kingdom. Agency directors were viewed as setting the emotional tone for PRPs working in their agencies (Yeomans, 2013). My aim was to examine the emotion management of the self and others from these senior-level perspectives. The research questions driving this study were: how do participants view their professional identities? How do participants understand and manage professional relationships within their own firms? What are the 'feeling rules' that apply to different situations and contexts? And what are participants' expectations of their employees in these different contexts? My observations in physical open spaces enabled me to gain personal insights of agency culture.

In this study, participants' experience of occupational socialisation in business and PR practice shaped their identities as entrepreneurs. Most participants saw their main responsibility as 'doing the best work for the client', reinforcing an identity of agency-based PR as an 'entrepreneurial profession' which is focused on selling creative ideas. As discussed in Chapter 3, an entrepreneurial profession appeals to 'the rhetoric of entrepreneurship, competition and efficiency to account for the value of what they do'. This is in contrast to other occupations that are driven by a public service remit (Muzio et al., 2008, p. 5). While the normative influence of feeling rules (or social norms) prescribed by the profession is regarded as a potential source of conflict by emotional labour theorists (Bolton, 2005), here, the potential sources of conflict (i.e. in norms and values) were likely to arise from client and employee relationships.

Gherardi (2015, p. 649) argues that gender plays into the entrepreneuring process, with the work-family balance being one of the 'major narratives in the field', particularly for women, because it is commonly assumed that women are doing most of the balancing. For some participants, the need to harmonise personal well-being with the demands of clients and employees involved complex emotion management to maintain equilibrium in these relationships. For some female participants, issues related to being a woman were encountered as sources of conflict in their daily interactions. Being a woman could be the basis for feeling isolated from senior, male board members; feeling excluded and patronised by a male-dominated professional membership organisation; as well as experiencing a lack of authority with a junior male colleague. Junior colleagues, and women in particular, were perceived by some participants as struggling to find a voice in the presence of senior male colleagues. Issues related to being a woman were also denied by two female participants, suggesting an alignment with the discourse of gender neutrality of business (Lewis, 2006).

Participants were involved in often frustrating struggles to develop existing client business as well as compete or re-tender for new accounts, sometimes through protracted tendering processes as a consequence of sector regulations. However, a surprising theme to emerge from this study was participants' unwillingness to venture into potentially 'fruitless' relationships with clients. This was partly an attempt to reduce over-servicing and doing work for little reward, but also an attempt to limit difficult emotional exchanges that could potentially lose 'whole teams'. Given the evident pressures on all agencies to develop or win new business, this may reflect confidence in the

PR role in the larger agencies and the desire to maintain happy teams, as well as a desire among directors of smaller PR firms for a healthier work-life balance. Agency directors of small firms reported winning new business through referral and enjoying long-term relationships with their clients. However, there were issues such as high staff turnover in the PR industry and a skill shortage which meant that directors were also keen to retain good staff and not expend resources on clients who were likely to be a poor 'fit' with the agency's values. Managing expectations and reducing emotional risk in client relationships were features of this concern and there were clear attempts to formalise relationship processes in order to achieve this. Therefore, the unexpected absence of key personnel could present a palpable feeling of anxiety; such was the potential risk to agency business.

Millennial employees were viewed favourably by participants as particularly 'bright' and 'smart'. For some participants, retaining good staff involved working collaboratively and performatively alongside their teams, getting their 'hands dirty', and being visible in physical open spaces, as well as having policies that included opportunities for flexible working. Nonetheless, agency directors had expectations of 'appropriate' employee attitudes and ways of communicating, and these expectations were made explicit through mentoring, coaching, and briefing sessions to support and develop good client relationships. Being 'switched on and engaged' expressed the type of disposition that was desired by participants in their staff relating to them as directors, as well as in client relationships. Expressing the 'right' emotions such as passion and enthusiasm for the brand is a crucial part of client service that PRPs learn through everyday experience and perform through embodied dispositions including attitude, dress, and demeanour appropriate to different contexts (Witz et al., 2003).

Finally, I perceived a shifting 'PR logic' (Fredriksson et al., 2013, p. 194). This new 'PR logic' included placing greater emphasis on relationships with SMIs than the news media in some client sectors. A highly competitive milieu, characterised by, for example, the speed of technological innovation, structural changes within the PR/marketing services and news media industries as well as client sectors, meant that agency directors were working within an unstable set of environmental circumstances and relationships.

References

Acker, J. (1992) From sex roles to gendered institutions. *Contemporary Sociology*, 21 (5), pp. 565–569.

Aldridge, M. (1998) Identity and mythology in contemporary UK press journalism. *Media, Culture & Society*, 20, pp. 109–127.

Arcy, J. (2016) Emotion work: Considering gender in digital labor. *Feminist Media Studies*, 16 (2), pp. 365–368.

Bernstein, E. S. and Turban S. (2018) The impact of the 'open' workspace on human collaboration. *Philosophical Transactions of the Royal Society B*, 373: 20170239.

Available from: http://dx.doi.org/10.1098/rstb.2017.0239. Accessed 28 October 2018.

Bloch, C. (2010) Negative acts and bullying: Face-threatening acts, social bonds and social place. In B. Sieben and Å. Wettergren, eds. *Emotionalizing Organizations and Organizing Emotions*. Basingstoke, Palgrave Macmillan, pp. 126–146.

Bolton, S. C. (2005) *Emotion Management in the Workplace*. Houndsmill, Hampshire, Palgrave Macmillan.

Bolton, S. C. and Muzio, D. (2008) The paradoxical processes of feminization in the professions: The case of established aspiring and semi-professions. *Work, Employment and Society*, 22 (2), pp. 281–299.

Budgeon, S. (2013) The contradictions of successful femininity: Third-wave feminism, postfeminism and 'new' femininities. In R. Gill and C. Scharff, eds. *New Femininities: Postfeminism, neoliberalism and subjectivity*. London, Palgrave Macmillan, pp. 279–292.

Burkitt, I. (2014) *Emotions and Social Relations*. London, Sage.

Burne James, S. (2018) Aggressive procurement teams continue to dog the industry claims PRCA. *PR Week*, 10 January. Available from: https://www.prweek.com/article/1454112/overly-aggressive-procurement-teams-continue-dog-industry-claims-prca. Accessed 28 October 2018.

Butler, J. (1990) *Gender Trouble: Feminism and the subversion of identity*. New York and London, Routledge.

Chung, H. (2017) Work autonomy, flexibility and work–life balance. Canterbury, Kent, ESRC/University of Kent. Available from: https://kar.kent.ac.uk/65922/1/Flexible%20working%20report.pdf. Accessed 8 April, 2019.

Davies, C. (1996) The sociology of professions and the profession of gender. *Sociology*, 30 (4), pp. 661–678.

Duffy, E. and Hund, E. (2015, July–December) 'Having it all' on social media: Entrepreneurial femininity and self-branding among fashion bloggers. *Social Media + Society*, 1 (2), pp. 1–11.

Eagleton-Pierce, M. (2016) *Neoliberalism: The key concepts*. Abingdon, Oxon, Routledge.

Edwards, L. (2008) PR practitioners' cultural capital: An initial study and implications for research and practice. *Public Relations Review*, 34 (4), pp. 367–372.

Edwards, L. (2014) Discourse, credentialism and occupational closure in the communications industries: The case of public relations in the UK. *European Journal of Communication*, 29 (3), pp. 319–334.

Edwards, L. (2015) *Power, Diversity and Public Relations*. Abingdon, Oxon, Routledge.

Edwards, L. (2018) *Understanding Public Relations: Theory, culture and society*. London, Sage.

Fitch, K. and Third, A. (2010) Working girls: Revisiting the gendering of public relations. *PRism*, 7 (4). Available from: http://www.prismjournal.org/index.php?id=gender. Accessed 5 October 2018.

Fitch K. and Third A. (2013) Ex-journos and promo girls: Feminization and professionalization in the Australian public relations industry. In C. Daymon and K. Demetrious, eds. *Gender and Public Relations: Critical perspectives on voice, image, and identity*. London, England: Routledge, pp. 247–268.

Fletcher, J. (1999) *Disappearing Acts: Gender, power, and relational practice at work*. Cambridge, MA, MIT Press.

Fournier, V. (1999) The appeal to professionalism as a disciplinary mechanism. *Sociological Review*, 47 (2), pp. 280–307.

Fredriksson, M., Pallas, J., Wehmeier, S. (2013) Public relations and institutional theory. *Public Relations Inquiry*, 2 (2) pp. 183–203.

Gherardi, S. (2015) Authoring the female entrepreneur while talking the discourse of work-family life balance. *International Small Business Journal*, 33 (6), pp. 649–666.

Gill, R., Kelan, E. and Scharff, C. (2017) A postfeminist sensibility at work. *Gender, Work and Organization*, 24 (3), pp. 226–244.

Harrington, J. and Rogers, D. (2018) PR Week UK top 150 consultancies 2018: Growth rate eases. *PR Week*, 23 April. Available from: https://www.prweek.com/article/1462603/prweek-uk-top-150-consultancies-2018-growth-rate-eases. Accessed 28 October 2018.

Hirst, A. and Schwabenland, C. (2018) Doing gender in the 'new office'. *Gender, Work and Organization*, 25 (2), pp. 159–176.

Hochschild, A. R. (1983) *The Managed Heart: Commercialization of human feeling.* Berkeley, University of California Press.

Holbrook, M. B. and Hirschman, E. C. (1982) The experiential aspects of consumption: Consumer fantasies, feelings and fun. *The Journal of Consumer Research*, 9 (2), pp. 132–140.

Holmes, J. (2006) *Gendered Talk at Work: Constructing gender identity through workplace discourse.* Malden, MA, Oxford, and Victoria, Blackwell.

Holmes, P. (2018) PRovoke18: With talent the number one challenge, firms get creative. Available from: https://www.holmesreport.com/latest/article/provoke18-with-talent-the-number-one-challenges-firms-get-creative. Accessed 28 October 2018.

Husserl, E. (1973 [1939]) *Experience and Judgment: Investigations in a genealogy of logic.* London, Routledge.

Jenkins, J. and Finneman, T. (2018) Gender trouble in the workplace: Applying Judith Butler's theory of performativity to news organizations. *Feminist Media Studies*, 18 (2), pp. 157–172.

Kelliher, C. and Anderson, D. (2010) Doing more with less? Flexible working practices and the intensification of work. *Human Relations*, 63 (1), pp. 83–106.

Kleres, J. (2015) Emotional expertise: Emotion and the expert interview. In H. Flam and J. Kleres, eds. *Methods of Exploring Emotions.* London, Routledge, pp. 90–100.

Lahav, T. and Roth-Cohen, O. (2016) The changing blogosphere and its impact on public relations practice and professional ethics: The Israeli case. *Public Relations Review*, 42, pp. 929–931.

L'Etang, J. (2015) 'It's always been a sexless trade'; 'It's clean work'; 'There's very little velvet curtain': Gender and public relations in post-Second World War Britain. *Journal of Communication Management*, 19 (4), pp. 354–370.

Lewis, P. (2006) The quest for invisibility: Female entrepreneurs and the masculine norm of entrepreneurship. *Gender, Work and Organization*, 13 (5), pp. 453–469.

Lewis, P. (2008) Emotion work and emotion space: Using a spatial perspective to explore the challenging of masculine emotion management practices. *British Journal of Management*, 19, pp. S130–S140.

Meng, J., Berger, B. H. and Rogers, H. (2017) Managing millennial communication professionals: Connecting generation attributes, leadership development, and employee engagement. *Acta Prosperitatis*, 8, Riga, Turiba University, pp. 68–83.

Muzio, D. Ackroyd, S., and Chanlat, J.-F. (2008) Introduction: Lawyers, doctors and business consultants. In D. Muzio, S. Ackroyd, and J.-F. Chanlat, eds. *Redirections in the Study of Expert Labour: Established professions and new expert occupations*. Basingstoke, Palgrave Macmillan, pp. 1–30.

North, L. (2016) The gender of 'soft' and 'hard' news. *Journalism Studies*, 17 (3), pp. 356–373.

The PAD Research Group (2016) Not so 'innocent' after all? Exploring corporate identity construction online. *Discourse & Communication*, 10 (3), pp. 291–313.

Peachey, K. (2015) How the new rules on parental leave work. *BBC News*, 15 April. Available from: https://www.bbc.co.uk/news/business-32130481. Accessed 2 October 2018.

Pieczka, M. (2002) Public relations expertise deconstructed. *Media, Culture & Society*, 24 (3), pp. 301–323.

PR Moment (2017) Why is there a talent crisis in public relations? Available from: https://www.prmoment.com/events/why-is-there-a-talent-crisis-in-public-relations. Accessed 24 August 2018.

Public Relations and Communications Association (2018) *The PRCA Census 2018*. London, PRCA.

Rakow, L. F. (1986) Rethinking gender research in communication. *Journal of Communication*, 36, pp. 11–26.

Scheff, T. (1990) *Microsociology: Discourse, emotion and social structure*. Chicago, IL, Chicago University Press.

Sissons, H. (2015) Lifting the veil on the PRP-client relationship. *Public Relations Inquiry*, 4 (3), pp. 263–286.

Smith, B. (2010) The evolution of the blogger: Blogger considerations of public relations sponsored content in the blogosphere. *Public Relations Review*, 36, pp. 175–177.

Sudhaman, A. (2015) Pepsico points the way for PR industry's procurement puzzle. 10 December. Available from: https://www.holmesreport.com/latest/article/pepsico-points-the-way-for-pr-industry's-procurement-puzzle. Accessed 2 October 2018.

Sudhaman, A. (2017) Q1 2017: Procurement 'dominant' says Sorrell as WPP PR growth leads group. 27 April. Available from: https://www.holmesreport.com/latest/article/q1-2017-procurement-dominant-says-sorrell-as-wpp-pr-growth-leads-group. Accessed 2 October 2018.

Suleman, K. (2016) PR Week reveals the top 150 UK PR consultancies 2016. *PR Week*, 3 May. Available from: https://www.prweek.com/article/1393421/prweek-reveals-top-150-uk-pr-consultancies-2016. Accessed 2 October 2018.

Tait, A. (2018) Read it and weep: Why is replying to emails so hard? *New Statesman*, 18 January [online]. Available from: https://www.newstatesman.com/science-tech/technology/2018/01/read-it-and-weep-why-replying-emails-so-hard. Accessed 28 October 2018.

Thomas, A. (2016) Is pharmaceutical procurement fit for the future? *PR Week*, 14 March. Available from: https://www.prweek.com/article/1387229/pharmaceutical-procurement-fit-future. Accessed 28 October 2018.

Thomas, R., Hardy, C., Cutcher, L., and Ainsworth, S. (2014) What's age got to do with it? On the critical analysis of age and organizations. *Organization Studies*, 35 (11), pp. 1569–1584.

Verčič, D., Tench, R. and A. T. Verčič (2018) Collaboration and conflict between agencies and clients. *Public Relations Review*, 44 (1), pp. 156–164.

Waeraas, A. (2009) On Weber: Legitimacy and legitimation in public relations. In Ø. Ihlen, B. van Ruler, and M. Fredriksson, eds. *Public Relations and Social Theory*. New York and London, Routledge, pp. 301–322.

Wajcman, J. (2015) *Pressed for Time: The acceleration of life in digital capitalism*. Chicago, IL, and London, The University of Chicago Press.

Warren, S. and Fineman, S. (2007) 'Don't get me wrong here, it's fun here but…': Ambivalence and paradox in a 'fun' work environment. In R. Westwood and C. Rhodes, eds. *Humour, Work and Organization*. London and New York, Routledge, pp. 92–112.

Waterloo, S. F., Baumgartner, S. E., Peter, J., and Valkenburg, P. M. (2018) Norms of online expression of emotion: Comparing Facebook, Twitter, Instagram and WhatsApp. *New Media and Society*. 20 (5), pp. 1813–1831.

Williams, C. and Connell, C. (2010) 'Looking good and sounding right': Aesthetic labor and social inequality in the retail industry. *Work and Occupations*. 37 (3), pp. 349–377.

Witz, A. Warhurst, C., and Nixon, S. (2003) The labour of aesthetics and the aesthetics of organization. *Organization*, 10 (1), pp. 33–54.

Wouters, C. (2007) *Informalization: Manners and emotions since 1890*. London, Sage.

Yeomans, L. (2010) Soft sell? Gendered experience of emotional labour in UK public relations firms, *PRism* [Online], 7 (4). Available from: http://www.prismjournal. org. Accessed 17 July 2017.

Yeomans, L. (2013) Gendered performance and identity work in PR consulting relationships: A UK perspective. In C. Daymon and K. Demetrious, eds. *Gender and Public Relations: Critical perspectives on voice, image and identity*. London, Routledge, pp. 87–107.

Yeomans, L. (2016) Imagining the lives of others: Empathy in public relations. *Public Relations Inquiry*, 5 (1), pp. 71–92.

7 Conclusions

Introduction

I began this book with the premise that emotional labour represents a large proportion of the practice of public relations (PR), and it could be considered as a defining feature of professionalism. While emotional labour is common to many occupations that require face-to-face or voice-to-voice contact, it is highly relevant to the work of public relations practitioners (PRPs), especially women who are employed at the lower and middle levels in PR firms, where the client's everyday demands influence the level of service provided. Unlike other business consultancy services, however, PR firms have other demands requiring emotion work: those of handling the news media, and increasingly, social media influencers (SMIs). These relationships are mediated within the agency setting, which itself has 'feeling rules' or socio-emotional norms which the practitioner must negotiate. Although technological developments are rapidly changing PR work (Sims, 2018), the need to manage relationships is unlikely to go away, even if these relationships are increasingly mediated online. Furthermore, mediated relationships prompt the requirement for different forms of emotional labour which I propose should be explored as developments in ICT are integrated in everyday PR routines (see page 144). Another purpose of this book was to address the emotional dimension of PR work, hitherto neglected by researchers, including those interested in the socio-cultural perspectives in PR scholarship. Therefore, this book contributes to a knowledge gap, as well as opening up avenues for further enquiry that further map the emotional terrain of PR practice. At the end of this chapter I make suggestions for how this work could be taken forward. I now summarise each chapter before presenting final thoughts and tentative theory on PR as emotional labour.

Chapter 1 introduced the book's central thesis in which I argued that emotional labour represents a large proportion of the practice of PR and in some situations, may be a defining feature of professionalism in PR. While emotional labour is common to many occupations that require face-to-face or voice-to-voice contact, it is relevant to the work of PRPs, especially women employed and the lower and middle levels of agencies where the client's demands influence the level of service provided. There are a number of good reasons to explore emotional labour in PR: the work is stressful, competitive, and in the United Kingdom, there is high annual staff turnover in agencies, as well as skill shortages. PR is also in the business of being positive, which may lead to a denial of pressures. Furthermore, unlike other business consultancy services, PR firms have other demands requiring emotion work: those of handling the media, and increasingly, SMIs. These relationships are mediated within the agency setting, which itself has explicit and implicit socio-emotional norms for the practitioner to negotiate. **Chapter 1** also positioned this book as contributing to socio-cultural PR scholarship. My stance is that of a critical-interpretive scholar examining both the broader, socio-cultural context of PR and the everyday 'lived experience' of agency practitioners whose everyday interactions I view as playing a part in structuring this context.

Chapter 2 introduced and critiqued Hochschild's (1983) emotional labour theory including the framework of 'feeling rules', 'surface acting', and 'deep acting' during service interactions that are considered to threaten the 'authentic self'. Turning to more recent literature, I explored Bolton's (2005) typology of workplace emotion. Bolton draws attention to 'performance' and 'identity' in understanding the motivations of professionals in willingly doing emotional labour in the pursuit of status and material rewards. Professionals, Bolton (2005) argues, enjoy more autonomy and less surveillance in their work. Rather than experiencing 'alienation from the self', professionals are more likely to experience the consequences of emotional dissonance arising from threats or contradictions to professional identity and status. While agreeing with Bolton that the complete 'transmutation of feeling' from private emotion to managed commodity may not be recognisable in the labour process for professionals, in that their work is not highly 'scripted', this raises questions that go to the heart of much theorising in PR scholarship: to what extent can PR be considered a 'profession' and what is professionalism? And what are the implications for PRPs when negotiating the interactional demands of 'always on' digital culture (Turkle, 2008; Wajcman, 2015). In this chapter I proposed an extended framework of emotional labour that focuses on 'embodied dispositions' (Witz et al., 2003); the shaping of emotional expression within physical open spaces; as well as through ICT-enabled interactions. Finally, I argued that consideration of gender and performativity is essential to address Hochschild's concern with female workers as the most suitable candidates for emotional labour. Chapter 4 builds on the theme of gender and PR to critically examine PR as a female-intensive occupation and the issues that arise from that.

Chapter 3 explored the structural aspects of society and culture that influence PR as a commercial service. Alongside other critical PR scholars, I regard neoliberalism and promotional culture as important explanatory frameworks for the institutionalisation and expansion of the PR industry during the past 40 years. An understanding of the social, cultural, and political trends arising from the neoliberal 'project' in the United Kingdom (Harvey, 2005) and free market policies of the 1980s and 1990s is fundamental to understanding agency/consultancy PR as among the new 'entrepreneurial professions' (Muzio et al., 2008). An entrepreneurial profession has a low barrier to entry and responds flexibly to the market. In becoming integrated within an expanding marketing services sector, PR is part of a promotional culture (Wernick, 1991) that shapes the public's relationship with institutions, increasingly through 'emotionalised' digital networks (Beckett and Deuze, 2016). Furthermore, the promotional industries that drive neoliberal economies are in increasing demand across the developing markets of Asia Pacific and Latin America. PR draws its power from the market in providing services that protect and enhance organisational or brand reputation by influencing public perceptions. The value of the PR service to the client is in expertise, but this expertise is often fragile, based on situational as well as personal characteristics, rather than an established body of scientific knowledge, despite advances in professional certification.

While the knowledge base that is required to practise PR successfully is changing rapidly as a consequence of digital capitalism and associated technological developments, PRPs within agencies continue to work performatively, drawing on personal and emotional resources to legitimise their practice through building strong relationships with clients and managing their expectations. Journalists, meanwhile, rely on PR sources for the supply of news stories, ideas, and research. Journalists' ever-increasing dependency on PR sources, at the same time, presents a threat to journalists' professional identities as independent reporters of facts and upholders of standards. This is particularly true at a time when journalism itself is undergoing a crisis of public trust and identity within a dynamic and 'emotionally-charged networked environment' populated by media actors (e.g. bloggers) who are better able to tune into audience tastes (Beckett and Deuze, 2016). Therefore, while PRPs need to build trust with their journalist contacts, media relations occupies a lower status in comparison to PR consulting (Zerfass et al., 2018, p. 95). In some client sectors, PRPs' emotional effort has been diverted to the demands of bloggers or SMIs as more powerful endorsers of PR messages, thus disrupting established media ecologies. From this depiction of the market for emotional labour in PR, I argue that PRPs are immersed in a continuous process of emotional labour to fulfil the demands of their management, their clients, and multiple media actors.

Chapter 4 pursued an understanding of emotional labour performed through gendered interactions in the workplace. An interdisciplinary review, which drew on gender theory, organisational theory, and the sociology of work, enabled me to examine ideas of gender (e.g. Rakow, 1986; Butler, 1990; Acker, 1992; Dow and Wood, 2006), emotional labour (Hochschild, 1983), discourse approaches to gender (e.g. Fletcher, 1998; Holmes, 2006; Bolton and Muzio, 2008; Marsh, 2009), masculine identity in occupations (e.g. Leidner, 1991; Alvesson, 1998; Simpson, 2004).

More specific to this study, I reviewed literature on the feminisation of PR (e.g. Grunig et al., 2000; Toth, 2001; Rakow and Nastasia, 2009), the construction of identities in PR work, including female identity (e.g. Fröhlich and Peters, 2007; Tsetsura, 2014), male identity (e.g. Elmer, 2010; Tindall and Waters, 2012), as well as intersectional approaches to identity (e.g. Pompper,

2013; Vardeman-Winter et al., 2013). Finally, I briefly examined questions arising from the gendered and emotional aspects of digital labour (e.g. Duffy, 2015; Arcy, 2016) and PRPs' use of social media as emotional labour (Bridgen, 2011).

In this chapter I argued that the feminisation of PR is a more complex phenomenon than it at first might seem. In terms of 'body count', there are more women than men working in PR but the larger concentration of women at the lower and middle levels of PR agencies has created a gender hierarchy, as both the industry and scholars have noted. Less acknowledged in the PR literature are the processes that construct and gendered institutions and organisations (Acker, 1992). These processes include decisions and procedures on who is included/excluded in terms of gender roles, the gendered discourses of the profession, as well as gendered performance and identity construction through PRP-client interactions. The gendered discourse of the PR professional project (Fitch and Third, 2010) suggests parallel struggles: a struggle, on the one hand, towards professional legitimacy (a 'respected' profession and a management function) which is enacted by professional membership associations, educators, and PRPs alike, in relation to *other professions*; and a more subtle gender struggle *within* the 'pink ghetto' through PRPs' day-to-day interactions with clients, journalists, colleagues, and online influencers. Postfeminist analyses, and an understanding of gender as performativity, enable an interrogation of the 'gender regime' in PR. Finally, digital emotional labour – identified as another area of gendered work – should be understood as the focus of PRP effort as online relationships increasingly define PR practice.

Chapter 5 reflected on my empirical exploration of practitioners' professional relationships from an emotional labour perspective (Yeomans, 2010, 2013, 2016). Participants in this study comprised four female and two male practitioners between the ages of 23 and 32. All were White graduates, from middle-class backgrounds and practised at agencies in two English cities. In this study, the emotional cues of senior colleagues and peers were interpreted as the 'feeling rules' (Hochschild, 1983; Bolton, 2005) of agency work that were internalised by practitioners, guiding their professional practice towards a 'client first' orientation (Kaiser et al., 2008). Learning on the job and observing others helped to shape not only practitioners' technical skills but also their relational skills so that they became relevant to the specific problem or situation. The process of developing and honing the relevant relational skills through interactions with clients, journalists, and others, in turn, helped to generate 'emotional capital' (Cahill, 1999; Illouz, 2007) as an embodied form of PR 'expertise' (Pieczka, 2002, p. 32). I argued that this embodied expertise supported the notion of an 'emotional intelligence' model of professionalism, more so than a 'knowledge' model (van Ruler, 2005). 'Being a PR professional' meant drawing on multiple identities to negotiate relationships. Different identities were enacted in order to meet the different expectations of how PR professionals should conduct themselves (Fournier, 1999), as well as to achieve recognition and status rewards for the practitioner (Bolton,

2005). Practitioners drew on multiple identities during interactions: a 'pro-fessional' identity (e.g. 'behaving well'), their social identities (e.g. as friendly people, even 'personalities'), as well as gender. Participants working in small, regional agency offices had a particular need to draw on different identities with different clients, because frequent, informal communication was part of the service offer within this context (Mart and Jackson, 2005) and personal 'chemistry' played an important role in service differentiation (Mart and Jackson, 2005; Pieczka, 2006; Sissons, 2015). Practitioners' identities were also shaped by structural notions of the individual as 'entrepreneur of the self' (Gordon, 1987, p. 300); as competitors in the labour market for PR jobs; as cultural intermediaries in promotional culture (Hodges and Edwards, 2013); and as consumers in their own right within the culture.

I argued that 'managing expectations' was *central* to practitioners' emotion management strategies due to the highly contingent nature of PR work where 'results' (largely defined as positive media coverage for the client) could not always be guaranteed. The performances of 'empathising' and 'educating' in PR agency work served to highlight the importance of gendered 'relational practice' (Fletcher, 1998). Much of the work of male and female PR consult-ants constituted 'relational practice', which, in turn, drew on practitioners' different identities. This raised questions about whether the emotion man-agement skills required of practitioners in their everyday work is perceived as women's work and therefore not a 'real job' (Tsetsura, 2011). A popular perception that PR is feminine work (sustained by 'PR girl' stereotypes) may explain why the male practitioners in this study re-framed their relational work in masculine terms, a practice found in other occupations where there is a female majority (Alvesson, 1998; Lupton, 2000; Simpson, 2004).

In this study, deep and surface acting were commodified aspects of the self in PR work (Hochschild, 1983). In addition, female practitioners learned to both deny their gender and their feelings to be perceived as 'serious' and 'professional'. However, in contradiction to Hochschild's concerns surround-ing the alienation of the self through repeated 'deep acting' performances, it would appear that commodified performances in PR agency work formed part of professional identity development: successful practitioners learned to exert control over their social interactions rather than be victim to them. Such processes, as argued earlier, support an emotional intelligence (EI) model of PR professionalism whereby the practitioner develops their own 'brand' and becomes known for their client handling skills that will earn the client's re-spect and trust. Through repeated performances of surface and deep acting in everyday social interactions, PRPs therefore become 'skilled emotion man-agers who are able to juggle and synthesize different types of emotion work dependent on situational demands' (Bolton, 2005, p. 289).

Chapter 6 critically examined professional relationships in PR, grounded in the experiences and understandings of eight directors and partners of PR agencies in the United Kingdom. My aim was to examine the emotion man-agement of the self and others from these senior-level perspectives. Building on the work presented in Chapter 5, I viewed agency directors as responsible for setting the emotional tone for PRPs working in their agencies. My observations of social interactions in physical open spaces enabled consideration of the emotional mood of the PR firm. In this study, participants' experience of occupational socialisation in business and PR practice shaped their identities as entrepreneurs. Most participants saw their main responsibility as 'doing the best work for the client', reinforcing an identity of agency-based PR as an 'entrepreneurial profession' which is focused on selling creative ideas (Muzio et al., 2008). As discussed in Chapter 3, an entrepreneurial profession appeals to 'the rhetoric of entrepreneurship, competition and efficiency to account for the value of what they do'. This is in contrast to other occupations that are driven by a public service remit (Muzio et al., 2008, p. 5). While the normative influence of feeling rules (or social norms) prescribed by the profession is regarded as a potential source of conflict by emotional labour theorists (Bolton, 2005), here, the potential sources of conflict (i.e. in norms and values) were likely to arise from client and employee relationships.

Gherardi (2015, p. 649) argues that gender plays into the entrepreneuring process, with the work-family balance being one of the 'major narratives in the field', particularly for women, because it is commonly assumed that women are doing most of the balancing. For some participants, the need to balance personal well-being with the demands of clients and employees involved complex emotion management to maintain harmony in these relationships. For some female participants, issues related to being a woman were encountered as sources of conflict in their daily lives, revealing patriarchal attitudes (Fitch and Third, 2010) as well as processes of exclusion and competing jurisdictional claims to PR expertise (Edwards, 2014, 2018). Being a female agency director could be the basis for feeling isolated among male colleagues; feeling excluded and patronised by a male-dominated professional membership organisation; as well as experiencing a lack of authority with a junior male colleague. Junior female executives were perceived by some participants as struggling to find a voice in the presence of senior male colleagues. Contrariwise, two female participants considered issues related to being a woman as irrelevant, suggesting an alignment with the belief in the gender neutrality of business (Lewis, 2006), as well as a belief that gender equality had been achieved (Fitch and Third, 2010; Fitch, 2015; Gill et al., 2017).

Reflective of contemporary industry reports (e.g. Holmes Report, 2018), participants in this study were involved in often frustrating struggles to develop existing client business as well as compete or re-tender for new accounts, sometimes through protracted tendering processes as a consequence of sector regulations. However, a surprising theme to emerge from this study was participants' unwillingness to venture into potentially 'fruitless' relationships with clients. This was partly an attempt to reduce over-servicing and doing work for little reward, but also an attempt to limit difficult emotional exchanges in situations where there were conflicting values, or a lack of understanding of the PR role (discussed in Chapter 5). Given the evident pressures on all agencies to develop or win new business, this may reflect confidence in the PR role in the larger agencies and the desire to maintain happy teams, as well as a desire among directors of smaller PR firms for a healthier work-life balance. Agency directors of micro and small firms reported winning new business through referral and enjoying long-term relationships with their clients. However, there were issues such as high staff turnover in the PR industry which meant that directors were also keen to retain good staff and not expend resources on clients who were likely to be a poor 'fit' with the agency's values. Managing expectations and reducing emotional risk in client relationships were features of this concern and there were clear attempts to formalise relationship processes in order to achieve this. Therefore, the unexpected absence of key personnel could present a palpable feeling of anxiety; such was the potential risk to agency business.

Millennial employees were viewed favourably by participants as particularly 'bright' and 'smart'; yet millennials brought their own demands and expectations of the workplace, with implications for retention in an industry with a skill shortage. For some participants, retaining good staff involved working collaboratively and performatively alongside their teams, getting their 'hands dirty' and being visible in physical open spaces, as well as having policies that included opportunities for flexible working. Nonetheless, agency directors had expectations of 'appropriate' employee attitudes and ways of communicating, and these expectations were made explicit through formal and informal mechanisms: mentoring, coaching, and briefing sessions to support, maintain, and develop good client relationships. Being 'switched on and engaged' expressed the type of feeling rule that was desired by participants in their staff relating to them as directors, as well as in client relationships. Expressing the 'right' emotions such as passion and enthusiasm for the brand is a crucial part of client service that PRPs learn through everyday experience and perform through embodied dispositions including attitude, dress, and demeanour appropriate to different contexts, including the open office of the agency itself (Witz et al., 2003).

In sum, a shifting 'public relations logic' was underway (Fredriksson et al., 2013, p. 194). A new 'PR logic' (which refers to 'taken-for-granted activities, rules, norms and ideas'), for example, placed greater emphasis on relationships with SMIs than the news media in some client sectors. This highly competitive milieu, characterised by, for example, the speed of technological innovation, structural changes within the PR/marketing services and news media industries as well as client sectors, meant that agency directors were working within a fluid and fragile set of environmental circumstances and relationships.

Public relations as emotional labour: a theory

Emotional labour, professionalism, and the PR profession

At the beginning of this book I argued that emotional labour could be considered a defining feature of professionalism. By this I mean that a multiplicity of relationships are the central focus of PR work, not only because PRPs have to manage professional relationships within the agency setting, they also advise client organisations on their stakeholder relationships and how best to communicate with stakeholders (see Figures 7.1 and 7.2). In order to become trusted advisers, PRPs use legitimisation strategies (Waeraas, 2009; Merkelsen, 2011), of which emotion management is part, first, to convince clients of their expertise in PR and, second, to justify their client's actions to stakeholders through corporate responsibility programmes and corporate reputation campaigns. An EI model of professionalism is therefore highly relevant as a model of professionalism in PR. The EI model as defined by van Ruler (2005, p. 161) is 'the development of experts who gain value for their clients by their commitment and their personality, their creativity and their enthusiasm for a cluster of tasks negotiated with the client' (van Ruler, 2005, p. 161). The model is characterised by a 'general learning potential and empathy' (p. 164) or the ability to acquire particular knowledge for particular situations and use it appropriately. Hughes (2010) positions EI as a defining feature of the processes of *informalisation* (Wouters, 2007), whereby society and organisations have increasingly relaxed social controls in order to manage complexity. Thus, EI shifts the focus away from the 'feeling rules and scripts' of emotional labour to individuals developing competences that rely on self-regulation. This 'individualisation of emotion' requires people be true to their authentic selves and emotionally reflexive, expressing themselves in ways that are 'appropriate', even though this brings the added pressure of negotiating complex situations without explicit guidelines (Hughes, 2010, p. 41). Chapter 5, which examined professional relationships from the perspectives of PRPs working in regional agencies in two English cities, provided further credence to recognition of an EI model within the regional, small business context. From this study, I characterised PRPs as 'skilled emotion managers'. The importance of 'the presentational self' (Bolton, 2005) and emotional reflexivity imbued PRPs' constructions of professionalism, how they learned to become PR professionals, and accounts of their everyday professional interactions. In Chapter 6, which examined professional relationships from the perspective of directors across a spectrum of agency types, an 'attitude above skill' thinking prevailed, particularly in the recruitment of junior account executives. A 'switched on and engaged' disposition meant that junior executives who demonstrated this disposition were likely to be receptive to learning the necessary technical and emotional skills through agency-based coaching and mentoring in order to perform the tasks required for the job.

An EI model of professionalism shows that professionalism is an interactive process that uses personal resources including emotional capital (Illouz, 2007) to navigate the identities and manage the expectations of others. The process of professionalism not only includes reading and interpreting comments and non-verbal communication in fluid, potentially political situations; it is also continuous. It involves all work-related social interactions to convince the agency practitioner's bosses, colleagues, client, journalist, and other contacts of their professional expertise, thereby reinforcing legitimacy (Waeraas, 2009), and in doing so earning their trust. Further, Fournier (1999) echoes this argument when she states that professional competence is as much about appropriate personal conduct than it is about the acquisition of scientific knowledge.

However, the earlier theorising may be countered by strong arguments that an EI model of professionalism is highly undesirable in progressing the PR 'professional project' (van Ruler, 2005). First, PR is already stigmatised by an image of 'spin', 'fake news', and manipulation, and it continues to defend its position as having a social purpose (CIPR, 2017; Mitchell, 2018). PR scholars are therefore particularly invested in progressing the value of PR to organisations and society through promoting the acquisition of training and education that help to raise professional (i.e. ethical) standards. However, although theory-based professionalisation lends weight to legitimising the profession, Merkelsen (2011) argues that one has to examine who benefits from such legitimisation. Is it the public, academia, the client, or the profession itself? A second argument against an EI model of professionalism is that it is untenable in a profession that increasingly requires 'hard' knowledge of algorithms, big data, and data management skills (Zerfass et al., 2017; Holmes Report, 2018). There is a danger, however, that in the PR trying to be more like marketing, which values numbers and data, or indeed, more tech-savvy, that it becomes caught up with the management 'myth of rationality' (Wehmeier, 2006) and loses sight of its focus on relationships, instead getting drawn into quantifiable views of relationships, rather than the more messy and complex human side.

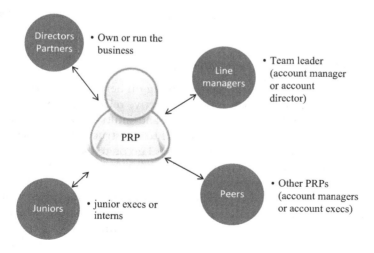

Figure 7.1 PRP professional relationships: emotional labour and identity management within a small PR agency.

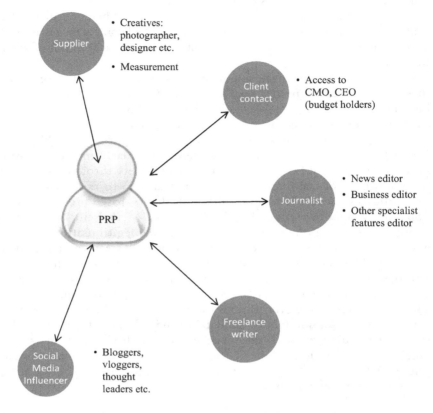

Figure 7.2 PRP professional relationships: emotional labour and identity management (external to agency).

Emotional labour and the feminisation of PR

As Pierce (1995, p. 179) has argued, drawing on her emotional labour study of male and female legal workers, the interactive relationship between structure, behaviour, and identity is dynamic and multi-layered, and gender is integral to this process. Gender is integral to the structuring process of PR, which is also dynamic and multi-layered, as I go on to explain. In the United Kingdom, PR is a female-intensive occupation. It is segregated by gender, both vertically (according to hierarchy) and horizontally (according to client sector). I have argued throughout that PR consulting/agency practice suggests an 'emotional-intelligence' model of professionalism which draws on the 'presentational self' (Bolton, 2005), embodiment (Witz et al., 2003), and identity performances (Tindall and Waters, 2012; Yeomans, 2013) that align with the client to form strong social bonds (Scheff, 2000). However, an EI model of professionalism is open to exploitation both from within and outside the profession. As discussed, work that is characterised as 'relational practice' (Fletcher, 1998) not only gets 'disappeared' in organisations but also is interpreted as gendered practice. Although the 'ability to manage one's own feelings and handle the feelings of others' contributes to a skills gap within the wider UK service economy (Winterbotham et al., 2018, p. 77), it has a double edge: first, relational practice is gendered feminine. This means it is categorised by society as part of women's natural skill set, rather than *learned* skills. Second, relational practice is likely to be undervalued unless it is accompanied by technical skills (Grugulis and Vincent, 2009). Furthermore, if PR is perceived as 'a pink ghetto' then its value as a 'real job' may be called into question (Tsetsura, 2011). Thus, the stereotype of women as 'natural born communicators' (Fröhlich, 2004), while championing feminine relational styles (Holmes, 2006), based on their 'difference', presents a paradox.

In consigning the relational skills of everyday practice to women occupying the lower and middle levels of agency structures, the patriarchal ordering of the PR profession is sustained (Fitch and Third, 2010; Golombisky, 2015). It is sustained by enabling particularly ambitious men, who are 'tokens' within a female-dominated office, to have a smooth ride on the so-called 'glass escalator' through the hierarchy (Williams, 1995, p. 87), or to bypass it all together, to achieve senior managerial or director status. Although participants in Yeomans' (2010, 2013) study, discussed in Chapter 5, did not construct PR as a 'woman's job', participants' narratives highlighted the tensions between the client sectors, including their ascribed gendered features (e.g. 'serious' B2B work and 'fluffy' consumer work), as well as expectations of gendered identity performance during client and journalist interactions. Thus, agency-client interactions encourage the reproduction of ascribed gender roles (Hochschild, 1983), according to situational demands. Turning to the experiences of female agency directors discussed in Chapter 6, patriarchal attitudes were encountered in some agencies and within PR professional membership associations. Women's networking associations, for some, offered alternative sources of support. However, these associations involve exclusive membership to senior women only, heightening notions of successful, goal-orientated neoliberal feminism (Yeomans, 2019), rather than inclusive places to encourage junior women's confidence and development, as well as sources of collective resistance. At the same time, being a woman in an entrepreneurial leadership role, for others, also suggested an alignment with 'invisible' and 'gender neutral' entrepreneurial identities (Lewis, 2006). These processes suggest a subtle, unacknowledged gender struggle within the PR profession. Individualised, competitive struggles that are approved and advocated within a neoliberal framework further delineate the market orientation of PR agency work (Rottenberg, 2014, 2018).

A final point here is that while face-to-face interactions show signs of diminishing in PR work, gendered, relational work continues through voice-to-voice interactions as well as online. Future scenarios of intensified *intra*personal, *individualised* interactions (Weyher, 2012), and, importantly to the discussion of gender, *who* is undertaking them, and *when*, in a 'hyper-modern' consumer culture (Zerfass et al., 2017) are likely to provide fertile ground for future emotional labour studies.

Emotional labour, promotional culture, and identity work

The significance of *identity work* involved in agency practitioners' emotional labour also suggests a further concept: that of the practitioner as 'entrepreneur of the self' (Gordon, 1987). Within the context of promotional culture, PRPs are theorised as cultural intermediaries (Curtin and Gaither, 2005; Hodges, 2006; Pieczka, 2006; Hodges and Edwards, 2013) who are actively engaged in the process of linking consumer lifestyles with products within neoliberal economies. Further to the concept of the PRP as 'cultural intermediary', I argue that *millennial* PRPs also align with the neoliberal notion of 'individuality as an enterprise, of the person as an entrepreneur of the self' (Gordon, 1987, p. 300 cited in du Gay, 1996, p. 72). As part of the enterprise culture, there is an expectation that the entrepreneurial self is reflexive or critically self-aware (du Gay, 1996). Wee and Brooks (2010, p. 47) note that debates on reflexivity concern, first, the extent to which actors *are* self-reflexive, and second, the 'possibility for actors to actively to fashion their identities'. The evidence in my studies suggests that not only did *some* agency PRPs have a heightened awareness of the need to adapt to different social contexts (perhaps partially due to their involvement in the research process on the topic of relationships) but it would appear that, to varying extents, they were also aware of the market value of such reflexivity. Wee and Brooks (2010, p. 50) refer to this as the 'commodification of reflexivity'. Identity projects such as 'Young Communicator of the Year' awards are evidence of the drive to commodify the self in the labour market, both within the agency as well as externally. Competing for awards is nothing new, but as Adkins (2004, p. 193) argues, tendencies towards individualisation in the contemporary world are so strong that people are 'constantly compelled to create themselves as individuals'. Adkins (2004) proposes that a more integrative account of agency and structure is offered by Bourdieu's understanding of practice. Reflexivity, within Bourdieu's account, is part of the 'habitus' itself. It involves a *tacit,* almost automatic understanding of what is required to operate in the practice rather than involving a critical reflection on structural conditions: in other words, the notion of a 'detraditionalisation' of gender and other structural features such as class, Adkins argues, may be overstated. Therefore, while PRPs may be routinely aware of the need to adapt their style for different audiences (particularly clients), this competence or skill may not be interpreted by themselves or other actors as 'emotional capital' (Illouz, 2007). Thus, while the concepts of 'individualisation' and 'detraditionalisation' of society are presented by scholars such as Beck and Beck-Gernsheim (2002) as liberating the individual from gender and other social structures, these structures are often routinely reproduced as part of the everyday habitus or lifeworld of practitioners rather than critically reflected upon.

The taken-for-grantedness of everyday routines in PR is an important point. The (masculine) discourse of professional work within the PR industry continues to focus on debates concerning the requirement for 'hard' skills such as the ability to understand big data, measurement and evaluation, and 'return on investment'. It is assumed that 'hard' skills, in turn, provide PRPs with the legitimating tools (Wehmeier, 2006) to talk about the value of reputation management at board level. However by ignoring, or downplaying, the value of the so-called 'soft skills', the extent of emotional labour required to work in a PR agency may go unrecognised or unstated. Furthermore, if emotional labour and its features are not made explicit in PRPs' occupational socialisation, and PRPs are instead left to 'sink or swim' to develop their emotional competences (O'Brien and Linehan, 2018), then the 'mental health epidemic', identified in industry research, is unlikely to diminish (CIPR, 2019, p. 7). The fact that agency directors appeared to be investing time in protecting their staff from client conflicts and emotionally risky situations suggests that equipping staff with emotional competences is not a priority. In PR office environments where millennials' intellectual skills such as research, data management, and data analysis are prized, in addition to the key 'admission' criterion of writing content (Holmes Report, 2018), there may be an unwillingness to specifically address the 'dirty' work of emotional labour (McMurray and Ward, 2014).

Global PR in the digital age: a 'new repertoire' for managing professional relationships?

PR agency clients are not just local and national, but global, and the media they need to target also fall outside national boundaries. Wajcman's (2015, p. 146) argument that mobile phones may be 'ushering in a range of new communication patterns, social relationships, and corresponding forms of life', is equally true of how relationships are developing within the professional sphere. While email communication continues to absorb valuable client hours, mobile devices populated with news apps and multiple modes of messaging enable PRPs to be both 'present in time yet absent in the flesh' (Wajcman, 2015, p. 146).

As such, PR is entering a new 'relational economy' (Licoppe, 2004), structured by generational difference, a confluence of globalised business and ICT developments: digital devices and mobile apps; client reporting/project management systems; 24/7 news and around-the-clock client contact; and workers who 'co-evolve' with their devices (Wajcman, 2015, p. 146). Echoing Licoppe (2004) in discussing social relationships, it is possible to glimpse a 'new repertoire' for managing professional relationships, facilitated by ICTs. As suggested earlier, if PRP-journalist relationships are increasingly performed remotely, both as a preference of millennial generations, as well as a necessity, rendering PRPs as 'present in time, yet absent in the flesh' (Wajcman, 2015, p. 146), then what are the implications for emotional labour? The prevalence of email used as the norm for much client and journalist communication, together with messaging services to 'cut through' to clients, already suggests a more private, less social form of relationship. The example of Jessica's emotional labour in servicing clients across continents in real time 'I never want them to see the time difference as an issue' (see Box 7.1) illustrates how PR bodies and emotions are deployed in ever more intensive ways to reduce agency costs and maximise benefit to the client. From this example it is possible to imagine human PR relationships becoming more business-focused and less social, less personal yet more connected, reliant on different modes of messaging, and involving vicarious empathy or perspective-taking (Yeomans, 2016) in efforts to simulate trusting, face-to-face, real-time relationships.

Another future scenario is where the 'seamless service' across time zones is provided in part or in full by machine learning: a robot with a built-in empathy code taking account of cultural nuances that are relevant now. As McStay (2018, p. 2) writes 'empathic media', or emergent media technologies, have the capacity 'to sense and discern what is significant for people, categorise behaviour into named emotions, act on emotional states, and make use of people's intentions and expressions'. McStay (2018, p. 8) outlines many uses of different empathic media technologies. For example, 'voice-first' artificial intelligence, such as Amazon's Alexa, illustrates how machine learning

---

Box 7.1 Presence and absence in the PR agency

An illustration of one PR 'future' was offered at Agency A, where Jessica serviced clients in the United States. She started work in the office at 12 noon and worked up to 10 hours a day, with a break for an evening meal. Her 'flexible' working hours enabled her to dedicate herself entirely to US clients through conference calls involving 10–12 people scheduled in 30-minute blocks, or through shorter video calls on her mobile phone. Much of her time was spent talking through projects with her B2B clients 'four to six hours a day'. Jessica's aim was to provide a seamless service: 'I never want them to see the time difference as an issue' therefore, exceptionally, she could be joining calls at 11.00pm. Media relations was less easy but 'only a sliver' of her work, which was largely spent on content writing for social media, and strategy work. 'I've pitched journalists in the US, but it's awkward. They might ask why a US reporter would call back to the UK. But it's not impossible'.

(Interview, March 2016)

algorithms can be trained to 'get to know people and their life contexts better'. An Alexa upgrade will enable the device to detect the frustrated, whispered speech of its users and whisper its response back (Simonite, 2018). As voice assistants developed for the home replace smartphones as easier devices to use (Simonite, 2018), it is possible to imagine how an empathic assistant like Alexa can be used in more complex business relationships where a 'voice first' relationship is required, initially to assist with internet conference calls, and, eventually, to host them.

Future research directions in emotional labour/emotion management in PR agencies

Based on the earlier discussion, future research into emotional labour in PR could examine how PRPs interact with the pre-designed 'scripts' of new technologies (as enablers or constrainers of emotion management), as well as the physical spaces PRPs and technologies occupy in which to undertake relational work. Such developments place an emphasis on theories such as actor network theory (Latour, 2005) that enable researchers to take a micro-sociological approach to study PRPs in action (Verhoeven, 2009) as they reflect on and interpret tasks and relationships in varying temporalities and spaces (Wajcman, 2015).

As suggested in Chapter 6, it is not just social and cultural interactions that are important but the 'interior monologue' (Scheff, 2000) that takes place in the deceptively simple act of providing an emotionally attuned email response, with recipient expectations that it will be swift and decisive (Tait, 2018). Psychosocial perspectives of PRP emotion management could prove fruitful in revealing how such emotional demands are negotiated. Longer periods of time spent in the field, employing ethnographic approaches, could provide deeper insights using video and photographs (e.g. Sissons, 2015), as well as autoethnographic accounts generated from participant observation and practitioner/participant diary-keeping on video or mobile phone. Future projects could explore PR's professional relationships based on the 'lived experiences' of clients and media actors.

Final thoughts: addressing the bigger picture of PR and the 'emotional turn' in society and culture

In the introduction to this book, and in subsequent chapters, I have argued that the socio-emotional dimension of PR work is missing from PR scholarship. This is partly because PR scholarship has only latterly addressed concepts that enable PR to be analysed in ways that question its role in society and culture (e.g. Ihlen et al., 2009; Edwards and Hodges, 2011; Ihlen and Fredriksson, 2018). However, even within this body of work, there is a failure to address the so-called 'emotional turn' which has prompted a wealth of studies in the social sciences and cultural studies over several decades (e.g.

Hochschild, 1983; Putnam and Mumby, 1993; Ahmed, 2004; Wulff, 2007; Greco and Stenner, 2008; McStay, 2018).

PR is one of the defining phenomena of the cultural landscape in the late twentieth and early twenty-first centuries. Not only is PR institutionalised (Fredriksson et al., 2013) within the broader structures of business and government, emotional processes are deeply embedded in promotional techniques, for example, to influence consumer purchasing decisions, address stakeholder concerns about corporate social responsibility and corporate reputation, and galvanise publics to donate money through emotional appeals (Cronin, 2018). Furthermore, the growth of social media platforms has enabled individuals who are not employed as PRPs to 'do' promotion (and emotion) in multiple ways. As we have seen in the foregoing chapters, women emulate celebrity appearance as 'aesthetic entrepreneurs'; using their smartphones to monitor and refine their online selves (Elias et al., 2017); fashion bloggers promote their passion for brands, competing for 'likes' and shares on Instagram (Duffy and Hund, 2015). And within competitive workplaces that celebrate collective and individual success, employees may habitually post and share promotional stories on social networking sites (SNS) such as LinkedIn and Twitter. Unpaid, digital labour in the form of promotional work shared by individuals through millions of posts on SNS contributes to the emotionalisation of society and culture. Edwards' (2012) theorisation of PR as 'flow' could well apply to the processes of emotionalisation, as this does not assume PR's attachment to an organisational function. These processes, which include SNSs, connect individuals acting as 'citizen-PRPs' in leading online issues-based petitions, as well as individualised 'entrepreneurs of the self' in branding their 'life projects'. Considering the broader promotional context in which PR is embedded, emotional labour/emotion management is but one micro-level aspect of the rich, emotional terrain of PR, a terrain which is deserving of much more attention. Therefore, I call for further studies that address the significance of PR in the emotional/affective turn in society and culture, as well as those outlined for emotional labour/emotion management.

References

Acker, J. (1992) From sex roles to gendered institutions. *Contemporary Sociology*, 21 (5), pp. 565–569.

Adkins, L. (2004) Reflexivity: Freedom or habit of gender? In L. Adkins and B. Skeggs, eds. *Feminism after Bourdieu*. Oxford and Malden, Blackwell Publishing, pp. 191–210.

Ahmed, S. (2004) Affective economies. *Social Text*, 22 (2), pp. 121–139.

Alvesson, M. (1998) Gender and identity. Masculinities and femininities at work in an advertising agency. *Human Relations*, 51 (8), pp. 969–1005.

Arcy, J. (2016) Emotion work: Considering gender in digital labor. *Feminist Media Studies*, 16 (2), pp. 365–368.

Beck, U. and Beck-Gernsheim, E. (2002) *Individualization*. London, Sage.

Beckett, C. and Deuze, M. (2016, July–September) On the role of emotion in the future of journalism. *Social Media + Society*, 2 (3), pp. 1–6.

Bolton, S. C. (2005) *Emotion management in the workplace.* Houndsmill, Hampshire, Palgrave Macmillan.

Bolton, S. C. and Muzio, D. (2008) The paradoxical processes of feminization in the professions: The case of established aspiring and semi-professions. *Work, Employment and Society,* 22 (2), pp. 281–299.

Bridgen, L. (2011), Emotional labour and the pursuit of the personal brand: Public relations practitioners' use of social media. *Journal of Media Practice,* 12 (1), pp. 61–76.

Butler, J. (1990) *Gender Trouble: Feminism and the subversion of identity.* New York and London, Routledge.

Cahill, S. E. (1999) Emotional capital and professional socialization: The case of mortuary science students (and me). *Social Psychology Quarterly,* 62 (2), pp. 101–16.

CIPR: Chartered Institute of Public Relations (2017) PR challenged to 'define social purpose' at CIPR national conference. 1 November. Available from: https://newsroom.cipr.co.uk/pr-challenged-to-define-n-social-purpose-at-cipr-national-conference/. Accessed 15 November 2018.

CIPR: Chartered Institute of Public Relations (2019) State of the profession 2019. London, CIPR. Available from: https://www.cipr.co.uk/sites/default/files/11812%20State%20of%20Profession_v12.pdf. Accessed 8 April 2019.

Cronin, A. M. (2018) *Public Relations Capitalism: Promotional culture, publics and commercial democracy.* Palgrave Macmillan.

Curtin, P. and Gaither, T. K. (2005) Privileging identity, difference and power: The circuit of culture as a basis for public relations theory. *Journal of Public Relations Research,* 17 (2), pp. 91–115.

Dow, B. J. and Wood, J. T. (2006) The evolution of gender and communication research: Intersections of theory, politics, and scholarship. In B. J. Dow and J. T. Wood, eds. *The Sage Handbook of Gender and Communication.* Thousand Oaks, CA, London, and New Delhi, Sage, pp. ix–xx.

Duffy, E. (2015) The romance of work: Gender and aspirational labour in the digital culture industries. *International Journal of Cultural Studies,* 19 (4), pp. 441–457.

Duffy, E. and Hund, E. (2015, July–December) 'Having it all' on social media: Entrepreneurial femininity and self-branding among fashion bloggers. *Social Media + Society,* 1 (2), pp. 1–11.

Edwards, L. (2012) Defining the 'object' of public relations research: A new starting point. *Public Relations Inquiry,* 1 (1). pp. 7–30.

Edwards, L. (2014) Discourse, credentialism and occupational closure in the communications industries: The case of public relations in the UK. *European Journal of Communication,* 29 (3), pp. 319–334.

Edwards, L. (2018) *Understanding Public Relations: Theory, culture and society.* London, Sage.

Edwards. L. and Hodges, C. E. M. eds. (2011) *Public Relations, Society and Culture: Theoretical and empirical explorations.* London and New York: Routledge.

Elias, A. S., Gill, R., and Scharff, C. (2017) Aesthetic labour: Beauty politics in neoliberalism. In A. S. Elias, R. Gill, and C. Scharff, eds. *Aesthetic Labour: Rethinking beauty politics in neoliberalism.* Basingstoke, Palgrave Macmillan, pp. 3–49.

Elmer, P. (2010) Re-encountering the PR man. *Prism,* 7 (4). Available from: http://www.prismjournal.org/fileadmin/Praxis/Files/Gender/Elmer.pdf. Accessed 28 October 2018.

Fitch, K. (2015) Feminism and public relations. In J. L'Etang, D. McKie, N. Snow, and J. Xifra, eds. *The Routledge Handbook of Critical Public Relations.* Abingdon, Oxon, Routledge, pp. 182–199.

Fitch, K. and Third, A. (2010) Working girls: Revisiting the gendering of public relations. *PRism*, 7 (4). Available from: http://www.prismjournal.org. Accessed 5 October 2018.

Fletcher, J. (1998) Relational practice: A feminist re-construction of work. *Journal of Management Inquiry*, 7 (2), pp. 168–186.

Fournier, V. (1999) The appeal to professionalism as a disciplinary mechanism. *Sociological Review*, 47 (2), pp. 280–307.

Fredriksson, M., Pallas, J., and Wehmeier, S. (2013) Public relations and neo-institutional theory. *Public Relations Inquiry*, 2 (2), pp. 183–203.

Fröhlich, R. (2004) Feminine and feminist values in communication professions: Exceptional skills and expertise or 'friendliness trap'? In M. de Bruin and K. Ross eds. *Gender and Newsroom Cultures: Identities at work.* Cresskill, NJ, Hampton Press, pp. 65–77.

Fröhlich, R. and Peters, S. B. (2007) PR bunnies caught in the agency ghetto? Gender stereotypes, organizational factors, and women's careers in PR agencies. *Journal of Public Relations Research*, 19 (3), pp. 229–254.

du Gay, P. (1996) *Consumption and Identity at Work.* London, Thousand Oaks, CA, and New Delhi, Sage.

Gherardi, S. (2015) Authoring the female entrepreneur while talking the discourse of work-family life balance. *International Small Business Journal*, 33 (6), pp. 649–666.

Gill, R., Kelan, E., and Scharff, C. (2017) A postfeminist sensibility at work. *Gender, Work and Organization*, 24 (3), pp. 226–244.

Golombisky, K. (2015) Renewing the commitments of feminist public relations theory from Velvet Ghetto to social justice. *Journal of Public Relations Research*, 27 (5), pp. 389–415.

Gordon, C. (1987) The soul of the citizen: Max Weber and Michel Foucault on rationality and government. In S. Whimster and S. Lash, eds. *Max Weber: Rationality and modernity.* London, Allen and Unwin, pp. 293–316.

Greco, M. and Stenner, P. eds. (2008) *Emotions: A social science reader.* Oxford, Routledge, pp. 1–21.

Grugulis, I. and Vincent, S. (2009) Whose skill is it anyway? Soft skills and polarization. *Work, Employment and Society*, 23 (4), pp. 597–615.

Grunig, L. A., Toth, E. L., and Hon, L. C. (2000) Feminist values in public relations. *Journal of Public Relations Research*, 12 (1), pp. 49–68.

Harvey, D. (2005) *A Brief History of Neoliberalism.* Oxford, Oxford University Press.

Hochschild, A. R. (1983) *The Managed Heart: Commercialization of human feeling.* Berkeley, University of California Press.

Hodges, C. (2006) 'PRP culture': A framework for exploring public relations practitioners as cultural intermediaries. *Journal of Communication Management*, 10 (1) pp. 80–93.

Hodges, C. M. and Edwards, L. (2013) Public relations practitioners. In J. Smith Maguire and J. Matthews, eds. *The Cultural Intermediaries Reader.* London, Sage, pp. 89–99.

Holmes, J. (2006) *Gendered Talk at Work: Constructing gender identity through workplace discourse.* Malden, MA, Oxford, and Victoria, Blackwell.

Holmes Report (2018) 2018 Global Communications Report. Available from: https://www.holmesreport.com/ranking-and-data/global-communications-report/gcr-2018-research. Accessed 28 October 2018.

Hughes, J. (2010) Emotional intelligence: Elias, Foucault, and the reflexive emotional self. *Foucault Studies*, 8, pp. 28–52.

Ihlen, Ø., van Ruler, B., and Fredriksson, M. (2009) *Public Relations and Social Theory: Key figures and concepts.* New York and London, Routledge.

Ihlen, Ø. and Fredriksson, M. (2018) *Public Relations and Social Theory: Key figures, concepts and developments*, 2nd ed. New York and Abingdon, Oxon, Routledge.

Illouz, E. (2007) *Cold Intimacies: The making of emotional capitalism.* Cambridge and Malden, MA, Polity Press.

Kaiser, S. Müller-Seitz, G., and Cruesen, U. (2008) Passion wanted! Socialisation of positive emotions in consulting firms. *International Journal of Work Organisation and Emotion*, 2, (3), pp. 305–320.

Latour, B. (2005) *Reassembling the Social: An introduction to actor-network-theory.* Oxford, Oxford University Press.

Leidner, R. (1991) Serving hamburgers and selling insurance: Gender, work and identity in interactive service jobs. *Gender and Society*, 5 (2), pp. 154–177.

Lewis, P. (2006) The quest for invisibility: Female entrepreneurs and the masculine norm of entrepreneurship. *Gender, Work and Organization*, 13 (5), pp. 453–469.

Licoppe, C. (2004) 'Connected' presence: The emergence of a new repertoire for managing social relationships in a changing communication technoscape. *Environment and Planning D: Society and Space*, 22 (1), pp. 135–156.

Lupton, B. (2000) Maintaining masculinity: Men who do 'women's work'. *British Journal of Management*, 11, special issue, pp. S33–S48.

Marsh, S. (2009) *The Feminine in Management Consulting: Power, emotion and values in consulting interactions.* Basingstoke, Palgrave Macmillan.

Mart, L. and Jackson, N. (2005) Public relations agencies in the UK travel industry: Does size matter? *PRism*, 3 (1). Available from: http://www.prismjournal.org/vol_3_iss_1.html. Accessed 2 May 2018.

McMurray, R. and Ward, J. (2014) 'Why would you want to do that?' Defining emotional dirty work. *Human Relations*, 67 (9), pp. 1123–1143.

McStay, A. (2018) *Emotional AI: The rise of empathic media.* London, Sage.

Merkelsen, H. (2011) The double-edged sword of legitimacy in public relations. *Journal of Communication Management*, 15 (2), pp. 125–143.

Mitchell, S. (2018) PR communications council announces single focus in 2018: Social purpose. *Ethical Marketing News*, 3 March. Available from: http://ethicalmarketingnews.com/%E2%80%8Bpr-communications-council-announces-single-focus-2018-social-purpose-pr. Accessed 15 November 2018.

Muzio, D., Ackroyd, S., and Chanlat, J.-F. (2008) Introduction: Lawyers, doctors and business consultants. In D. Muzio, S. Ackroyd, and J.-F. Chanlat, eds. *Redirections in the Study of Expert Labour.* Basingstoke, Palgrave Macmillan, pp. 1–30.

O'Brien, E. and Linehan, C. (2018) The last taboo? Surfacing and supporting emotional labour at work. *The International Journal of Human Resource Management*, 29 (4), pp. 693–709.

Pieczka, M. (2002) Public relations expertise deconstructed. *Media Culture and Society*, 24 (3), pp. 301–323.

Pieczka, M. (2006) 'Chemistry' and the public relations industry: An exploration of the concept of jurisdiction and issues arising. In J. L'Etang and M. Pieczka, eds. *Public Relations: Critical debates and contemporary practice.* Mahwah, NJ, and London, Lawrence Erlbaum Associates, pp. 303–327.

Pierce, J. (1995) *Gender Trials. Emotional lives in contemporary law firms.* Berkeley, CA, University of California Press.

Pompper, D. (2013) Interrogating inequalities perpetuated in a feminized field: Using critical race theory and the intersectionality lens to render visible that which

188   *Conclusions*

should not be disaggregated. In C. Daymon and K. Demetrious, eds. *Gender and Public Relations: Critical perspectives on voice, image, and identity*. London, Routledge, pp. 67–86.

Putnam, L. L. and Mumby, D. K. (1993) Organisations, emotions and the myth of rationality. In S. Fineman, ed. *Emotion in Organisations*, London, Sage, pp. 36–57.

Rakow, L. F. (1986) Rethinking gender research in communication. *Journal of Communication*, 36, pp. 11–26.

Rakow, L. F. and Nastasia, D. I. (2009) On feminist theory of public relations: An example from Dorothy E. Smith. In Ø. Ihlen, B. van Ruler, and M. Fredriksson, eds. *Public Relations and Social Theory: Key figures and concepts*. New York and Abingdon, Oxon, Routledge, pp. 252–277.

Rottenberg, C. (2014) The rise of neoliberal feminism. *Cultural Studies*, 28 (3), pp. 418–437.

Rottenberg, C. (2018) Catherine Rottenberg – How neoliberalism colonised feminism – and what you can do about it, 24 May. Available from: https://braveneweurope.com/catherine-rottenberg-how-neoliberalism-colonised-feminism-and-what-you-can-do-about-it. Accessed 28 October 2018.

van Ruler, B. (2005) Commentary: Professionals are from Venus, scholars are from Mars. *Public Relations Review*, 31 (2), pp. 159–173.

Scheff, T. J. (2000) Shame and the social bond. *Sociological Theory*, 18 (1), pp. 84–99.

Simonite, T. (2018) Amazon wants Alexa to hear your whispers and frustration. *Wired*, 20 September. Available from: https://www.wired.com/story/amazon-alexa-upgrades-whisper-alexa-guard/. Accessed 28 October 2018.

Simpson, R. (2004) Masculinities at work: The experiences of men in female dominated occupations. *Work, Employment and Society*, 18 (2), pp. 349–368.

Sims, M. P. (2018) GCR18 Pace of change in PR industry accelerates. 30 April. Available from: https://www.holmesreport.com/research/article/gcr18-pace-of-change-in-pr-industry-accelerates. Accessed 28 October 2018.

Sissons, H. (2015) Lifting the veil on the PRP-client relationship. *Public Relations Inquiry*, 4 (3), pp. 263–286.

Tait, A. (2018) Read it and weep: Why is replying to emails so hard? *New Statesman*, 18 January. Available from: https://www.newstatesman.com/science-tech/technology/2018/01/read-it-and-weep-why-replying-emails-so-hard. Accessed 28 October 2018.

Tindall, N. T. J. and Waters, R. D. (2012) Coming out to tell our stories: Using queer theory to understand the career experiences of gay men in public relations. *Journal of Public Relations Research*, 24, pp. 451–475.

Toth, E. (2001) How feminist theory advanced the practice of public relations. In R. L. Heath, ed. *Handbook of Public Relations*. Thousand Oaks, CA, London, and New Delhi, Sage, pp. 237–246.

Tsetsura, K. (2011) Is public relations a real job? How female practitioners construct the profession. *Journal of Public Relations Research*, 23 (1), pp. 1–23.

Tsetsura, K. (2014) Constructing public relations as a women's profession in Russia. *Revista Internacional de Relaciones Públicas*, 8, (4), pp. 85–110.

Turkle, S. (2008) Always on/always on you: The tethered self. In J. E. Katz, ed. *Handbook of Mobile Communication Studies*. Boston, MA, MIT University Press, pp. 121–138.

Vardeman-Winter, J., Tindall, N., and Jiang, H. (2013) Intersectionality and publics: How exploring publics' multiple identities questions basic public relations concepts. *Public Relations Inquiry*, 2, pp. 279–304.

Verhoeven, P. (2009) On Latour: Actor-network-theory (ANT) and public relations. In Ø. Ihlen, B. van Ruler, and M. Fredriksson, eds. *Public Relations and Social Theory*. New York and London, Routledge, pp. 166–185.

Waeraas, A. (2009) On Weber: Legitimacy and legitimation in public relations. In Ø. Ihlen, B. van Ruler, and M. Fredriksson, eds. *Public Relations and Social Theory*. New York and London, Routledge, pp. 301–322.

Wajcman, J. (2015) *Pressed for Time: The acceleration of life in digital capitalism*. Chicago, IL and London, The University of Chicago Press.

Wee, L. and Brooks, A. (2010) Personal branding and the commodification of reflexivity. *Cultural Sociology*, 4 (1), pp. 45–62.

Wehmeier, S. (2006) Dancers in the dark: The myth of rationality in public relations. *Public Relations Review*, 32, pp. 213–220.

Wernick, A. (1991) *Promotional Culture*. London, Sage.

Weyher, L. F. (2012) Re-reading sociology via the emotions: Karl Marx's theory of human nature and estrangement. *Sociological Perspectives*, 55 (2), pp. 341–363.

Williams, C. (1995) *Still a Man's World*. Berkeley, University of California Press.

Winterbotham, M., Vivian, D., Kik, G., Huntley Hewitt, J., Tweddle, M., Downing, C., Thomson, D., Morrice, N. and Stroud, S. (2018) *Employer skills survey 2017*. London, Department of Education/IFF Research. Available from: https://assets. publishing.service.gov.uk/government/uploads/system/uploads/attachment_ data/file/746493/ESS_2017_UK_Report_Controlled_v06.00.pdf

Witz, A. Warhurst, C., and Nixon, S. (2003) The labour of aesthetics and the aesthetics of organization. *Organization*, 10 (1), pp. 33–54.

Wouters, C. (2007) *Informalization: Manners and emotions since 1890*. London, Sage.

Wulff, H. (2007) *The Emotions: A cultural reader*. Oxford and New York, Berg.

Yeomans, L. (2010) Soft sell? Gendered experience of emotional labour in UK public relations firms, *PRism*, 7 (4). Available from: http://www.prismjournal.org. Accessed 2 October 2018.

Yeomans, L. (2013) Gendered performance and identity work in PR consulting relationships: A UK perspective. In C. Daymon and K. Demetrious, eds. *Gender and Public Relations: Critical perspectives on voice, image and identity*. London, Routledge, pp. 87–107.

Yeomans, L. (2016) Imagining the lives of others: Empathy in public relations. *Public Relations Inquiry*, 5 (1), pp. 71–92.

Yeomans, L. (2019) Is 'a new feminist visibility' emerging in the UK PR industry? Senior women's discourse and performativity in the neoliberal firm. *Public Relations Inquiry*, 8 (2), [in press].

Zerfass, A., Moreno, Á., Tench, R., Verčič, D., and Verhoeven, P. (2017) *European communication monitor 2017. How strategic communication deals with the challenges of visualisation, social bots and hypermodernity. Results of a survey in 50 countries*. Brussels, EACD/EUPRERA, Quadriga Media Berlin.

Zerfass, A., Tench, R., Verhoeven, P., Verčič, D., and Moreno, A. (2018) *European Communication Monitor 2018. Strategic communication and the challenges of fake news, trust, leadership, work stress and job satisfaction. Results of a survey in 48 countries*. Brussels, EACD/EUPRERA, Quadriga Media Berlin.

Appendix
Researching emotions: from theory to methodology

Emotions in society and culture: perspectives and key concepts

Introduction

The concept of emotion in the literature reveals a complex field that is influenced by a range of disciplines: there is no single theory of emotion. Calhoun and Solomon ask us to exercise caution in asking, 'What is an emotion?' as if 'emotions were a set of homogenous phenomena' (1984, p. 24). Kagan (2007, p. 1) concurs that 'the answers offered are riddled with ambiguity and do not enjoy the more consensual, transparent meanings of such concepts as velocity and heat'. Emotion is therefore a contested concept. Social and cultural perspectives, which contextualise this study, conceive emotions as socially constructed and emerging through social interaction: they are a product of socialisation within a culture (learning how to feel and interpret) and participation in social structures, and are subject to flux and change, depending on different social interactions in different social and cultural contexts. Within organisations, socio-cultural perspectives are concerned with the everyday constructions of emotion and meaning by organisational members. However, it is also important to examine the wider literature on emotion, since psychological and biological perspectives contribute to Hochschild's social theory of emotion discussed in Chapter 2. Furthermore, 'common sense' or popular understandings of emotion are likely to influence practitioners' discourse.

I begin by examining common sense understandings of emotion that shape everyday discourse. Such discourse associates emotion with biology; they are 'feminine' and have to be 'contained' or controlled rather than accepted as integral to what it means to be human. This 'containment' of emotion is particularly relevant to the professional context where the norms of emotional constraint are likely to differ according to status, gender, and context (Domagalski and Steelman, 2007). The norms of emotional expression are important to understanding occupational culture (Bloch, 2012). The discussion then moves on to debates surrounding the categorisations of emotion, including the problem of labelling emotions in isolation from their social contexts. The distinctions between the terms 'emotion' and 'affect' are then discussed, including the limitations of using the terms 'positive affect' and 'negative affect' in social situations (Hochschild, 1983, p. 202). There follows a brief discussion of the organisational behaviour (OB) literature on emotion, and its functionalist emphasis, before introducing the social theories of emotion that form the basis of my analyses.

Being in control: the limits of 'common sense' views of emotion in Western culture

Western 'common sense' understandings of emotion are first, that they are biologically based and second, feminine (Petersen, 2004). Petersen suggests these are the commonly accepted notions of emotion that are part of the mindset of Western culture and identified through popular discourse. Further to this, he argues that psychological perspectives 'prevail' (2004, p. 3). The first prevailing common sense view is of *human biology* as a driver of emotion. This perspective encompasses the *physical* (and observable) arousal and flow of emotions experienced in the body both in face-to-face and large-scale social settings, while the *cognitive psychological* understanding of emotion is concerned with subjective perceptions and evaluations of objects and the emotions that they arouse within the individual. The 'human biology' literature is explored further under the 'emotion versus affect' subsection later in this chapter.

The second prevailing common sense view, according to Petersen, is that emotion is subjective and feminine. Writing from a *cultural perspective,* the anthropologist Catherine Lutz broadens out the discussion on emotion by placing it firmly within Western ethnocentrism (2007, p. 21). Emotion is associated with subjectivity and the individual. In US culture, Lutz notes that 'emotions are treated as the private property of the self' and cannot be judged by others based on observations (Lutz, 2007, p. 27). Feelings are private: they 'belong' to the individual. The general, common sense view of controlling one's emotions is therefore culturally bound, and quite often associated with femininity. Lutz's study of emotion found that American women more than men talked about the need to control their emotions as if attempting to counter social stereotypes of women as 'irrational, weak and dangerous' (Lutz, 2008, p. 65). However, a feminist reading of 'control' is that women are expected to act on their emotions passively and privately instead of taking action against a possible social injustice or problem that they experience. Lutz (2008) argues that in Western societies still largely dominated by male values, where cool rationality is prized, giving vent to strong feelings is not seen as in women's best interests. Although, in an era of the Trump US presidency, characterised by unpredictable emotional outbursts on Twitter, the idea of 'cool rationality' as a male value could be contested, women are nevertheless subject to gender stereotypes of emotion (i.e. women are more emotional compared to men). Women are penalised for showing too much emotion, or not enough, and this is particularly true in evaluations of women leaders (Brescoll, 2016).

A common sense, 'container' view of emotion – where emotion is regarded as belonging to the individual and subject to self-governance – is highly relevant to an examination of public relations (PR). Public relations practitioners (PRPs), and women in particular, need to be mindful of the professional and cultural norms of emotion management within the workplace in handling relationships with colleagues, clients, and journalists. Indeed, as Bourne (2016) argues, drawing on the work of Lury and Ward (1997, p. 87), the emotional purpose of PR is to assuage the 'producer anxiety or uncertainty' of organisational decision-makers in remaining relevant to consumers. Hence emotion management is highly pertinent to PR in its role of establishing organisational legitimacy on behalf the client, as well the 'never ending' pursuit for relevance itself (Bourne, 2016, p. 123).

Emotional discourses are often contrasted with opposing discourses; hence the contrasting discourses on 'emotion' and 'thought' are often expressed in the psychological terms 'affect' and 'cognition'; the romantic and philosophical 'passion' and 'reason'; and the everyday terms 'feeling' and 'thinking' (Lutz, 2007). She writes: 'Encoded in or related to that contrast is an immense portion of the Western world view of the person, of social life, and of morality' (Lutz, 2007, p. 21). While emotion is associated with the body and thought with the mind, for someone to be *unemotional* connotes a lack of *humanity;* yet to *have feelings* presents the view of emotions as being natural, even primitive forces and therefore a sign of weakness, even a 'character defect' (Lutz, 2008, p. 63). Lutz (2007, p. 21) observes that within the Western, predominantly psychological, world view, both thought and emotion are conceived as 'features of the individual' and *contained* within the 'boundaries of the person' and as such are 'construed as psychological rather than social phenomena'.

Studies of metaphors of emotion within the English language demonstrate that the 'container' view is embedded within language, so that popular metaphors of anger, for example, refer to bodily feelings of 'heat' within a pressurised container that are susceptible to 'boiling' (Kövecses, 2000, p. 22). To what extent lay views of emotion determine or influence scientific theory, or vice versa, is the subject of debate; however, Kövecses' studies suggest that expert (i.e. psychological) theories of emotion build on and focus on aspects of language-based folk models of emotion (Kövecses, 1991).

A fairly limited, individual view of emotion (a 'container' view) has led numerous theorists to categorise observable human emotions, starting with facial expressions through to more recent studies in neuroscience, which identify, through brain scans and the mapping of neural circuits, the biological source of primary emotions (Damasio, 2006, pp. 131–134). The next section examines how emotions have been categorised by some theorists in order to distinguish between the so-called 'basic' or primary emotions and those that emerge within social situations.

Categorisations of emotion

A *theory of affects*, proposed by the social psychologist Silvan Tomkins (1962), considers eight 'primary' emotions arising from facial expressions: shame, interest, surprise, joy, anger, fear, distress, and disgust. Tomkins' theory, based on facial expressions and influenced by Darwin, has reduced in significance mainly because many privately held emotions are not directly communicated through facial expressions (Kagan, 2007); and yet Tomkins' work provides imaginative, discursive renditions of emotions – in contrast to the cognitive accounts of emotion that do little to communicate how and through which social situations feelings are experienced (Sedgwick and Frank, 1995).

In *The Sociology of Emotions*, Turner and Stets (2005, pp. 14–15) present a table of 20 categorisations of primary emotions. For example, within the table, Plutchik (1980) identifies a slightly different set of eight basic or 'primary' emotions from Tomkins. These are: acceptance, surprise, fear, sadness, disgust, anticipation, anger, and joy: mixtures of these emotions are called 'secondary' and 'tertiary' emotions because of their distance from the basic emotions. Kemper (1987), meanwhile, identifies four universal emotions as 'primary': fear, anger, depression, and happiness. Similarly to Plutchik, Kemper's secondary emotions emerge from the individual experiencing one or more of the primary emotions. The combination of fear and anger, as examples of primary emotions, can lead to hate, jealousy, and envy, as examples of secondary emotions. Kemper argues that secondary emotions emerge from the context of experiencing one or more of the primary emotions and are thus socially constructed, so that for example, the primary emotions of fear and anger can give rise to the social emotions of hate, jealousy, and envy.

Writing within the discipline of neuroscience, Damasio (2004) offers three further categorisations of emotion: background emotions, primary emotions, and social emotions. Background emotions constitute a 'state of being', depending on whether internal needs are being satisfied (such as state of health); primary emotions comprise the more familiar list of 'basic' emotions or 'emotions-proper' (p. 43) – fear, anger, disgust, surprise, sadness, and happiness. Social emotions, according to Damasio, include sympathy, embarrassment, shame, guilt, pride, jealousy, envy, gratitude, admiration, indignation, and contempt. Damasio posits that even the most primitive species such as worms exhibit intelligent social behaviours when faced with food scarcities and are not subject to cultural rules. However, Damasio also accepts that in many social situations, the so-called 'hard-wired' biologically based emotions of fear, anger, sadness, happiness, disgust, and surprise only become activated through social observation and interaction.

With the exception of Tomkins among this select list of theorists, categorisations of emotion do not shed light on how and when emotions are expressed in different social situations; how those expressing emotion discursively understand them; or how emotions may be used as a resource. The labels we give to emotions are also problematic: 'depression' (Kemper) could be read as 'sadness' (Plutchik), but equally, 'depression' may be felt while 'sadness' is an outward expression of depression.

A social constructionist perspective approaches the concept of emotion somewhat differently. Social constructionists such as Gordon (1981), Harré (2003), and Lutz (2003) share the view that vocabularies of emotion, or the labels we use to represent emotional expression, are learned through socialisation within a specific cultural and social context, and are therefore unlikely to be universal. For example, Harré cautions against making assumptions about a word such as 'anger' without proper 'attention to the local moral order' (Harré, 2003, p. 147). Therefore, the emotions acceptable to be displayed within a professional setting are likely to be governed by socio-cultural and professional norms. The social constructionist perspective including that of the professional setting is explored later in this Appendix.

'Emotion' versus 'affect'

Some of the difficulties that arise from categorisations and understandings of emotion may be attributed to the distinction between the terms *emotion* and *affect*. Gorton's (2007, p. 4) detailed discussion of the various perspectives in the literature presents a fluid picture where 'emotion' and 'affect' are used interchangeably to refer to the feelings that we negotiate 'in the public sphere' (emotion) and experience 'through the body' (affect). More precisely, according to Probyn (2005, p. 11), 'emotion refers to cultural and social expression, whereas affects are of a biological and physiological nature'. A further distinction, between emotion and *feelings*, is proposed by the influential and popular neuroscientist Antonio Damasio (2000, 2004, 2006) who regards an emotion as a physical response to stimuli of which one is not necessarily conscious, whereas feelings are something that one is consciously aware of happening – in other words thoughts (cognitions) are used to evaluate the emotions experienced.

Some theorists, however, insist on greater precision in the use of the terms emotion and affect. For example, Ducey (2007), following the ideas of Massumi (2002) and Spinoza, replaces Damasio's 'emotion' with 'affect', using Negri's definition of affect: 'the power to act' (Negri, 1999, p. 79), which refers to the body's capacity to affect and be affected. Therefore 'affects' are experienced both consciously and unconsciously, whereas feelings are the recognised outcomes of affects. Using these two terms, suggests Ducey, sociologists can more readily make the link between affects (level of intensity experienced in the body) to the significance of feelings that are experienced and exposed through language. Using this model, the experience of a negative 'affect' may be differentially expressed as 'anger' or 'frustration' according to the prevailing norms of the social context; thus, we can change how we interpret affects.

Other sociologists, such as Wettergren (2017, p. 819), regard affect theory (which she calls the 'unconscious counterpart of emotion') as unhelpful to the development of the sociology of emotion, due to its focus on 'the unspoken, bodily, pre-symbolic, unconscious, "drives" that influence social actors without their knowing'. She argues that the sociology of emotions most important task (echoing Lutz) is 'undoing the western modernist dichotomy between reason and emotion', while affect theory reinforces the dichotomy of the mind and body. This position is supported by the philosopher Robert Solomon, who argues against the 'myth' of emotions as being 'in the mind'. Drawing on Aristotle and the Stoics, Solomon (2007, p. 158) asserts that 'emotions arise, for the most part, in the nexus of our interpersonal relationships'. He notes that while a number of philosophers have attempted to adopt an anti-Cartesian position (referring to Descartes's dualism of mind and the body), few have succeeded, with the exception of phenomenologists such as Sartre, who saw consciousness as 'pure activity' and 'some of this activity is the having of emotions' (p. 155). Furthermore, a phenomenological position, as I have adopted in this book, 'highlights and celebrates' subjectivity and emotions, defined as 'acts of consciousness' (Solomon, 2007, pp. 156–157).

What emerges from critiques of psychobiological perspectives on emotion are different world views to that of social constructionism and social interactionism. The examination of emotions from both biological and psychological perspectives supports a 'container' view of emotion (or affect): that emotions start with the self; they are needs and drives held deeply within the individual that are aroused by external stimuli. As Burkitt (2014) argues in his critique of Damasio's understanding of emotions, developments in neuroscience sustain the view that external stimuli, while triggering certain emotions, are nonetheless non-specific objects, and 'rarely are these "objects" other people with whom we interact' (Burkitt, 2014, p. 82). That we can identify emotional response systems through functional magnetic resonance imaging scans and therefore 'know' the source of anger or fear, for example, by displaying visual patterns of arousal in the brain is compelling; however, the social situations (meanings and context) in which anger or fear is outwardly expressed or '*become* in social interaction' (Sieben and Wettergren, 2010, p. 6) receive less attention when viewed from a psychobiological perspective.

Having critiqued 'common sense' and psychobiological (i.e. highly individualised) perspectives of emotion, it is nevertheless important to bear these perspectives in mind when analysing the meaning structures of PRPs in discussing emotion management strategies, including the emotional language that emerges from practitioners' accounts of their everyday interactions. In the next section I introduce the literature on the sociology of emotion and the various strands within it, including the micro-sociological analysis that guides the approach in this book.

The sociology of emotion

One of the earliest volumes that set out a research agenda in the sociology of emotion was published by the US sociologist Theodore Kemper in 1990.

Kemper claimed that '1975 was the watershed year' in the new sociological sub-discipline (Kemper, 1990, p. 3). The 'watershed' was partly attributed to Hochschild's early theorising of the sociology of feeling and emotion which led ultimately to the publication of *The Managed Heart* (Hochschild, 1975, 1979, 1983) and partly attributed to other theorists, notably Collins (1975) and Scheff (1979). Kemper's 1990 volume was therefore an attempt to consolidate the sub-discipline within the American sociological tradition, in which all three mentioned theorists, as well as Kemper himself, played a major role. Another notable scholar included in Kemper's volume and of relevance to my research approach is Denzin (1990, p. 108), who strongly advocated a phenomenological approach to interrogate actors' 'lived emotional experience'. Denzin's vision was to:

> locate the human being within language and within emotionality. We must inquire into what kind of gendered emotional being this late postmodern period is creating [...] Our methods must always be interpretive, phenomenological, critical and biographical.
>
> (Denzin, 1990, pp. 108–109)

Denzin (1990, p. 108) presciently described and criticised the trajectory of a large part of sociological theorising which turned 'emotions into variables that can be measured and studied [...] Indeed, lived emotional experiences cannot be meaningfully quantified'. Not being able to quantify something is a challenge to any researcher who is looking for legitimacy both within and outside academia; indeed, one of the questions I was asked by a practitioner when undertaking my research was 'how do you quantify emotional labour'? The point of the research discussed in this volume is not to measure how much emotional labour is experienced in PR, but to understand when, how, and why it is experienced.

Within the US literature, Turner and Stets (2005, 2006) have subsequently contributed to, as well as extensively reviewed, the sociology of emotion, broadening Kemper's initial work. Sociologists, according to the authors, are concerned with 'the dynamics of the self, interaction, social structure and culture' (Turner and Stets, 2005, p. 23). In *The Sociology of Emotion*, the authors group sociological theories of emotion into seven clusters: dramaturgical and cultural theories; ritual theories; symbolic interactionist theories; symbolic interactionist theories incorporating psychoanalytic ideas; exchange theories; structural theories; and evolutionary theories. The first four of these theory clusters are micro-sociological perspectives: exchange theories tend more towards social psychological approaches; structural theories as macro-sociological and evolutionary theories connected with sociobiology and brain evolution. The discussion in the following section is not linked exclusively to Turner and Stets' theory clusters but begins with a brief overview of micro-sociological analyses offered by Calhoun et al. (2007) which is helpful to understanding Hochschild's approach as well as the approach I adopt in this book.

Micro-sociological analyses

Calhoun et al. (2007) identify three major strands in micro-sociological analysis: symbolic interactionism is the most prominent strand, arising from the works of Mead (1934) and Blumer (1969) and linked to the pragmatist philosophy which posited that social order and all knowledge were achieved in 'practically situated action' (Calhoun et al., 2007, p. 25). A second strand of micro-sociology is founded in the European philosophy of phenomenology, arising from Husserl and developed into social phenomenology by Schütz (1970, 1972) and social constructionism by Berger and Luckmann (1966). Garfinkel's (1967) ethnomethodology represented a further step in this line of thought to understanding the everyday experiences of ordinary people and how they construct knowledge or account for social reality. Calhoun et al. (2007, p. 25) call this a 'bottom up approach' to the study of culture. A third, distinctive strand, which focuses on interpersonal interaction, is represented by the work of Goffman (1959), in understanding how people present themselves to others.

The first two clusters of theory in Turner and Stets' (2005) review, *dramaturgical and cultural theories* and *ritual theories*, draw inspiration from the works of Goffman, the first cluster emphasising 'performance' and the role of culture in shaping interactions; the second examines the rhythm of interactional processes. Hochschild's social theory of emotion (1983) is included in the first of these two clusters. The third and fourth clusters, labelled as *symbolic interactionist theories* and *symbolic interactionist theories incorporating psychoanalytic* ideas, draw initially on the work of George Herbert Mead and Charles Horton Cooley.

Within the interactionist perspective, emotion is the product of ongoing narratives with the self, and the self in relation to others (dialectics). Katz (1999, p. 329) provides an example of the interactionist perspective:

> …when one is aware that others are observing the flowering of one's emotions, one is likely to take care to shape the message about the typically invisible aspect of one's identity that will become visible […] people often struggle to provide a visible script, a cultural explanation that will make sense of what observers will see.

Thus, from a social interactionist perspective, emotions are sense-making functions and link to a person's ideas of self-identity. As such, outward expressions of emotion such as crying or laughter can metamorphose – 'rise and decline in the vibrant flow of social life' (Katz, 1999, p. 3). In *How Emotions Work*, Katz (1999) drew on Mead's symbolic interactionism and Schütz's notion of 'intersubjectivity', which refers to the social knowledge that is common to, and constituted by, individuals who share the world of everyday life: the 'lifeworld', based on the assumption that others have the same 'consciousness and will, desires and emotions' (Schütz, 1970, p. 310).

While Hochschild is not referenced by Turner and Stets (2005) in their discussion of interactionist perspectives, it is clear from Hochschild's own work (discussed in Chapter 2) that the interactionist perspective was a primary influence in generating her social theory of emotion management, specifically the work of Gerth and Mills (1964) who was influenced by Mead (Hochschild, 1983, p. 223). Yet, if emotion is regarded as a 'signal function' (Hochschild, 1983, p. 22), a communicative or relational practice, then the analysis of socially constructed emotions that reveal structures of power, gender, race, and so on is key to accessing meaning among cultures and specifically occupational cultures within organisations. Therefore, while 'the interactionist model is used most widely internationally' (Wettergren, 2017, p. 821) in the study of emotions, my belief is that Schütz's notion of 'intersubjectivity' of individuals who share the occupational 'lifeworld' adequately accommodates the two perspectives of social constructionism and social interactionism. The following section explores the study of emotion within organisations, beginning with a critique of the OB literature and leading on to constructionist approaches to emotion in organisations.

Emotion in organisations

OB research on emotion

Much of the literature on emotion in organisations has emerged within the field of OB. Writing in 2011, Ashkanasy and Humphrey (2011, p. 214) observed an 'explosion' of interest in emotion within work settings during the previous 15 years. In their extensive review of the OB literature on emotion and affect, they attribute the initial interest in emotion in organisational settings to the work of Hochschild (1983) and subsequently to Weiss and Cropanzano (1996) with the publication of *Affective Events Theory*.

The functionalist emphasis of OB means that it is associated with management problem-solving. Many of the studies presented in Ashkanasy and Humphrey's review attempt to quantify, measure, and show how emotion may be understood and utilised for management purposes. Emotional labour studies in OB measure the frequency, intensity, variety, and duration of surface and deep acting (e.g. Brotheridge and Lee, 2003); examine leaders using 'emotional labor tactics' (Ashkanasy and Humphrey, 2011, p. 219) such as deep acting to spread 'emotional contagion' among their followers (e.g. Humphrey, 2008; Humphrey et al., 2008); and link emotional display rules to organisational policies and the need for the emotional culture or 'climate' to be 'healthy' by keeping negative emotional events to a minimum (e.g. Kelly and Barsade, 2001; Härtel et al., 2002). From a functionalist perspective, emotional labour studies help organisations to understand: first, the psychological outcomes of emotional labour such as individual burnout, exhaustion, negative/positive affect; second, how leaders' awareness of surface/deep acting can be utilised to influence others; and third, characteristics of a positive and 'healthy' organisational culture including organisational policies that limit the demands for emotional labour from employees. The bias in mainstream OB towards psychology and functionalist, managerialist approaches within the studies reviewed by Ashkanasy and Humphrey (2011) suggests a marginalisation of a body of interpretive and critical accounts of socially constructed emotion as well as interactionist approaches in organisational settings that recognise power dynamics and the influence of social structure and culture in everyday life.

Constructionist approaches on emotion in organisations

The British sociologist Fineman (2010, p. 24) critiqued much of the research on emotion in organisations as 'more an inside-out affair than outside-in' meaning that emotions are conceived as 'within-person phenomena' to the detriment of societal issues. The 'problemetisation' of emotion, as already argued in this chapter, is missing in much of the research on emotion in organisations, which, as Fineman notes, is instrumental in orientation rather than critical. Fineman (2010) argues for a shift from the individual-psychological towards an understanding of the construction of emotion within the politicised contexts of organisations, a position that is taken by scholars contributing to Critical Management Studies (CMS), a few of whom are referenced in this volume (e.g. Collinson and Hearn, 1996; Alvesson and Willmott, 2002).

'Emotionologies' defined as 'politico–ideological constructs' refer to institutionally approved 'stocks of knowledge, vocabularies, feeling and display rules', or emotional discourses that are deemed as appropriate emotions, and are often reflected through the media (Fineman, 2010, p. 27). An example of this is the way that society feels towards specific social groups, for example, asylum seekers, but also occupational groups such as bankers, estate agents, and PRPs. Therefore a micro-level study of an occupational group such as PRPs should take account of the ways in which PRPs emotionally construct their work *in relation to* the macro-level professional and societal discourse(s) about PR consultants. Fineman (2010, p. 28) argues not only for an understanding of structural 'emotionologies', but an understanding of organisational settings that are 'often supporting a dynamic of competing or contradictory emotions'. Competing emotionologies, according to Fineman (2010), are undertheorised. Sieben and Wettergren (2010, p. 3) put this in another way:

> [...] a theory of emotions promises to account for the link between social structure and individual actors. This may enhance our understanding of the ways in which social structures are not only maintained and reproduced, but also altered, in social interactions through the mechanisms of power and status (Collins 1990; Kemper 2006), as well as well as through mechanisms of group conformity (Goffman 1959), the emotional

orientation in the complex social landscape and the construction and internalization of social roles, identities and self-perceptions.

By way of illustration, Brook (2013) theorises and emphasises the link between actors and social structure using a dialectical conceptualisation of emotional labour, proposing that workers' subjective and collective 'personal meanings' are in a continuous dialogue and contest with management's dominant 'social meanings', for example, of what it means to be 'professional' or 'caring'. Within many contemporary service settings, a recruiting organisation's typical job advertisement constructs the ideal emotional worker using phrases such as 'outgoing, engaging personality', 'passionate about delivering an excellent customer service', and 'ability to remain calm under pressure'. These same phrases apply to a range of catering and hospitality roles through to marketing, PR, and event management roles. Thus, emotional labour starts with the job application as the first point of negotiation, challenging jobseekers' identities and self-perceptions about meeting increasingly uniform emotional demands as well as any technical skill that might be required.

The social construction of emotion and socialisation

A social constructionist view of emotion emphasises the learning of emotional vocabularies and behaviour through socialisation within a society or culture. Socialisation is defined as 'the comprehensive and consistent induction of an individual into the objective world of a society or a sector of it' (Berger and Luckmann, 1966, p. 150). Society, according to Berger and Luckmann, is an 'ongoing dialectical process' experienced by the individual as an 'objective and subjective reality' (p. 149). 'Primary socialisation' happens in childhood whereby an individual becomes a member of society through a process of internalisation in which the individual understands the meaning of events through socialising agents such as parents. According to Scheff (1990) the emotion of 'shame' is crucial in the socialisation of emotions primarily because it is associated from an early age with the emotions of grief, anger, and fear within specific social contexts – for example, anger (or loss of emotional self-control) about a child's behaviour, leading to feelings of shame that one is angry in relation to the social norms governing angry outbursts. The social norms and taboos that became institutionally embedded and served to regulate emotional self-control during social interactions were of central concern to Elias in his theorising of the civilising process. For Elias, the sociohistorical process of civilisation in Western society simultaneously increased human interconnectedness and, yet, gave modern individuals the 'capacity to have a detached attitude towards themselves and their relationships with others [...] and hold back their emotions to an unhealthy degree' (Smith, 2001, pp. 21–22). There was, for example, a 'decisive role played in this civilizing process by a very specific change in the feelings of shame and delicacy' in everyday standards of behaviour. Elias describes 'sociogenic fears', referring to the moving threshold of socially acceptable behaviour and the fear of being disapproved of, as 'one of the central problems of the civilizing process' (Elias, 1936 in Goudsblom and Mennell, 1998, p. 41). Shame, conceived by Scheff (2000, p. 84) as the 'master' emotion, is discussed in the following pages. My selection of shame as warranting particular attention owes to its relevance to occupational contexts. The relevance of shame and its variants, including embarrassment, to PRPs is similar to that of any professional who is concerned with status and establishing a trustworthy professional identity; no one in a professional situation wants to be put in an embarrassing position with a client.

Turning to 'secondary socialisation', this is defined as 'any subsequent process that inducts an already socialized individual into new sectors of the objective world of his society' (Berger and Luckmann, 1966, p. 150). Such a 'sector' or institution of society is the workplace. In their case study of management consulting firms (which share some characteristics with PR firms such as relatively flat hierarchies and client work), Kaiser et al. (2008) investigated the experiences of novices and the way their emotions, especially positive emotions, were socialised. In Kaiser et al.'s case study, internal socialisation agents were predominantly 'superiors, colleagues and subordinates'. Of these three groups, superiors, including individual mentors, frequently acted as 'powerful role models' for young professionals, not only in conferring technical expertise but also introducing novices to other high-ranking colleagues, thus enabling novices to feel 'comfortable' within the firm. Further, clients were also reported to have a strong influence among the novices interviewed. The level of importance accorded to clients as external socialisation agents was related to the extent of the '"client first" orientation' of consulting firms (Kaiser et al., 2008, p. 314). The authors concluded that some novices struggled to keep up their enthusiasm for solving client problems, leading to feelings of exhaustion or stress in extreme cases and possibly displays of inauthentic positive attitude, echoing Hochschild's emotional labour critique of the 'feeling rules' prescribed by management in organisations. Emotional labour studies that are constructionist in approach view management 'feeling rules' as socialising attempts that are inculcated among new recruits through induction schemes and continuous training. However, these socialising attempts may be embraced, subverted, or resisted, as recent emotional labour studies have demonstrated.

While a *discourse perspective* of emotion is not the primary analytical approach in this volume, it warrants attention because a focus on language is one of three major lines of argument in the constructionist approach (Gergen and Gergen, 2003). Meaning structures are derived from the analysis of language and discourse. Discourse constructs the outward expression of emotion as fluid and temporary rather than 'an enduring state of mind' (Edwards, 2005, p. 237). In discussing emotional discourse, the social psychologist Wetherell (2005, p. 24) observes that emotion talk is part of discourse activity, which in itself is a 'form of work' or social action: 'To report on an emotion or a feeling is also very commonly a rhetorical activity and the display of emotion does some interactional business'. Discourses, then, are framed by the specific contexts in which they are deployed as Wetherell observes: 'to speak at all is to speak from a position' (p. 23); in other words, emotion talk is linked to the presentation of self with a specific audience in mind.

Analyses of actors' emotion talk, while enabling emotive language to be explored in detail, require an understanding of primary and secondary emotions to interpret what is actually being expressed both verbally and non-verbally within social and cultural conventions. For example, Turner and Stets (2005) cite the work of Lewis (1971) who examined feelings of shame denial in therapist-patient interactions. While individuals exhibited outward signs of shame such as blushing in recalling a negative experience, they labelled their feelings as 'foolish' or 'stupid'. Within the emotional conventions of the workplace, both men and women might 'draft' and re-draft inner emotional states (Dennett, 1991) to re-formulate anger into frustration or even exhibit a denial of anger to enable their feelings to be re-directed towards more positive outcomes. This latter point is particularly relevant to understanding the *choice of emotional language* employed by PRPs to provide acceptable, controlled accounts of the feelings they experience within professional contexts and organisations – in other words, the emotional labour that is involved in their everyday practice. Emotional labour and its concepts are discussed in greater depth in Chapter 2.

Shame: a salient social emotion

Shame, as already argued, is perhaps the most salient of social emotions in that it is connected to experiences of the self in different social situations. Interestingly, Tomkins (1962) lists shame as a primary emotion (based on facial expressions) whereas Damasio (2004), writing from a neuroscience perspective, places it within the list of secondary or social emotions. Thomas Scheff, who is cited as a leading sociologist in his work on the emotion of shame (Katz, 1999; Turner and Stets, 2005; Bericat, 2015), identifies shame as the 'premier' or master emotion (Scheff, 2000, p. 84) and in common with Tomkins (1962), he considers shame as a category in its own right, located among the basic or primary emotions. He argues that although shame is not explicitly labelled or defined within the sociological literature, it has often been tangentially discussed. Scheff critically reviews the work of six sociologists who have studied the social dimensions of shame – Simmel (1904), Cooley (1922), Elias (1978, 1982, 1983), Sennett and Cobb (1973), Lynd (1958), and Goffman (1967), as well as the work of a psychologist/psychoanalyst Helen Lewis (1971) who argued that shame arose from threats to the 'social bond'.

Of the sociologists' work reviewed, Goffman (1967) is considered by Scheff to have made the most important contribution to the centrality of emotion in sociology. His work on the presentation of self, embarrassment and avoidance of embarrassment in everyday, social relationships, and the idea of 'facework' is discussed in Chapter 2. Goffman, according to Scheff, built on the work of Cooley and the concept of the 'looking-glass self' which became a 'leading trope for understanding the self' in the first part of the twentieth century (Katz, 1999, p. 142). Similarly to Hochschild's critique of Goffman, however, Scheff notes that Goffman defines the emotion of shame as behavioural and physiological, while ignoring the inner experience of feelings. In developing a sociological theory of shame which, drawing on Lewis (1971), he defines as a 'threat to the social bond' (Scheff, 2000, p. 95), Scheff turns to the psychoanalytic literature. Scheff observes that within the psychoanalytic literature, the discussion of shame (as opposed to 'drives') is somewhat marginalised, but he singles out Helen Lewis (1971) as particularly influential in identifying shame discourse (or shame 'markers') in verbatim transcripts of hundreds of psychotherapy sessions. She argued that every person feared social disconnection from others, but also in relation to the 'interior monologue in which we see ourselves from the point of view of others' (Scheff, 2000, p. 95).

Scheff (2000, pp. 96–97) goes on to define shame as a 'large family of emotions that include many cognates and variants, most notably embarrassment, humiliation, and related feelings such as shyness that involve reactions to rejection or feelings of failure or inadequacy'. Drawing primarily on Goffman's (1967) theory of 'face-threatening acts' (also Scheff, 1990 and Clark, 1990), Charlotte Bloch (2010) identified from the analysis of interviews with victims, five main categories of negative acts and bullying in the workplace: scolding; ignoring; challenging professional identity and feelings of pride; negative gossip; and humour. For example, damaged social bonds arising from others contesting aspects of face resulted in interviewees' experience of isolation and feelings of humiliation, shame, revenge, resentment and being attacked, as well as a downgrading of the 'situated self'.

As I have emphasised in this appendix, shame is found in almost all social interaction and is connected to other strong, negative emotions such as anger, fear, and grief. Shame, anger, and humiliation may well be the emotions that professionals seek to avoid in their everyday relationships as they navigate potential face-threatening acts. The nature of the PRPs' work means that all relationships are important because they are part of the service offer to clients. Thus, practitioners are likely to seek secure social bonds, which Scheff refers to as 'attunement' whereby 'actors attend both to their own self and voice and to the other's self and voice i.e. there is a balance between nearness and distance to self and the other' (Bloch, 2010, p. 132). As Burkitt (2014) argues from his study of NHS nurses, emotional attunement is a form of empathetic communication which is necessary in order to interpret situations correctly and make accurate, on-the-spot assessments, particularly in crisis situations. The need for PR professionals to make such assessments may also help explain their motivations to perform emotional labour, for example, maintaining effort to keep channels of communication open with 'difficult' journalists so that when a news story breaks, the relationship, if somewhat asymmetric, is already established.

Methodology: researching emotion in PR agencies

The empirical studies, which comprise Chapters 5 and 6, adopted a social phenomenological approach, which is concerned with analysing what people mean when they talk about things in their everyday life (Aspers, 2006, 2009). Few scholars have published empirical approaches in social phenomenology, the closest to PR being the work of Svensson (2007) who explicated the *inter-subjective* (Schütz, 1970), or shared, common sense meanings in marketing work revealed through narrative analysis. The question 'what is marketing work?' was pursued with the aim of 'dereifying' the textbook marketing management approach which Svensson critiques for constructing marketing work 'beyond human life and social practice' (p. 272) and as a 'set of neutral (in terms of ideologies and values) tools' (p. 273). The phenomenological approach thus encourages the researcher to question assumptions of the professional lifeworld in order to make the meanings of everyday, taken-for-granted practice visible to those outside it. Furthermore, as I have already argued, following Denzin (1990), the social phenomenological approach is well suited to studies that adopt social constructionist and interactionist approaches to emotion.

Exploring professional relationships in PR (2008–2012)

My first study comprised PRPs who were based in two major English locations. These are referred to as City A and City B. I conducted studies with six participants in total, following the discussion in Creswell (2007, p. 126) in which samples ranging from three to ten participants are recommended for phenomenological research. A range of sampling strategies are available in qualitative research; however in phenomenology, it is important to investigate a phenomenon among those who have experienced it. To arrive at a suitable sample for study, providing rich insights, sampling was based on key criteria and stratification. Participants were recruited on the basis of the following criteria:

- reflective of the largest age grouping of workers in the PR agency sector. My actual sample participants were aged between 23 and 32, which were closely aligned to the largest age grouping when fieldwork was undertaken (CIPR, 2010).
- worked as PR consultants in a PR firm;
- provided services to clients and journalists in an account handling role; and were
- willing to participate in the research project during two phases of fieldwork, including diary-keeping during the first phase.

The sample may be described as stratified purposeful to enable comparisons to be made between male and female participants. Four female and two male

PR consultants were recruited through academic contacts and practitioner alumni. Identifying male participants who met the criteria was a difficult task. As well as being far fewer in number, male agency practitioners were more likely to ignore requests to participate than their female agency counterparts, or their male counterparts working in-house.

Within an established PR agency, a client account team will usually comprise junior account executives (entry level), account executives, account managers, and account directors. Account directors are usually the 'team leaders', have the main responsibility for client contact, and generally have more seniority in the job. The attributes of participants in this study are presented in Table A.1.

Phenomenological study primarily includes the collection of information through in-depth, long interviews of more than one hour (Creswell, 1998; Kvale and Brinkmann, 2009), although as has been shown in the work of Svensson (2007), other data sources might include non-participant observation and other qualitative methods. Interviews were the primary information source for this study. The data collection process is shown in Table A.2. A preliminary study was undertaken to test the interview protocol. This resulted in one adjustment to the questions, which was to include colleague relationships.

Table A.1 Attributes of PR practitioners

Position	Name[*]	Highest educational qualification/CIPR membership	Location	Length of PR experience at the time of first interview
Account director	John	MA degree	City A	10
Senior account manager	Pamela	BA degree	City A	4
Senior account manager[**]	Gill	BA degree	City B	5
Account manager	Emma	MA degree	City A	5
Senior account executive[**]	Alison	MA degree CIPR member	City B	2
Account manager	Graham	BA degree CIPR member	City B	1

Adapted from Yeomans (2013, p. 36)
[*]pseudonyms; [**]part of preliminary study.

Table A.2 Three-stage process of data collection

	Interview 1	Interview 2
1 Preliminary study	Participants 1 and 2	Participants 1 and 2
2 Main study	Participants 3–6	Participants 3–6
3 Re-contact all six participants	Request participants' comments on a generic 'description of practice' based on thematic analysis	

Interviews

The phenomenological interviewing approach highlights the need for a reciprocal, or collaborative, relationship between the interviewer and the participant, so that the interview itself is viewed as a 'social encounter' (Dingwall, 1997 cited in Fontana, 2003): here, the interview takes a dramaturgical turn in that impression management and role-playing take places on both sides. Reality is co-created to provide a coherent and cohesive account of everyday life. If the relationship between interviewer and participant is particularly successful, then it moves from 'I-thou' to 'we' (Seidman, 1991). A successful relationship is more likely to benefit from *sequential* interviews, as adopted here.

Semi-structured, face-to-face long interviews were held with six participants aged between 23 and 32 working as account handlers in different PR agencies based in two cities in the north of England. Interviews were undertaken between August 2008 and May 2011.

The first long interview within this study was used to establish initial face-to-face contact, build rapport, and elicit descriptions of the 'lifeworld' from participants' own perspectives (Kvale and Brinkmann, 2009). The research topics covered: biographical information, including education, family, and career history; motivations for working in PR; descriptions of typical workplace interactions, including colleagues, clients, and journalists; being a woman/man; being professional. Drawing on Hochschild (1983), participants were also asked to provide examples of where they had to consciously change their attitude towards a client to maintain a good relationship.

Follow-up, second interviews of between 20 and 50 minutes with each participant enabled me to clarify and develop my understanding of the participant's perspective, as well as negotiate meanings, using the first interview transcript and the online diary entries as the basis for subsequent conversations. Creswell suggests that sequential interviews entail 'self-disclosure on the part of the researcher [which] fosters a sense of collaboration' (1998, p. 83). Self-disclosure became imperative, particularly over the telephone in order to maintain a friendly, conversational style, keep the momentum going, and avoid awkward silences. Rapport was maintained by congratulating participants on their promotions and other achievements. I also reminded them of the importance of my topic and that interpersonal relations in PR were not discussed in the textbooks, which some could relate to as PR graduates. In the second face-to-face interview with Gill my self-disclosure regarding my role as an academic manager meant that Gill appeared more able to reveal her own difficulties in showing her frustrations in front of her team.

Positioning myself in the research process

I increasingly became aware, as the interviewing progressed over time, of performing emotional labour, since there was a need to negotiate identities and empathise with participants as part of this process. Kleinman (2002), citing her own research practice in the sociology of emotions, argues that Hochschild (1983) legitimised emotions in social research. Such 'legitimisation' has enabled researchers to reflexively access their feelings and attitudes throughout the research process to inform greater understanding of themselves and others. Therefore, where relevant in Chapters 5 and 6, I acknowledge 'how the interview gets negotiated and constructed in the process' (Fontana, 2003, p. 58). Throughout the research process I drew on multiple identities in the co-construction of meaning with participants: as a former practitioner; as a researcher and academic; as a woman in relation to other women and men in the study; as someone from an older generation as my participants; also my identity as a parent, which helped me to empathise with two participants in Chapter 6 when talking about the challenge of balancing work responsibilities with a young family.

Self-reflection and reflexivity

Following Polkinghorne (1989), a self-reflective account was used both as preparation for the interviewing and in the analysis (Moustakas, 1994). Within phenomenology, this process is known as 'bracketing' or 'epoché', terms derived from Husserl (1963/1913) that involve setting aside preconceptions and prejudices. Bracketing involves setting aside common sense judgements and looking at a situation as if for the first time. As Moustakas (1994) acknowledges, 'bracketing' or suspension of belief can prove a difficult task. For example, although I had never worked within a PR agency, I had worked in PR for 8 years and had been a PR lecturer for 13 years at the time when the interviews took place. Inevitably, I had acquired some of the language, attitudes, and tacit knowledge that are found within a PR agency environment. While this experience was useful in gaining access to and building rapport with participants, assumptions could easily be made if accounts of interactions and interpretations were not reflected upon. For example, my study participants referred to 'selling-in' stories to journalists. Although I believed I knew what this process involved, its meaning from an emotion management perspective warranted further exploration. Questioning the process of 'selling-in', adopting a 'deliberate naiveté' (Kvale and Brinkmann, 2009, p. 31), led to interesting revelations of the interactional 'games' used by PRPs and journalists, as well as associations with fear. Within my reflexive accounts, there is a conscientious effort to acknowledge my part in the co-created nature of the interviews.

Participants' CVs and online diaries

CVs were collected for this study to gain details of participants' educational backgrounds. This understanding of participants' biographies (or accounts of biographies) relates to Schütz's emphasis on the *lifeworld* and how an individual finds him/herself in a particular situation at a given point in time (Wagner in Schütz, 1970, p. 15). In terms of participant socialisation, for example, I could observe from the CVs that participants were graduates in the humanities, PR, media, or psychology and some had undertaken postgraduate studies; therefore, participants shared common cultural and social capitals (Edwards, 2008) which they were able to bring to their professional roles.

The benefits of the *participant diary* to a qualitative study are that detailed accounts of events and feelings as they are happening can be gathered; also 'the charting of events over time allows the identification of patterns and changes in diarists' accounts of [organisational] processes' (Symon, 1998, p. 114). In my study, brief descriptive diary entries, which were completed by participants online using SurveyMonkey, acted as prompts and enabled further discussion and reflection at the second interview, rather than being artefacts requiring discrete textual analysis.

Analysis of interview transcripts

The purpose of phenomenological research is to understand the *lifeworld* of participants in their own terms. Aspers (2009, p. 6), following a social phenomenological approach, recommends that in analysing transcripts, researchers should be looking for actors' meaning structures (what people mean when they use certain kinds of words); their own theories; what 'ideal types' they construct among themselves; and 'in what kind of practices they are involved'. These 'first order constructs' should result in a detailed description of the lifeworld that it recognisable by the participants in the study (Aspers, 2009). 'Second order constructs' combine these descriptions with explanatory theory. Aspers goes on to suggest that researchers should also seek to look for 'unintended consequences' of their research, in other words outcomes that may not be of direct relevance or concern to social actors but may be linked back to their meaning structures (Aspers, 2009).

I analysed 12 transcripts in total: first, to identify the meaning structures for each participant to produce an individual account of practice; and second, to produce a collective, or *intersubjective*, account of managing professional relationships. As each participant's construction of practice could be regarded as a 'case study' in its own right it was important to safeguard this individual account. In examining the 'meaning of learning' among university students, Greasley and Ashworth (2007), for example, demonstrated how each student embodied a distinctive approach to learning. In my study, this distinctiveness is brought out in the discussion under thematic headings in Chapter 5, particularly in relation to gender identities. Even where shared understandings exist, these understandings may vary slightly according to the interests and motivations of each participant. The coding of transcripts was carried out using NVivo 9 software which enables the researcher to code, categorise, and thematise all texts; in this case interview transcripts and memos on transcripts that were made during the analysis stage.

First-order themes and 'description of practice'

A total of 117 categories were identified from just under 400 coded items in total across 12 transcripts using NVivo 9 qualitative analysis software. The same 117 *categories* were clustered around *themes.* Some categories were labelled by topic according to the subject matter and others analytically, meaning that I placed my own interpretation on a word or statement (Richards, 2005, pp. 87–88). Other category labels arose *in vivo* directly from the texts analysed to create a category using the words of participants. A 2,500 word 'description of practice' document, itself a product of typifications as 'first-order constructs', was mailed to five out of the six participants in this study. (The sixth participant could not be traced.) Three out of the five participants responded by email with brief, supportive comments agreeing with the description as being an accurate picture of agency life. One commented that in hindsight he would stress that agency culture and processes played an important role in shaping how relationships were managed, including whether clients were challenged or not. A fourth participant returned the hard copy of the document with handwritten annotations that indicated her drive to emphasise the more difficult aspects of the job. One annotation de-emphasised the description of the activities involved in 'building rapport' (i.e. getting to know and socialising with the client), placing greater emphasis on adopting the mental attitude of 'empathising with the client' – an approach which, as discussed in Chapter 5, is an aspect of PRPs' emotional labour.

A second annotation corrected one statement to assert that agency directors also expected female, not just male, practitioners to 'challenge' clients. This point about challenging clients is interesting because it touches on sensibilities concerning the notion of 'professionalism' and offering what is termed PR *counsel* or advice to the client – as well as *who* is offering it. This, in turn, raises issues about the gendered, passive notion of providing PR as a *service* that complies with clients' demands (Tsetsura, 2009), or the more assertive notion of a profession where there is an expectation of challenge, as well as more subtle variations of these two opposing ideas or images. The perceptions of consumer PR as 'fluffy' in the description of practice prompted an irritated response from this participant, even though the perceptions had arisen directly from participants who had engaged in consumer PR. Again, this response can be construed as a challenge to this participant's professional self-identity.

The emotion management of professional relationships in PR: agency director perspectives (2016)

The central research objective of this study was to explore how PR agency directors managed and understood professional relationships. My aim was to further develop socially constructed knowledge of PR relationships, using an emotional labour perspective. This project enabled me to focus on specific relational features such as gender, professional status, and professional identities pertaining to agency directors and the clients, journalists, peers, and staff with whom they interact. For this study, I adopted a similar phenomenological approach to my earlier work, including an interview protocol adapted for agency directors, as well as thematic analysis. However, instead of using sequential interviews, as in the previous project, I combined interviews with non-participant observations, thus providing me with first-hand experience of interactions and emotions in different situations.

Interviews

For this study I identified agency directors as socialising agents: the 'emotional experts' (Kleres, 2015) who set the tone of their enterprises. Semi-structured interviews with eight agency directors and partners (six female and two male) were conducted between February and November 2016. Participants were directors or partners of PR firms. Five were based in London and three in other major UK cities. All interviews were a minimum of one hour's length, with six taking place on participants' office premises, while two interviews were undertaken by phone.

A purposive sample of eight participants was recruited from my LinkedIn network and through personal recommendation of a colleague. I selected participants based on their director or partner status within an agency. I had aimed for a gender balance but as there were fewer male directors in my network, the pool of male directors willing to participate in the study was relatively small; therefore only two were recruited. I had also aimed for a sample entirely consisting of London-based directors but again, due to the limited pool of personal contacts in London, I recruited from other major cities. I felt it important to recruit acquaintances, as it helped establish rapport from the start. However, recruiting participants was challenging, as several contacts did not reply to LinkedIn messages for up to a week or more. Securing the interviews confirmed that I was gaining privileged access based on past relationships, access which could otherwise have proven very difficult, if not impossible, without consistently involving a third party acting as gatekeeper. All participants were sent participant information sheets and consent forms, along with requests for access to undertake observations. Three participants responded allowing a full day's access to their offices, and one offered attendance at a meeting.

The agency types represented were diverse, from finance and regulatory through to business-to-business, consumer, healthcare, and communication skills development. The size of organisations represented was similarly diverse: from transnational organisations of around 1,000 employees (large), through to medium (fewer than 250), small (fewer than 50), and micro companies with fewer than ten employees (European Commission, 2018); I undertook follow-up phone interviews of 20 minutes with two of my research participants on the topic of gender relations, since initial interview slots did not allow sufficient time for this topic to be fully discussed. In order to fully understand the handling of international client conference calls at Agency A, I also conducted a 20-minute telephone interview with Jessica*, a further participant.

The audio-recorded interviews were transcribed using a professional transcription service due to the project being constrained by a single financial year's funding. As in the previous study, I adopted a process of open, inductive coding, focusing on emotions and relationships. This produced a total of 332 items of coded text across eight transcripts. Coded texts were clustered under 39 categories. Following a preliminary thematic analysis, I sent a descriptive 'account of practice' to all participants as part of a member checking/validation process (Creswell, 2007). This 3,500 word descriptive account of practice was intended as a basis for further dialogue with participants. After circulating this document, I received no further comments or corrections and assumed this to be due to participants' busy schedules, or as confirmation that they had no issues with the description of practice as they understood it (Tables A.3 and A.4).

Table A.3 Attributes of directors and partners

Name*	Position	Size of company	Highest educational qualification	Age category
Timothy	Director	Micro	BA	40–45
Jane	Partner	Medium	BA	40–45
Charlotte	Director	Medium	BA	40–45
Sarah	Partner	Medium	MA	50–55
Helen	Director	Small	BA	40–45
Mandy	Director	Small	BA	40–45
James	Director	Micro	BA	40–45
Pauline	Director	Small	BA	55–60

* pseudonyms used.

Table A.4 Attributes of PR firms where observations took place

	Agency A	Agency B	Agency C	Agency D
Size of agency by staff nos.	Small	Large	Small	Medium
Type of agency	Mainly B2B focus	Integrated comms/ consumer	Specialist sector	Corporate/ financial

Observations

Interviews were complemented by observational data gathered at four London-based PR agencies, amounting to 18 hours of observed interactions resulting in 20 pages of typewritten notes. I observed largely prearranged meetings and sat in shared office spaces to observe mundane interactions. All the meetings were internal and ranged from staff meetings, through to routine client account updates, director-level meetings, and an awards re-hearsal. I participated in informal discussions with a further 12 practition-ers. Participating in discussions enabled me to check on my understanding when practitioners discussed specific processes such as targeting the fashion media (see Box 6.2). I was not given access to meetings at which clients were present. Observational notes, sometimes recorded on a tablet and at other times handwritten, were further complemented by self-reflexive di-ary notes, which recorded personal responses after each visit. It is worth noting here that observing within agency settings enabled me not only to record my own emotional responses to office layouts, personal interactions, and general office 'feeling' but also to use these responses to draw out the theoretical dimensions of physical spaces and interactions, following Bloch (2012) in her work on academia. My analysis in Chapter 6 should therefore be understood as one that is interested in 'emotions' as much as 'emotional labour'.

Limitations and further work

The empirical studies described and discussed are both small-scale, in-depth qualitative studies undertaken in England, UK. These studies, in turn, offer rich knowledge of the PR field through in-depth analysis and interpretation, supported by concepts or data in the existing literature, discussed in Chap-ters 2–4 of this volume. My own 'stocks of knowledge' (Schütz, 1970, 1972), sensitivity towards the topic, and the interpersonal situation of the interview (Kvale and Brinkmann, 2009) also have a bearing on the co-creation process. Therefore, while this work cannot be generalised in the quantitative sense due to differences in 'ontological and epistemological assumptions, logics and goals' (Smith, 2018, p. 144), the rich data and conceptually based interpreta-tions offer insights from the agency 'lifeworld' that form the basis of tentative theory-building. Thus, the findings should be considered a starting point for further exploratory work, as outlined in Chapter 7.

The social phenomenological approach is relatively flexible and further research would benefit from further sampling as well as innovative methods. Furthermore, an ethnographic study of emotion and emotion management in PR could prove particularly valuable. However, such possibilities do not in-validate the research designs outlined, which are appropriate in contributing to an exploratory project unique within the field of PR.

References

Alvesson, M. and Willmott, H. (2002) Producing the appropriate individual. Identity regulation as organizational control. *Journal of Management Studies*, 39 (5), pp. 619–644.

Ashkanasy, N. M. and Humphrey, R. H. (2011) Current emotion research in organizational behaviour. *Emotion Review*, 3 (2), pp. 214–224.

Aspers, P. (2006) *Markets in Fashion: A phenomenological approach*. London and New York, Routledge.

Aspers, P. (2009) Empirical phenomenology: A qualitative research approach (the Cologne seminars). *The Indo-Pacific Journal of Phenomenology*, 9 (2), pp. 1–12.

Berger, P. and Luckmann, T. (1966) *The Social Construction of Reality: A treatise in the sociology of knowledge*. New York, Doubleday.

Bericat, E. (2015) The sociology of emotions: Four decades of progress. *Current Sociology*, 64 (3), pp. 491–513.

Bloch, C. (2010) Negative acts and bullying: Face-threatening acts, social bonds and social place. In B. Sieben and Å Wettergren, eds. *Emotionalizing Organizations and Organizing Emotions*. Basingstoke, Palgrave Macmillan, pp. 126–146.

Bloch, C. (2012) *Passions and Paranoia: Emotions and the Culture of Emotion in Academia*. Farnham, Surrey, Ashgate.

Blumer, H. (1969) *Symbolic Interactionism: Perspective and method*. Englewood Cliffs, NJ, Prentice-Hall.

Bourne, C. D. (2016) Extending PR's critical conversations with advertising and marketing. In J. L'Etang, D. McKie, N. Snow, and J. Xifra, eds. *The Routledge Handbook of Critical Public Relations*. Abingdon, Oxon and New York, Routledge. pp. 119–129.

Brescoll, V. L. (2016) Leading with their hearts? How gender stereotypes of emotion lead to biased evaluations of female leaders. *The Leadership Quarterly*, 27 (3), pp. 415–428.

Brook, P. (2013) Emotional labour and the living personality at work: Labour power, materialist subjectivity and the dialogical self. *Culture and Organization*, 19 (4), pp. 332–352.

Brotheridge, C. M. and Lee, R. T. (2003) Development and validation of the emotional labour scale. *Journal of Occupational and Organizational Psychology*, 76 (3), pp. 365–379.

Burkitt, I. (2014) *Emotions and Social Relations*. London, Sage.

Calhoun, C. and Solomon, R. C. (1984) *What Is An Emotion? Classic Readings in Philosophical Psychology*. New York and Oxford, Oxford University Press.

Calhoun, C. Gerteis, J. Moody, J., and Pfaff, S. (2007) *Classical Sociological Theory*, 2nd ed. Wiley-Blackwell.

Chartered Institute of Public Relations (2010) 2010 CIPR membership survey: The state of the PR profession: Benchmarking survey. London, CIPR/ComRes.

Clark, C. (1990) Emotions and micropolitics in everyday life: Some patterns and paradoxes of 'place'. In T. D. Kemper, ed. *Research Agendas in the Sociology of Emotions*. Albany, State University of New York Press, pp. 305–334.

Collins, R. (1975) *Conflict Sociology*. New York, Academic Press.

Collins, R. (1990) Stratification, emotional energy, and the transient emotions. In T. D. Kemper, ed. *Research Agendas in the Sociology of Emotions*. Albany, State University of New York Press, pp. 27–57.

Collinson, D. L. and Hearn, J. (1996) *Men as Managers, Managers as Men: Critical perspectives on men, masculinities and managements.* London, Thousand Oaks, CA, and New Delhi, Sage.

Cooley, C. H. (1922) *Human Nature and the Social Order.* New York, Scribner's.

Creswell, J. W. (1998) *Qualitative Inquiry and Research Design: Choosing among five traditions.* Thousand Oaks, CA, London, and New Delhi, Sage.

Creswell, J. W. (2007) *Qualitative Inquiry and Research Design: Choosing among five approaches.* Thousand Oaks, CA, London, and New Delhi, Sage.

Damasio, A. (2000) *The Feeling of What Happens: Body and emotion in the making of consciousness.* London, Vintage Books.

Damasio, A. (2004) *Looking for Spinoza: Joy, sorrow and the feeling brain.* London, Vintage Books.

Damasio, A. (2006) *Descartes' Error: Emotion, reason and the human brain.* London, Vintage Books.

Dennett, D. C. (1991) *Consciousness Explained.* Cambridge, MA, MIT Press.

Denzin, N. K. (1990) On understanding emotion: The interpretive-cultural agenda. In T. D. Kemper, ed. *Research Agendas in the Sociology of Emotions.* Albany, State University of New York Press, pp. 85–116.

Dingwall, R. (1997) Accounts, interviews and observations. In G. Miller and R. Dingwall, eds. *Context and Method in Qualitative Research.* Thousand Oaks, CA, Sage, pp. 51–65.

Domagalski, T. A. and Steelman, L. A. (2007) The impact of gender and organizational status on workplace anger expression. *Management Communication Quarterly,* 20, pp. 297.

Ducey, A. (2007) More than a job: Meaning, affect and training health care workers. In P. T. Clough, with J. Halley, eds. *The Affective Turn: Theorizing the social.* Durham, NC, Duke University Press, pp. 187–208.

Edwards, D. (2005) Emotion. In M. Wetherell, S. Taylor, and S. J. Yates, eds. *Discourse Theory and Practice: A reader.* London, Thousand Oaks, CA, and New Delhi, Sage and The Open University Press, pp. 236–246.

Edwards, L. (2008) PR practitioners' cultural capital: An initial study and implications for research and practice. *Public Relations Review,* 34 (4), pp. 367–372.

Elias, N. (1978, 1982, 1983) *The Civilizing Process: V. 1–3.* New York, Pantheon.

European Commission (2018) What is an SME? Available from: http://ec.europa.eu/growth/smes/business-friendly-environment/sme-definition_en. Accessed 23 October, 2018.

Fineman, S. (2010) Emotion in organizations – A critical turn. In B. Sieben and Å. Wettergren, eds. *Emotionalizing Organizations and Organizing Emotions.* Basingstoke, Palgrave Macmillan, pp. 23–41.

Fontana, A. (2003) Postmodern trends in interviewing. In J. F. Gubrium and J. A. Holstein, eds. *Postmodern Interviewing.* Thousand Oaks, CA, London, and New Delhi, Sage, pp. 51–65.

Garfinkel, H. (1967) *Studies in Ethnomethodology.* Englewood Cliffs, NJ, Prentice-Hall.

Gergen, M. and Gergen, K. J. (2003) The social construction of the real and the good. In M. Gergen and K. J. Gergen, eds. *Social Construction: A reader.* London, Sage, pp. 1–6.

Gerth, H. and Mills, C. W. (1964) *Character and Social Structure: The psychology of social institutions.* New York, Harcourt Brace and World.

Goffman, E. (1959) *The Presentation of Self in Everyday Life.* London, Penguin Books.

Goffman, E. (1967) *Interaction Ritual.* New York, Anchor.

Gordon, S. (1981) The sociology of sentiments and emotion. In M. Rosenberg and R. Turner, eds. (1990) *Social Psychology: Sociological perspectives.* New York, Basic Books, pp. 562–592.

Gorton, K. (2007) Theorizing emotion and affect: Feminist engagements. *Feminist Theory,* 8 (3), pp. 333–348.

Goudsblom, J. and Mennell, S. (1998) *The Norbert Elias Reader: A biographical selection.* Oxford, Blackwell.

Greasley, K. and Ashworth, P. (2007) The phenomenology of 'approach to studying': The university student's studies within the lifeworld. *British Educational Research Journal,* 33 (6), pp. 819–843.

Harré, R. (2003) The social construction of emotion. In M. Gergen and K. J. Gergen, eds. *Social Construction: A reader.* London, Sage, pp. 146–147.

Härtel, C. E. J., Hsu, A. C. F., and Boyle, M. V. (2002) A conceptual examination of the causal sequences of emotional labor, emotional dissonance, and emotional exhaustion: The argument for the role of contextual and provider characteristics. In N. M. Ashkanasy, W. J. Zerbe, and C. E. J. Härtel, eds. *Managing Emotions in the Workplace.* Armonk, NY, ME Sharpe, pp. 232–250.

Hochschild, A. R. (1975) The sociology of feeling and emotion. In M. Millman and R. M. Kanter, eds. *Another Voice: Feminist perspectives on social life and social science.* New York, Anchor Books, pp. 280–307.

Hochschild, A. R. (1979) Emotion work, feeling rules and social structure. *American Journal of Sociology,* 85 (3), pp. 551–575.

Hochschild, A. R. (1983) *The Managed Heart: Commercialization of human feeling.* Berkeley, University of California Press.

Humphrey, R. H. (2008) The right way to lead with emotional labor. In R. H. Humphrey, ed. *Affect and Emotion: New directions in management theory and research.* Charlotte, NC: Information Age Publishing, pp. 1–17.

Humphrey, R. H., Pollack, J. M., and Hawver, T. (2008) Leading with emotional labor. *Journal of Managerial Psychology,* 23 (2), pp. 151–168.

Husserl, E. (1963) *Ideas: A general introduction to pure phenomenology.* Translated from the German original of 1913 by W. R. Boyce Gibson. New York, Collier Books.

Kagan, J. (2007) *What is Emotion? History, Measures and Meanings.* New Haven, CT, and London, Yale University Press.

Kaiser, S. Müller-Seitz, G., and Cruesen, U. (2008) Passion wanted! Socialisation of positive emotions in consulting firms. *International Journal of Work, Organisation and Emotion,* 2 (3), pp. 305–320.

Katz, J. (1999) *How Emotions Work.* Chicago, IL and London, University of Chicago Press.

Kelly, J. R., and Barsade, S. G. (2001) Mood and emotions in small groups and work teams. *Organizational Behavior and Human Decision Processes,* 86 (1), pp. 99–130.

Kemper, T. D. (1987) How many emotions are there? Wedding the social and autonomic components. *American Journal of Sociology,* 93 (2), pp. 263–289.

Kemper, T. D. (1990) Themes and variations in the sociology of emotions. In T. D. Kemper, ed. *Research Agendas in the Sociology of Emotions.* Albany, State University of New York Press, pp. 3–26.

Kemper, T. D. (2006) Power and status and the power-status theory of emotions. In J. E. Stets and J. H. Turner, eds. *The Handbook of Sociology of Emotions.* New York, Springer, pp. 87–113.

Kleinman, S. (2002) Emotions, fieldwork and professional lives. In T. May, ed. *Qualitative Research in Action.* London, Thousand Oaks, CA, and New Delhi, Sage, pp. 375–394.

Kleres, J. (2015) Emotional expertise: Emotion and the expert interview. In H. Flam, and J. Kleres, eds. *Methods of Exploring Emotions.* London, Routledge, pp. 90–100.

Kövecses, Z. (1991) A linguist's quest for love. *Journal of Social and Personal Relationships,* 8 (1), pp. 77–97.

Kövecses, Z. (2000) *Metaphor and Emotion.* New York and Cambridge, Cambridge University Press.

Kvale, S. and Brinkmann, S. (2009) *Interviews: Learning the craft of qualitative research interviewing,* 2nd ed. Los Angeles, CA, London, New Delhi, and Singapore, Sage.

Lewis, H. (1971) *Shame and Guilt in Neurosis.* New York, International Universities Press.

Lury, C. and Warde, A. (1997) Investments in the imaginary consumer. In M. Nava, A. Blake, I. MacRury, and B. Richards, eds. *Buy This Book: Studies in advertising and consumption.* London, Routledge, pp. 87–102.

Lutz, C. A. (2003) Emotion: The universal as local. In M. Gergen and K. J. Gergen, eds. *Social Construction: A reader.* London, Sage, pp. 39–42.

Lutz, C. A. (2007) Emotion, thought and estrangement: Emotion as a cultural category. In H. Wulff, ed. *The Emotions: A cultural reader.* Oxford, New York, Berg, pp. 19–29.

Lutz, C. A. (2008) Engendered emotions: Gender, power and the rhetoric of emotional control in American discourse. In M. Greco and P. Stenner, eds. *Emotions: A social science reader,* Oxford, Routledge, pp. 63–71.

Lynd, H. M. (1958) *On Shame and the Search for Identity.* New York, Harcourt Brace.

Massumi, B. (2002) *Parables for the Virtual: Movement, affect, sensation.* Durham NC, Duke University Press.

Mead, G. H. (1934) *Mind, Self, and Society.* Chicago, IL, University of Chicago Press.

Moustakas, C. (1994) *Phenomenological Research Methods.* Thousand Oaks, CA, Sage Publications Inc.

Negri, A. (1999) Value and affect. *Boundary,* 2 (26.2), pp. 77–87.

Petersen, A. (2004) *Engendering Emotions.* Basingstoke, Palgrave Macmillan.

Plutchik, R. (1980) *Emotion: A psychoevolutionary synthesis.* New York, Harper and Row.

Polkinghorne, D. E. (1989) Phenomenological research methods. In R. S. Valle and S. Halling, eds. *Existential-Phenomenological Perspectives in Psychology.* New York, Plenum, pp. 41–60.

Probyn, E. (2005) *Blush: Faces of Shame.* Minneapolis, University of Minnesota Press.

Richards, L. (2005) *Handling Qualitative Data: A practical guide.* London, Thousand Oaks, CA, and New Delhi, Sage.

Seidman, I. (1991) *Interviewing as Qualitative Research: A guide for researchers in education and the social sciences.* New York, Teachers College Press.

Scheff, T. J. (1979) *Catharsis in Ritual, Healing and Drama.* Berkeley and Los Angeles, University of California Press.

Scheff, T. J. (1990) Socialization of emotions: Pride and shame as causal agents. In T. D. Kemper, ed. *Research Agendas in the Sociology of Emotions.* Albany, State University of New York Press, 281–304.

Scheff, T. J. (2000) Shame and the social bond. *Sociological Theory,* 18 (1), pp. 84–99.

Schütz, A. (1970) *On Phenomenology and Social Relations.* Chicago, IL, and London, University of Chicago Press.

Schütz, A. (1972) *The Phenomenology of the Social World.* London, Heinemann Educational Books.

Sedgwick, E. K. and Frank, A. eds. (1995) *Shame and Its Sisters: A Silvan Tomkins reader.* Durham, NC, and London, Duke University Press.

Sennett, R. and Cobb, J. (1973) *The Hidden Injuries of Class.* New York, Vintage Books.

Sieben, B. and Wettergren, Å. (2010) Emotionalizing organizations and organizing emotions – Our research agenda. In B. Sieben and Å Wettergren, eds. *Emotionalizing Organizations and Organizing Emotions.* Basingstoke, Palgrave Macmillan, pp. 1–22.

Simmel, G. (1904) Fashion. *International Quarterly,* 10, pp. 130–155 (Reprinted in the *American Journal of Sociology* 62, May 1957, pp. 541–559).

Smith, B. (2018) Generalizability in qualitative research: Misunderstandings, opportunities and recommendations for the sport and exercise sciences. *Qualitative Research in Sport, Exercise and Health,* 10 (1), pp. 137–149.

Smith, D. (2001) *Norbert Elias and Modern Social Theory.* London, Sage.

Solomon, R. C. (2007) *True to our Feelings: What our emotions are really telling us.* Oxford, Oxford University Press.

Svensson, P. (2007) Producing marketing: Towards a social-phenomenology of marketing work. *Marketing Theory,* 7 (3), pp. 271–290.

Symon, G. (1998) Qualitative research diaries. In G. Symons and C. Cassell, eds. *Qualitative Methods and Analysis in Organizational Research: A practical guide.* London, Thousand Oaks, CA, and New Delhi, Sage, pp. 94–117.

Tomkins, S. S. (1962) *Affect, Imagery, Consciousness,* 2 vols. New York, Springer.

Tsetsura, K. (2009) How female practitioners in Moscow view their profession: A pilot study. *Public Relations Review,* 36 (1), pp. 78–80.

Turner, J. H. and Stets, J. E. (2005) *The Sociology of Emotions.* New York, Cambridge University Press.

Turner, J. H. and Stets, J. E. (2006) *The Handbook of the Sociology of Emotions.* New York, Springer Science and Business Media.

Wagner, H. R. (1970) Introduction. The phenomenological approach to sociology. In A. Schütz, ed. *On Phenomenology and Social Relations.* Chicago, IL, and London, University of Chicago Press, pp. 1–50.

Weiss, H. M., and Cropanzano, R. (1996) Affective events theory: A theoretical discussion of the structure, causes, and consequences of affective experiences at work. In B. M. Staw and L. L. Cummings, eds. *Research in Organizational Behavior.* 18, pp. 1–74.

Wetherell, M. (2005) Themes in discourse research: The case of Diana. In M. Wetherell, S. Taylor, and S. J. Yates eds. *Discourse Theory and Practice: A reader.* London, Thousand Oaks, CA, and New Delhi, Sage and The Open University Press, pp. 14–27.

Wettergren, Å. (2017) Commentary: Sociology of emotions from an embedded perspective. *Journal of Sociology,* 53 (4), pp. 819–821.

Yeomans, L. (2013) Researching emotional labour among public relations consultants in the UK: A social phenomenological approach. *Romanian Journal of Communication and Public Relations,* 15 (3), pp. 31–51.

Index

Note: **Bold** page numbers refer to tables; *italic* page numbers refer to figures and page numbers followed by "n" denote endnotes.

.

Printed in the United States
by Baker & Taylor Publisher Services